THE POWER OF WORDS

Unveiling the Speaker and Writer's Hidden Craft

THE POWER OF WORDS

Unveiling the Speaker and Writer's Hidden Craft

David Kaufer

Suguru Ishizaki

Brian Butler

Jeff Collins

Foreword by Todd Oakley

LEA LAWRENCE ERLBAUM ASSOCIATES, PUBLISHERS

2004 Mahwah, New Jersey   London

Lawrence Erlbaum Associates, Inc., Publishers
10 Industrial Avenue
Mahwah, NJ 07430

Cover design by Kerry Ishizaki

Library of Congress Cataloging-in-Publication Data

The power of words : unveiling the speaker and writer's hidden craft/ David Kaufer …[et al.].
   p. cm.
  Includes bibliographical references (p.) and index.
  ISBN 0-8058-4783-9 (c. : alk paper)
  1. English language--Semantics. 2. English language--Spoken English. 3. English
  language--Written English. 4. Written communication. 5. Oral communication. I. Kaufer,
  David S.

PE1585.P69 2004
401'.43--dc21   2003049234

Books published by Lawrence Erlbaum Associates are printed on acid-free paper, and their bindings are chosen for strength and durability.

Printed in the United States of America
10   9   8   7   6   5   4   3   2   1

To Nancy and Dan,
D.K.

To My Family,
S.I.

To Michelle, Paul, and Sam,
B.B.

To Kathy,
J.C.

TABLE OF CONTENTS

Table of Contents

FOREWORD

By Todd Oakley

Language arts teachers are all too familiar with the technically correct but tedious and uninspired paper. My own experiences with the correct but ho-hum essay correlate most tellingly with an encomium assignment whereby a student sets out to praise her or his mother. The tell-tale sign of tediousness was always in evidence when the student inserted somewhere in the essay the familiar sentiment, *She was always there for me.*

Communicating to the student why the presence of such a sentiment hinders rather than enhances the persuasive effect of her or his writing is perhaps one of the most difficult tasks let to the writing instructor, because a good explanation of why this phrase does not prime the intended audience response demands attention to a middle-level of composition that neither rhetorical theory nor linguistics has been able to properly theorize and confirm. Traditional linguists, especially those espousing a "syntacto-centric" viewpoint, tend to feel most comfortable at micro-level of distributed forms, while rhetoricians — emboldened to think about the larger contingencies governing text production and consumption — feel most comfortable at the macro-level of genre and other cultural, historical, and sociological formations. But neither approach is sufficient in itself to explain why *she was always there for me* fails as sufficient trigger of audience approbation. Some rhetoricians familiar with the genre of the encomium will concede that the writer does manage to paint an impressionistic portrait of a parent attending to the child and that this word picture satisfies the genre expectation of mentioning the living subject's achievements. For linguists, who take face to face conversation as the default context (even as they use written strings as their main data source), this string is sufficient prompt-with the existential "there" serving as a sparse and efficient cue-for the hearer to get "the gist" of what she or he means. From the linguist's perspective, there is no real problem here (or no problem for which linguistics has any relevance). From the rhetorician's perspective, however, there is indeed a problem, but no clear consensus on why it is a problem.

The problem is neither with *grammar* nor *genre*. The phrase fits in the canon of grammatical acceptability, as it is a "well-formed" sentence. This sentiment fits within the epideictic genre, as it is a "well-formed" thought about a living person capable of properly orienting the reader regarding matters of personal virtue. The problem is *representational.*

The authors of this book subscribe to the view that rhetoric is a design art, and design arts deal explicitly with representations. Architects and engineers, for instance, plan artifacts using common representational elements (i.e., representations of space, motion, and time) in designing a planned artifact. And the artifacts they use to design new artifacts, e.g., sketches, blueprints, models, schematics, story boards, and so on-each have their own representational logic. In practicing her art, the designer must make the representation of her own intentionality fit with the representational capacities of these artifacts. The same is true with language: the writer practices her art effectively when she makes the representation of her own intentionality fit the representational capacities of artifacts she is using.

As outside observers, we can say that our fictitious uninspired writer uses the representational capacity of the chosen artifact that does not fit his or her intentionality. More technically, the construction fails to link up with an implicit "pragmatic scale" applied by sophisticated readers: "being there" for children is thought to be a minimum requirement of good parenting, and thus does not meet the threshold of achievement that would place in evidence virtues of the person praised.

It is this mezzanine level of representation linking grammar to genre that is in most need of development.

A major advance in the study of rhetoric and applied linguistics, this book fits within several traditions of inquiry that attempt to link the microcosm of grammar to the macrocosm of rhetorical effect but which have yet to reach the mainstream of rhetoric and composition studies. What is truly remarkable about this study is that it uses new technology in corpus linguistics to build a theory of the micro-units (or "strings" as the authors call them), such as *on the one hand, I think, goes without saying,* and so on. These strings prime readers to construct different representations that, in turn, guide readers through the macro-units of texts and text types. The authors recognized that a comprehensive survey of English as a priming instrument for audiences would require a catalog able to archive hundreds of thousands and even millions of strings. They thus designed special-purpose software to assist them in their data collection efforts. The result is a remarkable text analysis environment known as *Docuscope*. While most applied linguists base corpora either on genre or grammar, the designers of Docuscope, focused on writers building textual impressions at the point of utterance, take the unusual step of using genre based corpora to conduct factor analyses of English text types in order to confirm their hypothesis that a finite set of representational elements connect grammar and discourse. Exploring this hypothesis required the authors to be extremely systematic about language triggers across English. Rhetorical priming theory represents an important advance by offering a comprehensive catalog of these ubiquitous triggers of common representations.

The authors' catalog of these triggers consists of three clusters, six families, and eighteen dimensions, with the current catalogue exhibiting anywhere from one to fourteen distinct classes within a dimension. A short summary will suffice. The three clusters include *Internal, External,* and *Relational* perspectives. Inner perspective, in turn, contain two families—*present interior thinking* and *interior thinking projected into the past or future*—along six dimensions: *first person, inner thinking, think positive, think negative, think ahead,* and *think back.* Relational perspectives contain two additional families—*relating audience to representations* and *relating audiences to the linear medium of language*—along six dimensions: *reasoning, sharing social ties, directing activities, interacting, notifying, and linear guidance.* External perspectives consist of one family—*extended space*—along six dimensions: *word pictures, spatial intervals, motion, past events, time intervals, event shifts.* At the lowest level are more than ninety classes of priming strings for the representation such as *temporal passage, sense objects, motion intervals, scene shifting,* among others.

For the remainder of this forward I will briefly review specific developments in linguistics which stand to benefit from such a corpus outlined in this study and which, in turn, will deepen, sharpen and enhance the corpus itself.

The general thrust of this book is compatible with a brand of functional linguistics known as Cognitive Linguistics, a family of theoretical approaches including Cognitive Grammar, Construction Grammar, and Mental Spaces and Blending Theory, each of which will be discussed below. As a scientific framework, cognitive linguistics pursues three hypotheses: language is not an autonomous faculty, but arises from general cognitive operations; grammar is conceptualization; and language structure arises from language use (for review, see Croft & Cruse, in press). All three hypotheses, especially the third, are compatible with the aims and scope of this study.

Before describing these theories, let me say a few words about the nature of the strings themselves. As the authors note, a meaningful string of English is roughly 1-4 words in length, suggesting that meaning is not fully compositional, but rather emergent: the meaning of the whole is more than a function of the parts. The typical few-word-span of a string is an outcome of the computationally driven analysis; however, it should be pointed out that this mean length aligns with extensive study of spoken language conducted by Wallace Chafe and his associates at the University of California at Santa Barbara, developers of the *Corpus of Spoken American English.* According to Chafe (1994), 1-4 words in exactly the mean length of what he terms substantive intonation units. Intonation units are "spurts" of language that form functionally relevant segments separated by pauses and other prosodic phenomena, such as changes in frequency, duration, intensity, voice quality, and silence. On analysis, these intonation units comprise representations of meaningful events, actions, and states. In addition to substantive intonation units, Chafe catalogued the presence of regulative intonation units for managing the flow of discourse. Such units are consistent with the notion that rhetorical design knowledge consists of representational patterns for cueing readers to allocate attention to certain events, actions, and states. It would appear that the authors of this study have considerable empirical support from another corpus. One desideratum from this study would be substantial research on the relation between writing and speaking, now that we have extensive corpora for each.

One of the earliest (and most completely developed) of the cognitive linguistic theories is Ronald Langacker's Cognitive Grammar (1987, 1990). In contrast to formalist theories, cognitive grammar equates meaning with conceptualization;

conceptualization, in turn, is equated not just with abstract conceptions, but also phenomena such as sensory, emotive, and kinesthetic sensations. It is no accident, for instance, that the authors' theory specifies dimensions and classes denoting sensory perceptual experience. Cognitive grammar seeks to understand the "cognitive routines" indexed by language. A cognitive routine is a cognitive event sufficiently entrenched as to be primed by space and efficient linguistic triggers. The author's notion of a representation is compatible with Langacker's notion of a routine. Langacker's pivotal claim is that linguistic expressions and grammatical constructions embody "conventional imagery" and that grammar is simply a structured inventory of conventional units. Cognitive grammar is also a usage-based theory, meaning that these conventional units arise from specific communicative situation and the purpose of a grammar is to "construe the conventional imagery of a language for specific expressive purposes."

A principal claim of this theory is that meaning and form are intimately related and that linguistic constructions denoting the same ostensive "objective" state of affairs are in fact distinct representations. Consider, as Langacker does in several of his articles and books, the sentence *The roof slopes downward* as compared to *The roof slopes upward.* Assuming the same referential object, one can consider these sentences equivalent in meaning (as most formalist theories still do), but you would be missing a crucial point about our knowledge of language: the ability to construe perspective. The interesting fact about each version is not the existence of the roof or even its spatial orientation, but the implicit perspective of the speaker. With the first utterance, the speaker is representing the roof from an "elevated" vantage point, whereas with the second utterance the speaker is representing the roof from a level vantage point. Of course, the reasons for expressing it one way or the other are indefinite, but the principle is the same: the grammar reflects meaningful differences.

The theory of rhetorical priming presented in this book does not aim to reveal such specific meaning differences; however, it is worth noting that an analysis provided by the theory classified roof as a sense object. The mere classification as such suggests that conceptualization of perspectives is an important taxonomic category already present in the corpus. After all, sense objects are always sensible to someone from some specific viewpoint. The point is not that the authors' is a theory of cognitive grammar, far from it. Rather, the point is that their theory is highly compatible with the aims and scope of cognitive grammar, and just as the corpus would benefit from the results and implications of cognitive grammar research so would cognitive grammar benefit from the heuristic power of a theory of rhetorical priming.

Another notable cognitive linguistic theory is Construction Grammar. Like cognitive grammar, construction grammar equates grammar with conceptualization but focuses more specifically on syntax. In contrast to the formalist enterprise of treating syntax as pure form, construction grammar, construction grammarians—most notably Charles Fillmore, Paul Kay, Laura Michaelis, Ivan Sag (in press) and Adele Goldberg (1995)—define constructions as form-meaning pairings existing independently of particular verbs. While there are innumerable lexical constructions, such as *let alone, even,* and negative polarity items such as *few/a few,* and *just,* there is a finite set of syntactic structures that carry meaning independent of the words in the sentence. For example, Goldberg argues that sentences like *Sam threw the ball over the fence, David sneezed the napkin off the table,* and *Todd waived the student into his office,* are manifestations of the same caused motion construction, a construction with the schematic meaning of X causes Y to move Z. Similarly, distinct utterances like *The blacksmith hammered the metal flat* and *She kissed him unconscious* evidence the same resultative construction, with the schematic meaning of X causes Y to become Z.

The aims of a theory of language as an instrument of rhetorical priming has much in common with construction grammar, for both theories seek a systematic treatment of language triggers to reveal what is ordinary about language structure. The authors' theory is only a short distance away from tagging such constructions, as the present technological environment already specifies a number of classes and dimensions consistent with construction grammar. For instance, an analysis of caused motion would likely reveal a strong correlation of sense object and motion interval, space interval, or scene shifting between the direct object and object of the preposition of a finite clause. Likewise, an analysis of resultative constructions would likely reveal a strong correlation of sense object and sense property classes in the final clause complement. A rapprochement of construction grammar and rhetorical priming theory would be mutually beneficial. For construction grammar, the authors' powerful text analysis environment provides an empirical method for determining the distributional range of these constructions. Are they more common in writing than in speaking? Do some constructions appear more frequently in specific genres? For rhetorical priming theory, it would make systematic analysis a host of new strings types possible, thus extending the corpuses already impressive reach.

The last notable variety of cognitive linguistics covered here is Mental Spaces and Conceptual Blending theory developed by Gilles Fauconnier and Mark Turner. As the title of their newest book *The Way We Think* (2002) suggests, conceptual blending's scope is more ambitious than cognitive or construction grammars, as it offers a general model of meaning construction in which a small set of partially compositional processes operate in analogy, metaphor, counterfactuals, and many other semantic and pragmatic phenomena (Coulson & Oakley, 2000; Fauconnier & Turner, 1998). In this theory, understanding meaning involves the construction of blended cognitive models that include some structure from multiple *input* models, as well as emergent structure that arises through the processes of blending. Conceptual blending theory describes a set of principles for combining dynamic cognitive models in a network of *mental spaces* (Fauconnier 1994), or partitions of speakers' referential representations.

Mental spaces contain partial representations of the entities and relationships in any given scenario as perceived, imagined, remembered, or otherwise understood by a speaker. Elements represent each of the discourse entities, and simple frames represent the relationships that exist between them. Because the same scenario can be construed in multiple ways, mental spaces are frequently used to partition incoming information about elements in speakers' referential representations. To illustrate, suppose an architect in the course of describing her first model of the renovated house utters the following sentence to her clients: *Here, the flat garage roof has been replaced with a roof sloping downward toward the valley.*

One virtue of mental space theory is that it explains how the addressee might encode information at the referential level by dividing it into concepts relevant to different aspects of the scenario. A central insight of mental space theory was that radically different types of domains functioned similarly in the way they licensed the construction of mental spaces. In this example, the speaker sets up at least two distinct mental spaces: A speaker's Reality space, which references the actual house and site for renovation, and a Representation space for a model of what the real house might be in the near future. The access principle, for example, that allows speakers to refer to an element in one space by describing its counterpart in a linked mental space, operates similarly whether the linked spaces are a belief and a reality space, a past and a present space, or a picture and a reality space. In this example, the locative deictic *here* accesses both the future reality space of the real house through the representation space, whereas, the subject *the flat roof* applies only to the present speaker's reality space, while the adverbial *sloping downward toward the valley* accesses content in both spaces but from the elevated vantage point established in the representation space.

This brief analysis suggests that speakers or writers alike use specific representational elements akin to the strings discussed in this study to prime hearers or readers to construct sufficiently similar mental models. Many times, the mental models that get created have special properties and characteristics captured in the theory of blending.

Conceptual blending theory is a development of mental space theory intended to account for cases in which the content of two or more mental spaces is combined to yield novel inferences, such as the following sentiment intimated to me a few weeks ago:

Had Gore won Florida, we would not have invaded Iraq.

The two domains at play in this sentence: US Electoral Politics and Armed Conflict, with the rhetorical goal being to highlight the causal link between a close election and a war. Fauconnier (1997) suggests that examples like above prompt for the construction of a *blended space* that inherits partial structure from two or more different *input* spaces. The inputs are thus the 2000 Presidential Election space and the Iraq War space.

The blended space inherits some structure from the Election space, namely that hotly contested election results in Florida which gave Bush the required margin of victory, along with selected structure from the War space, namely the implication the United States' decision to invade Iraq was a direct consequence of conservative Republican policies and procedures different from the policies and procedures endemic to the Democrats represented by Gore. The disanalogy between the Bush's and Gore's foreign polices represented in the this space (and primed simply by mentioning Gore's name) lead to counterfactual blended space in which President Gore takes a very different position toward Iraq (and possibly our allies). In the blend, but not the input spaces, the 2003 war in Iraq does not occur. Conceptual blending processes proceed via the establishment and exploitation of mappings, the activation of background knowledge, and frequently involve the use of mental imagery and mental simulation. Blending processes are used to conceptualize actual things such as *hanging chads,* possible things such as *President Gore,* fictional things such as *Winnie the Pooh,* and even impossible things such as a *present-day President Gore.* Interestingly, even though cognitive models in blended spaces are occasionally bizarre, the inferences generated inside them are often useful and lead to productive changes in the conceptualizer's everyday knowledge and inferencing capacity. In fact, entertaining such counterfactual notions as a present-day President Gore is a very common mode of reasoning in the social and political sciences (see Turner, 2001). Although conceptual blending theory was motivated by creative examples that demand the construction of hybrid cognitive models, the processes that underlie these phenomena are actually widely utilized in all sorts of cognitive and linguistic phenomena (see Coulson, 2001 for review).

Let us now returning to the opening example, *She was always there for me.* A brief computational analysis with Docuscope shows traits from all three clusters: *she* is relational, *was always* is interior, and *there* is exterior. More specifically, this expression exhibits traits of inner thinking, linear guidance, and extended space. Still more specifically, the dimensions of this expression encompass first person, cohesion, and spatial interval. And at the lowest level of specificity, this expression functions along representational classes of first person ("me"), confidence ("was always"), cue back ("she"), spatial interval ("there").

It is evident that this expression encompasses all three representational types and is therefore, stretched "thin" to prompt concrete audience experiences. Although cognitive grammarians refrain from making any normative claims of linguistic propriety, they would be quick to note that such an expression is maximally schematic with respect to what entities are to be profiled. In particular, the locative there, though meaningful, does not sufficiently prime readers to construe a concrete relation between subject and predicate within clausal boundaries.

It merely gestures toward a writer's intention without fulfilling it. Mental spaces theory adds perhaps an additional component to the analysis extending it beyond the scope the expression itself. There are at least two distinct mental spaces in operation here. First, a mental space representing the writer's design goal (a goal the reader should likewise recognize easily). In this space, he is a writer trying to say something interesting to the reader about another person. The other space represents particular facets of the subject under discussion. One important feature of mental spaces theory is the asymmetry of attention paid to any given space at any given moment in ongoing discourse. Only one mental space can be rhetorically in focus at any given time. A distinct problem with such vague assertions is that lack of focused attention paid to the very mental space to which the writer wants the reader to attend; instead, the reader is likely to attend to the space representing the goals *of* the design (i.e., "the writer is attempting to persuade me to care about person x") rather than the goals *in* the design (i.e., "person x is virtuous because…").

At present, mental spaces and blending theory, construction grammar, and cognitive grammar provide some of the more fruitful areas of linguistic and cognitive research into the rich contexts involved in the interpretation of texts. By the authors' own account, their theory is about how speakers and writers trigger interpretation and not on the full richness of an interpretation once settled. And yet, as the corpus studies reported in their last chapter begin to show, understanding the constellation of triggers that constitute a text or group of texts can usefully constrain its space of interpretation. For this reason, this book offers investigators concepts and method for testing their theories about language and interpretation over a broad range of texts in a manner heretofore elusive to standard corpora (as they do not code for representational strings) and beyond the grasp of the lone investigator (as he or she can only read one text at a time).

This short forward provides merely a hint of the riches in store for the rhetorician, compositionist, or linguist as each explores the material covered in these pages. This study brings together corpus linguistics and rhetorical theory to provide text scholars with a broad palette of representation forms found frequently in a broad range of text types. First and foremost, it suggest that Interior, Exterior, and Relational perspectives are pervasive representational elements of the English language and that effective written communication must provide sufficient prompts that prime readers to construct meaning. For the first time, text scholars have available to them a catalogue of a significant portion of the priming strings available to writers and readers. *The Power of Words: Unveiling the Speaker and Writer's Hidden Craft* is a signal achievement in text scholarship whose publication is most welcome.

PREFACE

Calling the atmosphere of an office "cool" conveys a different experience for a listener or reader than calling it "cold." Calling a drink "flavored" marks a judgment perceptibly different from calling it "flavorful." Words in use prime an audience's experience and different words prime different experience. This is hardly news, but it is newsworthy that analysts of language have yet to systematize facts like these into a more general understanding about the priming potency of words and strings in the English language. Although the simple examples of "cool" and "flavored" might suggest otherwise, these potencies cannot be explained, or dismissed away, as connotative meanings. The English string "would often come" primes an audience toward the past whereas the string "would like to come" primes toward the future. Yet the priming potency of neither string involves the strict meaning, literal or connotative, of any the individual containing words. For this reason, language priming though English strings represents, in our view, an autonomous, systematic, and largely unexplored focus for the pragmatic study of language behavior.

According to its vernacular meaning, the word *prime*, used as a transitive verb, means, "to prepare; make ready; or instruct beforehand." Cognitive and social scientists use *prime* as a term to indicate preconditioning a subsequent behavior through training or suggestion. In studies of text comprehension, for example, reading researchers (Schwanenflugel & White, 1991) have showed that readers can be preconditioned to make faster decisions about completing a verb phrase like "climbed the" with "stairs" when the prior text is thematically about a house and preconditioned to complete it with "mountains" when the prior text is about the outdoors.

In the context of this book, we use priming in its vernacular sense to describe a speaker or writer's implicit knowledge relating strings of English and ways of predisposing audience experience through language. Skilled speakers and writers who create art, not simply meaning, through language must learn to notice and act on the priming potencies of language in use. Learning to listen and read for words as priming tools (not as completed meanings or interpretations) helps speakers and writers acquire the expertise to guide experience for others through the linear medium of language. This is the kind of language learning Richard Lanham (1986) has referenced as learning to "look at" language as a close reader and writer. It is also the kind of learning that in previous work we have associated with controlling language to design the readers' experience (Kaufer & Butler, 2000).

We present original research that develops this approach to language. We present a theory of language as an instrument of rhetorically priming audience and a catalog of English strings to flesh out the theory. Our catalog seeks to reflect the range and variety of audience experience that contiguous words of surface English can prime. Our project is to create a comprehensive map of the speaker and writer's implicit knowledge about predisposing audience experience at the point of utterance.

In the first chapter of Part I, we explain why studying language from the standpoint of priming, not just meaning, is vital to nonquestion-begging theories of close reading and to language education in general. In the remaining chapters of Part I, we detail the steps we took to prepare a catalog study of English strings for their properties as priming instruments. We describe the properties of the English strings we classified. We describe our methods of classification, including the assistance of computer-supported coding that has allowed us to catalog over 500 million unique English strings across a range of audience experience categories. We describe the tensions between our catalog classifications as a fixed coding catalog and as an organic social system, as we recruited students in writing classrooms over a three-year period to help us catalog strings for their priming potency and to help check our previous catalog entries.

In Part II, we describe in detail our catalog of priming categories and we include enough examples to help readers see how individual words and strings of English fit into the catalog. We divide the universe of priming strings into three perspectives: internal, relational, and external. Priming from internal perspectives reveals the mind, interior thought, affect, or subjectivity of the speaker, writer, or a person or character referenced. Priming from relational perspectives creates ties between the speaker or writer and the audience or ties between persons and characters they might reference. Priming from external perspectives reveals the state of the world outside mind, elaborated descriptively within a scene or extended over time. Taken together, these perspectives cover a large and comprehensive catalog of the priming potencies of English strings.

In Part III, we describe how we have applied our catalog of English strings as priming tools to conduct textual research. For example, Jeff Collins (2003) has demonstrated that the string families we report in this book aggregate to create reliable and stable "factors" or "choice points" for writers across broad corpora of written English. The corpora he used were comprised of 15 genres within American English and the texts' publication was separated by decades (1960s, 1990s). Yet the usages of the string families by the authors of the texts were confirmed consistently to distribute themselves along the boundaries of text genre. There is thus some powerful but still preliminary evidence that the families of English priming categories we report here begin to converge on the writer's hidden craft of organizing variable experience for audiences. This hidden craft relates rhetorical choice in the small to audience experience over larger rhetorical artifacts.

When used as a coding scheme for various multivariate statistical applications, our catalog successfully illuminates important differences between written genres. We have used it in pedagogy to explore the genres of Shakespeare and presidential inaugurals. In research, we have used our catalog to generate new understandings on the longstanding Federalist Paper controversy concerning whether Alexander

Hamilton or James Madison wrote specific papers that each claimed to have authored individually. We have used the catalog to note interesting differences in writing styles among career authors, like newspaper columnists. We use the last section of the book briefly to overview these expanding areas of application.

Although most of our focus is to present a comprehensive catalog of rhetorical priming categories for English, we are also interested in making a theoretical case for a systemic and understudied micro-layer of language through which speakers and writers control the audience experience. Hopper (2002) has referred to this intersection of small-language segments and audience experience as "micro-rhetoric." Our intent here is to explore some of the vast range of micro-rhetoric as it expresses in short contiguous strings of contemporary and standard American English. The idea of syntax, the ordering of words that interfaces with meaning and pragmatics, is predominantly associated with sentence grammar. However, in this book, we marshal a small library of examples illustrating various orderings within English phrasing that serve the art of rhetoric at least as powerfully as they serve sentence grammar.

We understand that many of the details of micro-rhetoric we present are open to further discussion and revision. Our intention is to open and encourage that discussion.

ACKNOWLEDGMENTS

We wish to thank the many generations of student writers and designers who helped us build our archive of English strings and, more importantly, participated with us in learning about English from a writer and formal speaker's special vantage. Linda Bathgate, our editor at Lawrence Erlbaum, has been a voice of steady encouragement. Cheryl Geisler, Chris Neuwirth, Davida Charney, Susan Hagan, Roland Hsu, and colleagues in the Rhetoric Program and Department of English at Carnegie Mellon have provided us useful sounding boards. Communities of scholars at the US Air Force Academy, the Rensselaer Polytechnic Institute, and the University of Pittsburgh, Katz Graduate School of Business have helped in the evolution of our ideas. Jeff Collins would especially like to acknowledge Colonel Tom Bowie at the US Air Force Academy. We are also indebted to Pantelis Vlachos, who provided much crucial statistical consultation, Milu Ritivoi for his programming support, and Kerry Ishizaki for her interaction design consultation and the book design. Finally, we thank our families.

INTRODUCTION: WORDS AND THEIR POTENCY FOR PRIMING AUDIENCES

> Words, so innocent and powerless as they are, as standing in [the] dictionary, how potent for good and evil they become in the hands of one who knows how to combine them. —*Nathaniel Hawthorne*

Hawthorne's well-worn truism is notable not so much because it's true, but that, hundreds of years later, we still lack systematic accounts of all that lies behind its truth. In this book, we present original research that compiles and inventories some of the linkages between ordinary strings of English and their potency for priming audiences. We explore many unremarkable English strings that participate, alone and in combination, to guide audiences to construct remarkable micro-experience.

The path we journey in this book is challenging because a competent speaker or writer's knowledge of priming audience lies dormant as implicit knowledge, knowledge we can invoke only when prompted to do so. It also has remained ephemeral knowledge, knowledge with little documentation behind it. When we recognize the various ways words jumpstart audiences, it is usually only a momentary recognition, a recognition we quickly make and just as quickly toss aside as an idiosyncratic accident of language. Comedians with a ready eye and ear for language sometimes call up these accidents as a basis for humor. Great writers sometimes memorialize them when paying homage to the art of writing. Perhaps no author tried to externalize the internal wave and flow of writing than Mark Twain. In a letter dated October 15 1888, Twain mused on the writer's special feel for words to his correspondent, George Bainton. Bainton at the time was editing a self-help book for young writers, which was to be a compilation of solicited reflections on writing from noted authors of the day. In his epistle to Bainton (later published in Bainton's 1990 volume, pp. 85-88), Twain wrote an aphorism about writing that Bainton's volume helped make famous:

> The difference between the almost-right word and the right word is really a large matter — it's the difference between the lightning bug and the lightning.

This passage sheds useful light on the implicit knowledge of the writer to prime readers. It also sheds light on the large variation of reader experience that resides within the control of this hidden knowledge. Twain's observation illustrates in microcosm the focus of this book. In this volume, we address the wide variation in language experience controlled by our implicit know-how with words. Our theoretical approach is to conceptualize this know-how as a priming art speakers and writers tacitly rely on to direct audiences. Our methodological approach is to explore this priming art within a systematic inquiry, demonstrating how this primary art, far from random, can be classified across various hierarchical classes of priming experience that language affords.

We begin our investigation by comparing the knowledge of priming potencies with the knowledge compiled in standard dictionaries. As a lexicographer for the *Collins Cobuild Dictionary* (Sinclair, 1995), Channell (2000) hinted at the mountain of implicit knowledge about words and their priming effects she uncovered in the course of researching dictionary entries. As one example, she reported that the English verb phrase *set in* almost always primes the conveyance of a negative attitude (p. 41). One can say *hard times set in* but not (without irony) *good times set in.* Yet few dictionaries have a specific entry for *set in* and this particular priming effect.

Channell suggested that she became aware of the regularity of these curiosities only because she was involved in a "project (such as the compilation of a new dictionary), which involved looking in detail— and individually— at most of the lexis of current English (p. 41). In this book, we try to bring the dictionary writer's sense of words in combination to prime audiences into a new kind of catalog, a catalog that classifies seemingly unlike words and strings by their like priming potential on audiences. To understand the kind of catalog, consider that the word *headache* in English strongly primes a negative attitude. This suggests for a speaker or writer looking to prime a negative attitude, the verb phrase *set in* and the noun *headache* are compositional alternatives. From the standpoint of audience priming, they do a similar job and their association needs to be cataloged as such. This requires an understanding of priming families and their potential to interact in the construction of audience experience within small runs of language. This is the understanding we pursue in this book.

To make this discussion more concrete, let us examine some of the precise differences between knowledge about word meanings, as found in standard dictionaries, and the knowledge underlying a speaker or writer's know-how about priming an audience's experience through words and strings of English.

Take the English word *menace.* A dictionary will show that the word can function as a noun, verb, or adjective.

1. Jack was a menace to society. *(noun)*
2. He menaced her all the way home. *(transitive verb)*
3. He saw that Mary was watching him with a menacing look. *(adjective)*

The noun (string 1) classifies people and things that pose hazards. The verb (string 2) indicates threatening action. The adjective (string 3) suggests a threatening facial expression. The focus of the standard dictionary is to partition a word into a range of senses that explain the various usages of the word within sentences.

Now consider the word *menace* from within the writer's priming art. As a designer of audience experience, the experienced writer will notice the following composing options for menace:

A. Use *menace* to capture negative affect in the world brought to the audience's notice.
B. Use *menace* to make accusations about a person's character, or to report on such accusations.
C. Use *menace* to convey to the audience a world of threatening motions.
D. Use *menace* to capture physical descriptions that can cause an audience to feel or sense anger or intimidation swelling up in a character in the text.

Such priming knowledge allows the writer to elaborate the dictionary strings 1-3 into a range of audience experience:

4. Jack was a menace to society. *(accusation, person description, negative affect)*
5. He menaced her all the way home. *(motion, negative affect)*
6. He saw that Mary was watching him with a menacing look, eyes flaming. *(negative affect, visual description)*

The expert in the art of priming with *menace* knows that *menace* can blend with superlatives like best to build conceivably good-hearted characters with crusty exteriors:

7. He put on his best menacing look.

Example 7 illustrates why the writer's priming art, although involving the connotative meaning of single words (cf., Hart, 2000), delineates more than the properties of single word tone and connotation. The writer of this example, to be sure, had to exploit the denotation and connotation of *menacing*. Yet the writer had also to keep track that the overall experience conveyed in *his best menacing* look includes someone dissembling for fun, an understanding that far exceeds knowing the denotation or connotation of the single word *menace*.

Knowing menace from a dictionary allows the writer to differentiate discrete senses, filling in different sentence frames to differentiate the parts of speech and senses that follow from them. Knowing *menace* from the vantage of a priming art, by contrast, means knowing how to stretch the discrete dictionary senses into combinations that paint a continua of audience experiences — negative mood, accusation, threatening motion, intimidating physical description, crusty exterior, and so forth. The cumulative knowledge of A-D above serves a speaker or writer seeking to produce primings as experience builders.

Although a word's meaning is not the same as it priming potential, its meaning certainly supports and constrains that potential. Simply stated, a speaker or writer must control meaning as a prerequisite to controlling priming. One needs to know the meaning of *resistance* to understand the experience the war media report when they report *the troops met with resistance*. Meaning conditions priming. From the time of Austin (1962), who first distinguished utterance meaning from perlocution,* we have known that this truth does not entail that meaning is sufficient for priming, that what language primes audiences to think or do is *not* fully predictable from what it means. Note, for example, that mentioning *the troops met with resistance* makes resistance part of the meaning of the utterance but does not make the utterance come across as an act of resistance. Meaning is not sufficient for priming. Yet neither, as Austin (1962) and generations of speech act theorists following him understood, is it necessary. Many experiences can be primed through words whose conventional meaning does not intersect with the experience primed. Thus, for example, a string such as *I respectfully say in response* primes resistance to a previous utterance without any of its component parts carrying on the surface a resistant meaning.

In light of the complex interplay between meaning and priming, the dictionary remains a vital though contingent perch from which to peer out on the writer's priming art. As any experienced writer knows, there is a gulf between what a single word means and how a word contributes within a run of words to prime an audience. An expert at conventional Scrabble and Sunday crosswords, relying on dictionary knowledge of words and meanings, is not necessarily an expert at controlling words, in combination, to paint experience for audiences. Controlling words in combination involves knowing how to complete runs of words to pin down primary and blended experiences for audiences. We call this knowledge part of a phenomenological mental game we often experience when we write that we call *rhetorical scrabble*. The intuitive feel of this game was well expressed by bell hooks (2000), when she makes a reflection that would become a motivating epigraph for T.R. Johnson's (2003) *Rhetoric of Pleasure:*

> I am driven to write, compelled by a constant longing to choreograph, to bring words together in patterns and configurations that move the spirit. As a writer, I seek that moment of ecstasy when I am dancing with words…toward the infinite. (p. 3; cited in Johnson, p. 23)

---

* We assume for the moment that what we are calling primings overlap extensively with what Austin and other speech act theorists call perlocutions. This assumption is false in its details, as perlocutions in the speech act literature have never been operationally tied to contiguous strings, as we operationalize the units of priming. Still, what speech act theorists had to say about meaning/perlocution relationships remains fundamentally true for meaning/priming relationships, which is why the assumption helps us in the current discussion.

We offer rhetorical scrabble as a specific (and certainly not the only) metaphor to link hooks' insight to the choreography of words and the movement of a compliant* audience taking them in. More specifically, rhetorical scrabble involves running words together until a specific audience experience is pinned down. In conventional scrabble, one keeps laying down letters until legal words are completed. In rhetorical scrabble, the speaker or writer keeps laying down words until (in our coding judgment) a discernable experience for an audience schooled in the language is primed. Most single words of English and certainly the highest frequency function words (e.g., *the, an, with, for*) do not carry the intactness necessary to pin down a resolvable or unambiguous audience experience.

Just as conventional scrabble can keep open as options the completion of many different words, the speaker or writer's in-progress games of rhetorical scrabble can keep open many different audience experiences before one is actually pinned down. Laying a run of words down one path can pin down some audience experiences while continuing down an alternative path can pin down other experiences. For example, a speaker or writer beginning a sentence with the string *Mary hit it off,* primes a different audience experience when the phrasal verb *hit it off* is followed with the definite article *the* instead of the preposition *with.* Compare:

8. Mary hit it off the...
   (Mary in motion)
9. Mary hit it off with...
   (Mary and someone with positive feeling for each other)

In addition, a single English sentence can prime multiple audience experiences.

10. Mary hit it off with Bill and they walked hand in hand to the batting cage.
    (both positive feeling and motion)

Most of us probably recognize something resembling rhetorical scrabble as we relate the words we choose to the experience we create for audiences. We produce sentences in parts and we examine the parts for adequacy, where adequacy includes not only language correctness and appropriateness, but also the measured control of the audience's experience based on the priming potential of the words selected. Some of this general story about sentence composition reflects the findings of empirical research (Kaufer, Hayes, and Flower, 1986). However, in this book, we don't rely on rhetorical scrabble as a psychological reality whose

---

* Compliance is a mode of orientation to an incoming message rather than an act of passive acceptance towards it. In our view, close readers must first be compliant readers if they are to become skillfully resistant readers.

putative truth as cognitive theory makes or breaks our descriptive observations about language. Rather, in this book, we offer rhetorical scrabble as the heuristical construct we used to coordinate our descriptive observations relating language and audience experience.

As we read and listened to language to compile our catalog, we continually asked ourselves the following two questions: Given the strings the speaker or writer did produce, what are the continuations, at any point in the run, that the speaker or writer could have produced? How would have this alternative path changed, if at all, the audience experience primed? By mentally simulating games of rhetorical scrabble across utterances, texts, situations, and genres, we were able to compile an extensive catalog of priming categories that strings of English make available. The next section discusses more of the theoretical background of our undertaking.

I

Preliminaries

1

Priming Audience and Practices of Literacy

The implicit know-how of relating words and audiences is not an isolated skill. It is fundamental to reading and writing. In this chapter, we explain why literate skills of reading and writing include the hidden skill of using language to prime an audience's experience. We consider why an understanding of literacy as using language for audience priming is essential to non-question begging theories of close reading. We then turn to the significance of priming theory to writing education.

LANGUAGE PRIMING AND CLOSE READING

Focusing on the critic's perspective, the literary tradition has developed a concept of *close reading*. Close reading in this tradition involves what Lanham (1986) has called the know-how to look *at* a text. This skill of *looking at* language within reading is contrasted with conventional content reading, which, in Lanham's terms, involves looking *through* a text to its meaning. One can read a text for its plot, never stopping to look at its words and sentences. This is reading for understanding but not reading as a writer.

One begins to read as a writer when one looks beyond content to the author's choice making. Close reading relies on the oscillation between these two views, looking through language to its product—meaning—and looking at it to understand the workings of the instrument that provides the product. Close reading insists on never losing focus on the surface text, the actual words priming the reader, even as the reader interprets the words and transforms them into situated readings. In the literary tradition, the close reader, as normative model, can read as a writer, can spot the writer's magical tricks that allow readers to forget they are reading.

The Oxford critic I. A. Richards is widely credited for coining the term, using it synonymously with the term *practical criticism* in a book under that title first published in 1929 (I. A. Richards, 1950). Richards' idea of practical criticism is to urge readers to examine language not only as bearers of meaning but also as instruments that, in the hands of skilled authors, makes meaning possible.

Critics of the 1970s and 1980s either directly or indirectly attacked the idea of close reading by attacking the school of New Criticism, a literary tradition that prescribed that interpretations stay "within" the text. These critics alleged that such a narrow interpretative focus reduced interpretation to formal marks on the page. It was an error not unlike the error of mistaking a musical composition for the silent notation of a musical score. The critics Louise Rosenblatt (1978) and Wolfgang Iser (1978) argued for the existence of mediating entities between the formal text and reader interpretation, what Rosenblatt called a *transaction* between writer and reader and what Iser referred to as a *virtual* text mediating the surface text and the reader's understanding. Stanley Fish (1980) moved the balance between writer and reader closer to the reader's side of the equation. He contended that readers must bring their own cultural and historical background and, especially, the communities of interest to which they belong to the interpretation of a text. Fish contended that interpretations are made by individual readers, but even more by the institutionalized communities through which readers work and network.

Fish in many respects is surely right. His worries about overly narrow definitions of textual interpretation are justified. The reading experience is not limited solely to marks on the page. It always involves the reader and the communities of interest to which the reader belongs. Despite the many grains of truth in their position, Fish and his adherents have caused some small backlash of its own.

Recently, one prominent journal, *Research in the Teaching of English,* devoted an entire issue (August 2000) to the efficacy of so-called pure "textual" variables in learning to read and write. Michael W. Smith and Peter Smagorinsky, the editors of the journal, cited the need for the special issue as such:

> Twenty years ago, Stanley Fish (1980) asked what has become one of the most famous questions in the recent history of literary criticism: Is there a text in this class? His question resonated for us recently when James Robert Martin, one of our editorial board members, wrote us noting his unease with current literacy research in which, he said, "the text doesn't really matter" because of the author's focus on "the context, the social practices in which [the text] is embedded." (p. 5)

A recent critic of the idea that texts make an independent contribution to the reading experience is Mark Faust (2000), who rejected what he called the "dualism" between social experience and text in textual processing. Faust observed, "[R]eading is a process that produces different experiences with the same words at different times" (p. 21). The text and the social experience required to interpret it, according to Faust, cannot be pulled apart. Unfortunately, Faust explored no specific examples to argue his point, so let's provide one, and then study how well his point can be sustained:

11. There is late breaking news. *(written over the wire, December 7, 1941)*
12. There is late breaking news. *(read over radio, November 22, 1963)*
13. There is late breaking news. *(sent over the Internet, September 11, 2001)*

These examples focus precisely where Faust asks us to focus—the same words, different times, and undoubtedly different social experiences. But if we look closely, we know these experiences are different precisely because they accommodate a great deal of similarity in the textual experience that we can—contrary to Faust's thesis of indistinguishability between text and social experience—pull apart from the social experience of interpretation. Notice that each text in these examples relies on a lexical-grammatical string (e.g., *there is late breaking)* that primes audiences to perceive language being used to update them. Each textual string primes this update function and the social context of the update helps the reader complete the experience, and so the specific content, of the update. Faust is right to maintain that context and experience can guide language priming and channel these primings into specific reader interpretations Yet Faust is wrong to maintain that textual and social experiences are indistinguishable. Social context and experience can complete only what the small priming choices of textual experience help launch. We support Faust's point that textual interpretation requires words to be imbued with social experience. We disagree with his point that textual experience and social experience start from a non-identical source of origin.

We postulate interpretation as a logically, if not temporally, phased process, with early, upstream, and later, downstream, aspects. The part of the rhetorical art that concerns us most in this book is language experience as a priming art, an art of how words, in combination, initiate the audience's interpretation. An interpretative process won't end until the audience has had the chance to elaborate the words from the historical, cultural, and personal categories of experience they evoke. We call these elaborations downstream interpretation. An interpretative process won't get off the ground, however, without the speaker or writer's words jumpstarting the audience through initial primings, the primings serving as upstream input to the audience's fuller interpretation downstream.

We focus in this book entirely on the upstream, not the downstream, of interpretation. Although we don't pretend for a moment that close reading is fully captured in the upstream priming properties of words, we can't lose sight of the fact that close reading can't be adequately defined without including these initial primings as an indispensable part of the story.

5

In his own assessment of the difficulty of teaching close reading to undergraduates, McGann and his colleagues (2001) observed that students have great difficultly "negotiating" reading because of their "inclination to 'read' texts at relatively high levels of textual abstraction" with "a weakened ability to notice other close details of language — semantic, grammatical, rhetorical" (p. 147). McGann's point is that close reading requires noticing the language as well as interpreting it. Interpretation is a high art, visible and touted among critics. Noticing is a low craft, less visible and often hidden in theories of interpretation. Nonetheless, close reading requires the cooperation of the high art with the low craft. The close reader must build ties between the upstream of noticing language primings and the downstream of social elaboration. As a geologist builds bold theory from ordinary surface traces in the fossil record, the close reader understands that whatever mighty interpretations accrue downstream must at least "fit" the visible residues found upstream in the surface primings of language.

Close reading requires that deep comprehension be supported by surface-level primings. As B. R. Myers (2001) recently noted in his much-discussed "Reader's Manifesto," reviewers of contemporary fiction lose their credibility when they fail to tie their overall evaluations of texts to concrete prose passages. Consider strings 14 to 17, which reviewers have used to evaluate Michael Chabon's Pulitzer Prize-Winning novel, *The Amazing Adventures of Kavalier & Clay.*

14. It's absolutely gosh-wow, super-colossal — smart, funny.
    (*The Washington Post*)
15. A big, ripe, excitingly imaginative novel....echoes Ragtime...suggests John Irving. (*The New York Times*)
16. Some books you read for their plot, some for their style. When, like Chabon's, both are exceptional, you're in a rare place. (*USA Today*)
17. I'm not sure what the 'great American novel' is, but I'm pretty sure that Michael Chabon's sprawling, idiosyncratic, and wrenching new book is one. (*The New York Times Book Review*)

High praise indeed. Yet, according to Myers, it is also inflated praise if the reviewer, given the space, is not able to reproduce at least some choice examples of the prose effects Chabon musters to justify it. The "what" of close reading, Myers suggests, should include language visible on the page.

How does one learn close reading? How more specifically does one learn to integrate the surface noticing of language with the deep comprehension of language, guided by social context? This is a hard question to answer. Let us for the moment turn to Harvard for help. The Harvard Online Writing Center Website (2001) describes "close reading" as a "methodology that asks readers to pay close attention to a text in order to answer some question about that text."

The method seems clear enough. Yet, is it really? What does it mean to pay close attention to a text? A text is among the most complex information spaces that human civilizations have designed. What is the object of our attention when we pay attention? As it attempts to define close reading for students, the Harvard instructions beg the question of attention: "Pay attention to the text and you will discover the right things to pay attention to."

The question begging reveals itself almost this blatantly in the language the Harvard Online Writing Center Website uses to teach the method of close reading:

> What words or phrases in these passages do you think are important? Underline, highlight, or take notes so that you can locate these passages easily....Now examine these words and phrases closely. What strings emerge?

The Writing Center advises the student to survey where in the text it is fruitful to look and then to select one's specific focus. Unfortunately, the advice begs the question of attention, because students must bring a theory of noticing to the text to assure that their noticing will be well placed and rewarded. The Harvard Writing Center advice identifies skills of textual noticing equivocally: Knowing where to look is both a prerequisite and an outcome of learning to read closely. The advice unintentionally offers very little assurance: one can learn to read closely only if one already knows how.

Let's assume for the moment one can learn surface patterns of close reading through the experience of reading itself. As readers, we challenge ourselves when we constantly look at the small actions authors take and ask ourselves — why did the author take that action and not some alternative? As writers, we constantly find ourselves thrown into this challenge whether we like it or not. For as writers, we must make meaning and expose ourselves to all kinds of sentence possibilities that don't work very well before we find the ones that do. We write draft after draft, often understanding after reading a new draft that we have failed to give our readers the experience we are after. By serving as our own readers of our own drafts, we can often push ourselves to write something that we can agree is worth others reading too.

These observations reflect current conventional wisdom. Yet they leave unspecified what readers must actually do to acquire the skill to notice patterns of surface language associated with close reading. We suggest that readers probably pick up these patterns by playing some equivalent of a mental game we call rhetorical scrabble. We hasten to say "some equivalent" because we don't claim the details of rhetorical scrabble that go on in the head resemble the details as we describe them. What interests us about the game is not the assumption of its psychological reality but the assumption that it captures some of the felt experience of the speaker or writer seeking to combine words to prime the audience experience. As such, it has served us as a useful heuristic for collecting and categorizing English strings for their value as priming instruments.

In conventional Scrabble, one has some combination of the 26 letters of the alphabet. One takes turns with an opponent to use letters to make words. On every move, one's word-making is constrained by the letters all the players have placed on the board in previous turns. If one brings a reading knowledge of, say, 50,000 documented words of English, one must, on every move, search for which of the letters in one's hand completes one of the words in the documented set.

In rhetorical scrabble, one's target is not words but strings of words and their ability to prime categories of audience experience. Depending on the length of the text, writers play rhetorical scrabble across tens, hundreds, and thousands of sentences. The speaker or writer's genre and rhetorical plans affect the audience experience one wants to seed across a planned communication. Language users play rhetorical scrabble at the interface of a longer planning horizon for a message and the very immediate strings to be placed now before the audience's ears or eyes. Writers, working with an audience who is not physically present, usually play the game against themselves across drafts, seeing if they can create visible language that remains true to their plans and writing context and that adequately pins down the overall text experience they wish to afford readers.

Let us look specifically at how one plays the game. The game starts whenever the speaker or writer is at the point of composing contiguous language while considering longer-range communicative plans. When the game starts, the speaker or writer has a variety of different ideas about a communication's general effects on the reader and wants to figure how the next string of words can further those effects.

Let's assume a writer is working on a cover letter for a job application and wants to create a positive impression. Let's assume a prior text part where the writer has recently informed the reader that she is active as a community volunteer and now wants to describe her reason for volunteering. Let's say the writer has decided to implement this reason in a sentence beginning: "I wanted to make…" The internal board of the writer's rhetorical scrabble game may now look as follows:

Initial board: *I wanted to make…*

Rhetorical scrabble requires pinning down some words in order to reduce the search for the words to come. There are a very large number of arbitrary words following other arbitrary words. The writer's choice becomes usefully constrained when searching from a known word or string (e.g., I wanted to make….). There is of course no guarantee that the writer will have chosen the best opening sentence frame as a constraint. Research in revision suggests that inexperienced writers have a very difficult time giving up on their opening run, even when encouraged to make global revisions over all their sentences (Faigley and Witte, 1981; Flower, Hayes, Carey, Schriver, and Stratman, 1986). We suspect that novice writers often cling too long to unproductive sentence frames because their play at rhetorical scrabble is limited.

Let us now describe the writer's first response to the initial playing board. It will be to explore multiple alternative paths from "I wanted to make...." Imagine the writer creates a decision space that contains the following possible paths:

18. I wanted to make... myself *(reflexive path)*
19. I wanted to make... my *(possessive path)*
20. I wanted to make... a *(article path)*
21. I wanted to make... it *(situational-it path)*
22. I wanted to make... over *(make-over as extended verb path)*
23. I wanted to make... up *(make-up as extended verb path)*

Each pathway opens up a set of new options, each option opening up a new space of rhetorical primings the writer intends for the reader. In rhetorical scrabble, the writer explores pathways with the idea of understanding what priming actions will be strengthened, inhibited, layered, or separated, by choice of pathway. Writers must match these different pathways to their overall rhetorical goals.

For example, the initial board already features first person (I) and personal desire (want). Pathway 18 strengthens the tone of personal involvement and self-determination. A deeper search through this pathway reveals the options and primings more clearly:

24. make myself the *(best I can be? trite, do I want to join the army?)*
25. make myself a laughingstock *(not working)*
26. make myself at home *(not working)*
27. make myself conspicuous *(for public service? seems inappropriate)*
28. make myself heard *(sounds defiant)*
29. make myself interesting *(aren't I already?)*

This deeper exploration helps the writer see that choosing any path leading with *myself* will strengthen the impression of individual desire and self-determination. This might be fine in some writing contexts, but in this context, the writer is trying to make a case for her interest in humble public service. The *myself* continuations create rhetorical primings that are too ego-centered and self-absorbed, undermining the sense of self-effacement that the writer understands the larger context calls for.

Let us now fast forward and assume the writer is much deeper in the game and has decided that pathway 21 looks the most promising space for solutions. The situational *it* continuation inhibits some of the unwanted meanings the writer wants to dampen, as it turns the focus off the writer herself (unlike the reflexive and possessive continuations of 18 and 19) and on some situation detached from her personal ego. Assume then that the writer accepts this pathway and now explores her set of continuations from there. A deeper exploration of pathways from 21 reveals more moves to take:

30. make it the *(calls for a detached situation not yet composed)*
31. make it my business to *(personalization and possible defiance)*
32. make it a practice of *(calls for an abstraction not yet composed)*
33. make it a practice to *(calls for recurring goal not yet composed)*

Rhetorical scrabble is fraught with contingency, a contingency seldom acknowledged in traditional language references. Novice writers have difficulty experiencing this contingency as anything but frustration. Novices come easily to words but they come less easily to them as part of a rhetorical art. As a result, they tend to have a hard time seeing words as thrilling instruments that are always reaching beyond themselves — not infrequently beyond the intentions they are able to form to play the instrument as well as it can be played — into the reader's world of afforded experience. It is hard to develop a love of contingency if contingency itself is dismissed as a mistake of inexperience that good writers outgrow.

The truth seems more that experience teaches writers how to accept more contingency, taking larger risks, while managing it more effectively. Every move of rhetorical scrabble can close off paths for writers and open new ones. They often do both. With experience, writers learn the value of continuing to learn larger challenges and higher risks and rewards than they knew when they began. For example, in the previous example, the inexperienced writer may extend the sentence with string 33. The temptation of this continuation is that it is, arguably, easier to compose a goal that is true to one's experience (e.g., *I make it a practice to volunteer as a tutor each year*) than a principle (e.g., *I make it a practice of...*) that would leave the writer with new and unanticipated ideas to work out. However, with experience, the writer might take the harder path, knowing that taking the additional time to work out a personal principle about how volunteerism adds benefits that can outlast the writing task and transfer to other tasks of self-representation as well.

PRIMING WORDS VS. INTERPRETING THEM DOWNSTREAM

It is fashionable among cultural critics to resist looking at isolated words or strings of words because they are not, it is alleged, as rich as context, culture, and history to support interpretation. This of course is true. This truth is often used however to smuggle an unstated nonsequitor, which is to assume that the surface language used to prime audiences somehow competes with, rather than works alongside, contextual, historical, and ideological frames of interpretation. The fact of the matter is that surface primings routinely collaborate, rather than compete with, deep interpretation. The one initiates the interpretation process; the other helps bring to it some settled state of closure.

Although these inputs collaborate in interpretative processes, they are distinct and can be separated. There is, furthermore, value to their distinctiveness as a production strategy. Writers are able to generate words on the page quickly by focusing on the priming potency they are after. Getting words out in the air or on the page would be a slower and less efficient process if we had to interpret and evaluate the fine shadings of our words before words came out. Let's illustrate this subtle point through an interactive demonstration you, dear reader, can test on yourself.

Without peeking ahead, write five sentences that use the English preposition *for*. No informant we've asked has any trouble doing this. Now ask yourself how you use the word *for* in your repertoire as a writer. It's hard to imagine how a language user could fail to answer this question, as this is one of the most common words of English. The same writers who have no problem using *for* in their own practice have a very hard time explaining what they know. To explain what they know, they become readers and interpreters of the sentences they have written. Often this strategy doesn't work as well as they had thought because our reading knowledge of *for* and all the slivers of meaning to which it contributes are not systematically available to our conscious awareness.

If one consults an unabridged dictionary, like Webster's 2nd unabridged (1948, p. 984), one finds eleven meanings, involving senses such as; in consideration of which something is done or takes place (does it *for* John); indicates substitutes or compensations (eye *for* an eye); an extended subject, as in *(for* me to come is impossible); the cause motive or occasion of an act (did it *for* money); information that can be overridden *(for* all her flaws, she has a good heart); proportion *(for* one winner, there are a thousand losers); specification (he is tall *for* his age); and duration in time and space *(for* many years, *for* many miles).

If one consults the Collins CoBuild Dictionary (Sinclair, 1995; pp. 658-660, hereafter CCD), a dictionary based on concordance data from the 200 million-word Bank of English corpus, one finds 35 senses of the word *for,* listed here, with examples we have adapted for brevity.

[1] This gift is FOR Bill (FOR = beneficiary)
[2] I do work FOR Bill (FOR = employer)
[3] I speak FOR Bill (FOR = representation)
[4] I made the pick up FOR Bill (FOR = substitution)
[5] I feel FOR Bill (FOR = object of empathy)
[6] I feel contempt FOR Bill (FOR = object of affect)
[7] I make time FOR Bill (FOR = center of interest served)
[8] Bill is FOR hire (FOR = services available)
[9] Bill's knife is good FOR opening cans (FOR = purpose)
[10] Bill needed a job, FOR he was recently fired (FOR = reason)
[11] Bill needed a job FOR lack of work (FOR = reason)
[12] Bill couldn't walk FOR legs that failed him (FOR = cause)

[13] Were it not FOR Bill, we would have frozen (FOR = avoided contingency)

[14] Bill was married FOR 30 years (FOR = time duration)

[15] Bill drove FOR 30 miles (FOR = spatial extent)

[16] Bill got it FOR a dollar (FOR = rate of exchange)

[17] Bill planned it FOR Saturday (FOR = time shift to target of occurrence)

[18] Bill partied FOR his birthday (FOR = target occasion)

[19] Bill left FOR St. Louis (FOR = destination)

[20] The goal FOR Bill here is to make money (FOR = stakeholder/stakes)

[21] It is possible FOR Bill to come (FOR = introduce subject of infinitive)

[22] Bill was tall FOR his age (FOR = against expectations)

[23] Bill is FOR lower taxes (FOR = positive affiliation)

[24] Higher taxes were not FOR Bill (FOR = negative affiliation)

[25] It's FOR Bill to decide (FOR = responsibility)

[26] Bill is FOR bussing (FOR = agreement)

[27] Bill argued FOR bussing (FOR = support)

[28] Bill prepared himself FOR the cold (FOR = restricting the verb)

[29] For every winner there are two losers (FOR = ratio comparison)

[30] Pound FOR pound, Bill is the best (FOR = comparison across ranks)

[31] Agricola is Latin FOR farmer (FOR = definitional substitution)

[32] For more information, see the website (FOR = cross reference)

[33] Bill was all FOR it (FOR = strong endorsement)

[34] Bill was in FOR it (FOR = in trouble, facing punishment)

[35] Bill was visiting FOR the first time (FOR = how often)

If one placed each of these meanings in even richer contexts, say the social and historical contexts of particular audiences and readings, the meanings of *for* could proliferate further. In a recent political campaign, a candidate was attacked for lying when he said he was *for* a minimum wage. This is because he had once voted against a minimum wage when other factors had made the legislation undesirable. He responded to the attack by claiming that he was for a minimum wage, but to be understood as noncontradictory, he had to rely on voters coming up with a thirty-sixth construal of *for,* to mean supportive of as a general policy, all things equal.

Meanings and shadings proliferate as interpretative processes move upstream from the priming of words to the downstream of interpretive completion. As soon as our informants recognize the discrepancy between their "off the top of the head" knowledge of *for* and the dictionary's copious coverage of it, we ask them if the dictionary definitions help them understand the difficulty of defining the word. They always respond affirmatively. It is hard to articulate how *for* contributes to meaning because it covers such a vast territory of meaning across contexts. When we then ask informants if they feel they need to rely on the dictionary to use the word in sentences, they invariably say no.

Although not laboratory controlled, we take this informal demonstration experiment as at least suggestive that producers of the language don't need to wait on the fine discrimination of completed meaning downstream to feel a facile control of the production process upstream. They can control much of the language simply by controlling the major categories through which the language behaves as a priming instrument, an instrument that jumpstarts audiences in the right direction. To be sure, writers after precision must role-shift to the vantage of downstream reader during revision. The point is that this is a deliberate role-shift and writers don't need to see how their words play all the way downstream in order to get their audiences primed upstream.

Primings seem to depend on shallow representations that turn into much richer, more complex delineations when the writer assumes the role of downstream reader. Recent research in written production (Galbraith & Torrance, 1999) suggests that the writer's production can be influenced by meanings created downstream as the writer toggles back and forth between the writer and reader role. This toggling of roles permits the writer to respond not only to a surface priming interest but also to the interpretatively weighted outputs that flow downstream from the priming surface. It is not unlike the painter who can, in one moment, look down at the palette and see only a few basic colors to mix and, in the next moment, can look at the canvas and see hundreds of blended colors and shades. In the role of reviser-editor looking at a text and its downstream effects, we see endless shadings and slivers of meaning. In the role of the writer bringing ideas copiously and quickly to the page, we seem able to rely on a simpler palette of priming properties, relying on a restricted number of primary categories that alone and in combination are enough to jumpstart audiences in the right direction.

Accordingly, when we look to enumerate the meanings of the word *for* from the vantage of categories within the priming properties, we seem to experience a shallower and coarser-grained phenomenon than the one we encountered when sorting through the fine slices of meanings compiled from a concordance dictionary.

Having examined the copious breakdown of *for* as it flows downstream to slice fine grains of meaning and shading, let us now reconsider *for* from the vantage of a lightweight priming word. As a word priming audience experience, *for* seems to prime two key experiences for audiences — a goal of projecting ahead to the future and a positive affect that indicates a beneficiary of the projection. Thus, the priming rule regarding *for* might be something like: When a word or phrase X blends both the concepts of projecting ahead and positive affect, one can say *for* X.

This rule explains the priming in a sentence like:

34. This gift is for Bill
    (Bill as part of future projection; positive affect; caused by gift)

Many other usages with *for* differ in surface input through what Facconnier and Turner (2002) call *metonymic tightening* (see also Coulson and Oakley, 2000). Metonymic tightening means that when metonyms (words that stand for other words—Washington as a metonym for the federal government) are projected as part of a blended effect, there is pressure to tighten them within a syntactic series. For example, employees may not consciously think of their service as a direct benefit to their bosses, but the metonymic tightening in the following example suggests that English has come to tighten the verb *work* + *preposition for* (often in the sense of *on behalf of*) into a metonymic shortening of the complex employment contract.

35. I work for Bill.
    (Bill = metonymic shortening of the institution whose well-being and future is the speaker's responsibility)

While *for* can mean (in the listing of a dictionary entry) substitution, a writer can effectively prime this meaning merely by reporting an action and the person benefitting.

36. I made the pickup for Bill
    (The idea of "substitution" seems a later inference that is not part of the priming. The priming only seems to indicate that I did something and Bill benefitted from it. The inference of substitution comes into play when it is assumed that Bill could have made the pickup too—so the nature of my beneficence was to substitute my labor for his.)

Although concordance-based dictionaries, as we have seen, can list over 30 meanings of *for*, writers can jumpstart most, if not all, these senses just by controlling a handful of audience experiences that *for* primes and then leaving it to the readers' inference to fill in the remaining detail. In addition to its effects on future projection and positive affect, *for* also primes at most six other categories of audience experience—specification comparison, resistance, reason, temporal interval, and spatial interval. Consider the following:

37. He prepared for finals.
    (for as future projection and specification)
38. He is the best, pound for pound.
    (for as comparison across ranks)
39. For all his bad habits, I still like him.)
    (for as resistance to a counter-assertion)
40. I wanted to see her, for I miss her.
    (for signals the reason I want to see her)
41. He stayed imprisoned for five years.
    (for signals temporal interval)

42. She walked for ten miles.
(for signals spatial interval)

We found that English *for* relies on eight priming categories to jumpstart over 30 specific dictionary shades and meanings. We then asked ourselves, if one can find priming categories for English *for,* how many priming categories can one ultimately find if we tried to explore and catalog other English words and strings for their priming properties.

This was the daunting question we posed for ourselves when we embarked on a journey to understand how ordinary strings of English prime unordinary experience for audiences. We recognized that tracking function words like *for* would set us on a good path, for these are the most frequent and versatile words of English, with ubiquitous recurrence as playing pieces in rhetorical scrabble. If the priming categories we located across English strings could cover the range of major function words, we reasoned we would be on good grounds to think that our catalog of priming categories would clear a major hurdle for arguing some form of comprehensiveness if not completeness for our project.

Just as we have done with the word *for,* we let the reader witness in later chapters how the extremely versatile adverb *just* makes its way through our catalog of string categories of priming experiences. As competent language users, we have an implicit art with *just* that gives audiences a spectrum of jumpstarts for many varied interpretative paths downstream. We master the use of *just,* arguably, not because we study its dictionary meanings (most English language users surely have never looked it up) but because, like *for,* we corner the word within a small set of priming categories and control the word, implicitly, when we learn to control the categories to which *just* contributes as a priming action. The CCD (Sinclair, 1995), enumerates more than 20 concordance-derived senses of this nimble adverb. Our classification of priming categories presented later in this book captures most of the concordance senses of English *just* without—and this is significant—our ever having to isolate *just* as a stand-alone dictionary entry.*
Although we don't have direct evidence for this claim, it is tempting to speculate that to learn function words is simply to learn categories of priming rather than discrete meanings. We could then explain the versatility of such words for language production by explaining that such words, embedded in different strings, contribute, albeit barely visibly, to a much wider variety of priming experiences than so-called "content" words, the latter involving words more specialized in their meaning but less versatile as instruments of audience priming.

---

* All 20+ senses of *just* appear on pp. # 909–910 of the CCD.

LANGUAGE PRIMING AND LEARNING TO WRITE

Whatever the precise psychological details underlying our play at rhetorical scrabble, we can always ask what it would take to play it better. Our answer: Take the mental game out of the black box of private experience and turn it into a public art. We believe priming theory holds great promise for the way we think about teaching formal and planned public speaking and writing.

However this promise will never be realized if we can't find a way to make the priming aspects of language a more visible and public part of education. To appreciate the costs of invisibility, imagine what it would be like to play conventional scrabble were there no dictionaries to catalog the concept of "a legal word of English." No player would know exactly where a word started or stopped and so how to keep score. Yet we have no formal references that focus on the priming properties of language and how strings of English initiate priming experiences for audiences. One important goal of the catalog we present later in this book is to present work that points toward such a reference.

Let us now consider how language education might directly benefit from the kind of priming theory we seek to develop here. Thus far, no language references have been written to support play at rhetorical scrabble. We have no catalogs linking English strings to categories of audience priming and no systematic categorizations of priming categories that English makes available. These gaps leave rhetorical scrabble a more ill defined game than it need be for many experienced as well as novice writers. Imagine education in public speaking or writing focused on teaching students to craft priming experiences. Before students composed a single sentence for any speech or writing assignment, teachers and students could carry out extended discussions about the audience experiences they should be creating through their language choice.

To cite our own teaching practice as an example, consider the questions that we regularly ask our students as a way of trying to develop their forethought about a text as an artifact needing to prime various experiences for audiences. These questions, conveniently, preview the major categories of our catalog described later in this book.

Questions About the Need to Prime Audiences From an Internal Perspective:

To what extent will your reader need to experience your mind at work and to what extent do you need to show a subjective side? Do you need to let your feelings show? If so, will you need to reveal positive feelings, negative feelings, or both? To what extent will you need to keep thinking in the present and to what extent do you require the reader to follow your thoughts into the future or past?

Questions About the Need to Prime Audiences From a Relational Perspective

What ties will you establish with your readers? Will you keep your readers observers looking in on you without your acknowledging their presence? Or will you want to acknowledge that you have readers? If you acknowledge your readers, will you address them in second person *(you)* or will you let your reader stay a generalized other *(one, the reader)*? Will your acknowledged reader remain an observer or a participant with whom you interact? If an interaction partner, what kind of partner will your readers be and what kind of interaction are you seeking with them? Is your reader a weaker partner, there only to absorb what you know and she doesn't? If so, what expertise will you claim as your hook and leverage for writing? Is your reader a stronger partner, someone whom you must persuade? What appeals to get your reader to listen will you count on? Is the reader a more equal partner whom you want to reason with and ask for a decision or conclusion? If your reader is an equal partner in reasoning, what are the shared premises you need to build on? What generalizations and support will you use to keep him with you? Is your reader there to share an activity with you, to take instruction, follow procedures, or fill out forms? If so, what strategies will you use to support the activity?

Where do you imagine you'll need to enter the text to help your reader understand or follow you? Will you ever need to take the reader by the collar and address her directly? Do you have information to report that you require the reader to read and remember? What is that information and how will you report it? How will you keep your reader from getting lost? Purpose statement up front? Points numbered? Reported events sequenced?

Questions About the Need to Prime Audiences From an External Perspective

To what extent are your purposes served by immersing your readers in specifically detailed situations? Do you need to tell an extended narrative from the past? Will you need to slow your narrative in order to open up scenes? Will you need to cover a vast range of time or are you better served keeping your temporal range confined? What scale of compression will you go for? Are you covering minutes in pages or centuries in sentences? Will you need to open up scenes outside a narrative in order to illustrate a point? How much scene do you need to cover and how many scenes will you need?

Student writers can profit, we submit, when they learn that planned language and texts afford this range of forethought about audience experience. They further profit, we submit, when they are given a chance to respond to these questions, and to keep responding to them throughout the composing process. Through answering these questions, students can learn how their small language choices contribute

17

to the overall reader experience. Yet, our students would find these questions daunting were we not able to show them how ordinary words and strings (i.e., the language they know and, for the most part, control) structure the reader's experience from internal, relational, and external perspectives.

We have yet to evaluate our curriculum for widespread use, and we have not focused this book on education or sought to develop a refined educational model based on priming theory. We have rather used our educational experience as an example of our theory rather than a validated solution in its own right.

Most writing teachers, it seems fair to say, desire to have their students bring language awareness and forethought to their design of text. However, it doesn't happen when students have no scaffold with which to link the words and phrases they know with concepts and combinations of rhetorical action. For education, our long-term research goal is to locate a categorization of language that can serve as a scaffold for students who need to reshape their view of language from static meaning to the contingency of rhetorical action with words. Rhetorical scrabble and its internal workings have remained trade secrets in the mental life of our best writers, and this fact has made it hard to communicate to aspiring writers even the possibility — never mind the achievement — of using the words we freely share to develop what has remained a more elite skill than it need or should be.

2

Cataloging English Strings for Their Priming Potencies: A Report of a Research Study

In the remaining chapters of Part I, we detail a research study we undertook to prepare a catalog of English strings as priming instruments. We describe the properties we looked for when selecting strings for our catalog. We describe our method of categorizing strings, including the assistance of computer-supported coding. This has allowed us to catalog over 500 million unique English strings across a range of audience experience categories. We also describe the tensions we felt between viewing our catalog as a closed coding scheme and as an organic social system, with defined social conventions in the classroom that allowed students to confer over and recommend changes to the catalog, with their recommendations often binding on our changing the catalog.

PROPERTIES OF STRINGS SELECTED: WHAT WE CAN LEARN ABOUT AUDIENCE PRIMING FROM OUR STUDY

Let's consider some of the major properties of English strings we looked for when considering candidates for our catalog.

Contiguous, Reusable, and Functionally Unambiguous

The stings for our catalog had to be single words or a string of contiguous words. The string had to be long enough to complete a stable or functionally unambiguous priming experience for an audience. Many single words fit this description and many do not. High-frequency function words (e.g., *just, for, to, of, and*) are too ambiguous to contribute a univocal priming experience. We first focused our attention on strings more than single words to accommodate the inherently phrasal and textual character of language. Many single words eventually entered our catalog, but only after considering functions that were expressible in longer runs. After determining what seemed stable functions in multi-word runs, we systematically went through automatically generated word lists* of the 50,000 most frequent words of English. We found that, depending on the starting letter, a large percentage (from 10 to 30%) of single words are too ambiguous to carry univocal or distinctive functions on behalf of audience experience. Although the dominant organization of dictionaries and thesauri is the single word entry, the most important lesson of our exercise running through single-word dictionaries is that speaker and writers ply a rhetorical craft that relies on functions often spanning multiple word runs. This finding comports with the substantial independent evidence that writers do not compose one word at a time but compose in larger strings (Wray & Perkins, 2000). Altenberg (1990) estimated that up to 70% of our language performance in speaking or writing derives from formulaic strings rather than single words. This may seem a deflating observation for writing teachers who seek to inspire creativity by warning students to avoid "cut-and-paste" clichés of language in favor of original thought. When the formulas are truly clichés and idioms (e.g., *let the cat out of the bag, spill the beans*), that is, frozen from variability, the teachers' warning is not bad advice. However, although all frozen formulas and clichés are linguistic strings, the strings in English we describe in this book are seldom clichés or idioms in the narrow sense and accept wide variation. Moreover, in light of the mathematics of combination, a writer who learns strings to prime the audience experience has learned a much larger space for creative choice than the writer who knows all the single-word entries in the largest English dictionary but does not know how to combine these entries to prime for audience experience. Consequently, a thorough understanding of English strings and their effects on readers is invaluable for supporting one's own exploration, experimentation, and creativity with language.

Although low-frequency content words can pin down relatively stable textual experiences and priming actions, many single words of English are extremely unstable with respect to priming action. The priming ambiguity is often accompanied by a part-of-speech ambiguity, as many words can function as either nouns or verbs. Take the word *state* as in:

43. State of mind *(mood)*
44. They need to state their case *(part of verb phrase)*
45. State of Missouri *(place)*

---

* These word-lists are commercially available from many vendors, with different vendors carrying out their own in-house research on frequencies from corpus data. The word lists we used are available from WinterTree Software Inc.

46. He was in quite a state *(negative reference)*
47. State of euphoria *(positive reference)*
48. Head of State *(official title)*

The priming effect of *state* on a reader, as many single words of English, is widely variable. Although the word *state* has relatively frequent usage across English, it lacks the intactness or stability of priming action we required for our catalog.

Coupled with the constraint of functional unambiguity is the constraint of reusability or robustness. Ambiguity is a chronic problem of strings that are too short. The failure to be reusable or robust is the chronic problem of strings that are too long. Strings that exceed two or three words can fail to recur across texts. Just as we had to reject many single-word entries from our catalog study, we also had to reject long strings that were extremely stable but nonrecurring. A good example is a string we found in an e-mail warning from the maintainer of a campus online registration system:

49. Any efforts to clog the system at unauthorized times will result in the suspension of privileges.

Taken as a single speech act, this string is unambiguous as a warning or threat. That is to say, one will likely never come across this identical string as anything but a warning or threat. That's the good news. The bad news is that one is not likely ever to see this string in another text — period! The string is simply too rare to be repeated. The linguist Noam Chomsky (1957) discouraged the statistical study of language when he noted that the chances of hearing the exact same grammatical sentence (e.g., "colorless ideas sleep furiously") are next to zero. Chomsky overlooked the frequent recurrence of smaller 1 to 5 word English strings across English texts, which we have relied upon in our own research. However, his basic insight, namely that complete sentences seldom repeat verbatim across the language, is accurate. Sentence-length strings that are stable in terms of audience priming are typically nonrepeating and so nonrobust. Long strings enter the realm of authorial style and can leave behind altogether the reusable fund of language from which all speakers and writers are free to draw.

Understanding the limitations of English strings that are either too short or too long allowed us also to appreciate the significant gap between ordinary linguistic reuse and borrowing (which is common and necessary among writers) and plagiarism (which is frowned on as a crime of the writer). Linguistic borrowing is a requirement for learning how to be an original writer. Plagiarism is not. We are hardly the first to point out this mistake. As a line of scholars (Ede & Lunsford, 1990; Howard, 1999; Woodmansee, 1996; see also the collections of Buranen & Roy, 1999; Woodmansee & Jaszi, 1994) interested in rethinking authorship and intellectual property have observed, the idea of the "original" writer, untouched by linguistic reuse and borrowings, is a romantic myth. The appeal of the myth is to exaggerate the writer's "genius" by concealing the extensive role borrowing plays even in texts judged most original. All writers learn their trade by borrowing, extensively and implicitly, from the strings of others. Although one cannot minimize plagiarism as a crime, our culture at times seems, unreasonably, to extend the charge of plagiarism to any borrowing at all. Howard (1999) in particular noted the wide confusion between imitating the prose-one has read (what she called "patchwriting") with the charge of academic dishonesty. The sad and ironic result, according to Howard, is that we criminalize the very behavior that students must practice to learn to be authors.

Our research provided some insight into why we have a hard time appreciating the dependence of so-called "original" writing on the borrowing of precomposed strings. It is very hard for the human eye to see these borrowings, especially when they occur in short (2 to 5 word) runs. We learn to read for meaning, which often requires our rehearsing abstracted gists (e.g., "What is the author telling me?") that we accumulate over sentences and paragraphs. Unless we are engaged in close reading of the language, we do not stop to take in all the stings that prime the meaning to which we finally arrive. We see the edifice of meaning, in other words, without also seeing the borrowed expression that holds it up. We focus on the art of the writer, reluctant to think that such an original art could possibly rely on so many borrowed parts.

Can Cross Regular Syntactic Boundaries

English strings in our catalog can encode but also cross regular syntactic boundaries. They can but need not overlap with regular syntactical units, such as noun phrase, verb phrase, adverbial phrase, and so on. For us, the string, *felt self-important enough to* signals negativity even though it is not a well-formed grammatical unit. Priming units, in sum, need not be regular grammatical units. Candidacy as a priming element in our catalog of strings applied only to the string's rhetorical potency. It was not conditioned by the requirement that it be a well-formed constituent of grammar.

We thus relied on no explicit syntax or semantic theory to code English strings. Rather than assume that words or strings of words are "inserted" into pre-existing syntax, we follow Jackendoff (1999) in thinking of the lexicon as providing an interface between syntactic, conceptual, and experiential structures. During play at rhetorical scrabble, we hypothesize that writers do not experience syntax, semantics, and experiences as separate layers. They rather experience the interface of all these layers in relation to how the interface is working (or not working, as the case may be) to jumpstart an audience down desired pathways.

When words are seen as experiences for readers, the flexibility and expressive variety sought by the writer becomes a higher priority than preserving the regularity and parsimony sought by the linguist. Linguists refer to word stems and morphological endings deriving from a common stem as *lemmas*. The stem *take,* along with the words *takes, taking, took,* and *taken* constitutes a single lemma. For the lexicographer seeking to systematize the storage of words, lemmas are elegant constructions for thinking how words are stored. For the speaker or writer seeking to prime experiences for audiences, lemmas mask crucial representational information. A writer selecting the word *took,* for example, is able to continue a narrative structure. Selecting the word *taking* can continue an ongoing action or a motion. The present tense *take* and *takes* are good for present reportage (e.g., *John takes his hat and leaves)*. The same stems, with different endings, are not interchangeable from the point of view of audience priming. Word morphology, in other words, is not representation neutral but makes a large difference to what a speaker or writer can accomplish by way of priming. The differential effects of word morphology become even more pronounced when morphological suffixes change in the context of strings. The string *is subject to* indicates a contingency that tends toward the negative. However, when an — *ed* suffix is added, the string primes negative experience, shorn of contingency. Compare the following strings:

50. Jack is subject to colds.
    (contingency about negative happenings)
51. Jack is (all the time) subjected to colds.
    (negative happenings shorn of contingency)

Based on this evidence about the sensitivity of priming to morphological variation within words, we found we had to create strings at the grain size of literal words and stems and not generalized lemmas.

Despite the indifference of our strings to well-defined grammatical constituents, our interest in adjacency relations can and does overlap with relations that are well defined in the literature of corpus linguistics — namely, colligation, coherence collation, neighborhood collation, and semantic prosody. Colligation indicates syntactic as well as semantic dependence (e.g., *depend + on)*. Coherence collocation indicates an associative relation (e.g., *stamp + envelops)*. Neighborhood collocation indicates an empirical co-occurrence relation between words (e.g., *stamp + on the notarized letter)*. Semantic prosody indicates sequential tendencies within strings based on prior frequency expectations in the language (e.g., the word "cause" anticipates a negative more than a positive effect). (See Scott, 1998 for an operational understanding of these distinctions.)

Strings in our catalog can involve colligation, collocation, and semantic prosody relationships. They are not restricted to any one such relationship. The overriding concern for us was how the string primes the audience's experience, not the mechanism by which it came to hold together as a multiple word unit.

Context-Sensitivity

Context-sensitivity means that the experiences primed by an English string can shift as small strings move in and out of larger ones. Consider the following strings 52 and 53:

52. John should go to the store.
    (high insistence)
53. John is going to the store.
    (descriptive; no insistence)

In string 52, the writer seems to care that John go to the store. The telling cue is the word *should*, which in this string signifies the feeling of obligation or insistence that John run his errand. This string contrasts with 53, where the string *is going* expresses a more descriptive, less evaluative stance, with respect to John's errand. Were one to generalize, one might say from this contrast that English *should* indicates obligation and insistence and the English *auxiliary verb + going* indicates a narrower interest in description with no normative interest in obligation or insistence.

How far would these two generalizations take us? Not far at all, one will soon understand, once one starts playing rhetorical scrabble. Consider the same *should* and *auxiliary verb + going* expressions within different English strings:

54. I should be taking Jack to jail.
    (low insistence; written to mean that Jack won't be taken to jail)
55. I am going to take Jack to jail.
    (high insistence; written to mean that Jack will surely be taken to jail)

Our generalizations turn on their head. Contrary to our initial generalization, the *first person + should* now indicates low insistence. The writer of 54 may still feel that Jack deserves jail (the "ought to" sense of *should*) but the writer has lost the resolve to take Jack there (the "insistent" sense of *should*). Contrary to our second generalization, the *first person + am going* string now indicates the writer's high sense of obligation, insistence, and resolve.

What happened to our generalizations? They collided with some hard truths about learning English as a speaker or a writer. Even if one learns words through strings, the words themselves, like luggage in a plane's overhead compartment, shift in flight as they move in and out of longer strings. Our best dictionary writers understand these hard truths and enumerate as best they can the variability of meaning, shading, and tone as a word migrates from string to string.

Nonetheless, not even our best references can track the subtle lessons one learns when one plays rhetorical scrabble during real-time composing. For although fine dictionaries can embed entry words in the various strings that divide them by meaning and part of speech, no dictionary can teach the writer the subtle carry-overs and losses of tone, shading, and (what we are calling) primed experience that arises in the migration of words in and out of different strings. Writers only learn these subtle carry-overs and losses through the practice of close reading and writing and the contingent play of rhetorical scrabble. Short of this practice, the writer can't stay with a word long enough to incorporate it into one's priming art, an art of plasticity and feel for a word that is required to "control" it on behalf of a reader.

To think through a specific example of the plasticity and feel with words we have in mind, consider that to understand English *should,* one needs to understand that it retains its sense of obligation across strings 52 and 54 and only loses its sense of insistence in 54. The loss of insistence in 54 arises from the interaction of *should* with the first person and the fact that American prose has long allowed writers to use *I + should* formula (often with *probably*) to divorce themselves from their public duty when they feel a higher calling. On occasion, a merciful judge will warn a teenage first offender:

56. I should (probably) throw the book at you.
(but I won't and you, dear defendant, know that immediately — because you hear the "should" standing for narrow duty, which you know I have chosen in your case to subordinate to mercy).

The *I + should* string has a rich legacy in American letters and if one thinks that it stands only for a narrow duty overridden by a higher good, one had better think again. In his 1858 Freeport debate with Stephen Douglas, Abraham Lincoln takes the Republican position that the new territories should not permit slavery. However, he takes this position only from a reluctant sense of duty. His deep conviction, one he is willing to defer for the time being, is to eliminate slavery. He embeds the *I + should* string in a larger string to express his true conviction, not his duty:

57. I should be exceeding glad to see Congress abolish slavery....
("should now" indicates the obligation of the higher calling, not the duty).

Similarly, in the case of strings 53 and 55, one must understand not just the strings in which *auxiliary + going* vary. One needs to understand the interactions, the carry-overs and losses, as smaller strings move in and out of larger ones. Therefore, for example, one needs to understand that the string *auxiliary + going* retains the idea of projection into the future in the larger strings 53 and 55. However, when string 55 combines this projection with first person, a new element emerges — A speaker projects a future she can control without halting or hesitation. We understand this new emergent element revealing the speaker's resolve to make the future happen.

Experience-Based

Experience-based means that the English strings we collected do not enumerate discrete meanings, but rather prime experience for audiences with a continuous brush. Consider the following strings:

58. John smeared his rival. *(aggression, negative affect)*
59. John smeared oil on his arm. *(motion)*
60. John smeared venom over his rival. *(metaphorical extension blending aggression-motion)*

Dictionaries list *smear* with at least two senses. The first sense is evident in 58. The second, in 59. The first sense is speaking to defame or harm reputation. Politicians smear other politicians. Under this meaning, smeared is a transitive verb taking a direct object *(rival)*. The semantic case of the direct object is the target (or victim) of the smear. The second sense is spreading a pliable solid or liquid unevenly across a surface, often with an instrument. The second meaning takes two primary forms, using the semantic cases of location and instrument:

61. Graffiti artists *smear* paint *(instrument)* on a wall *(location)*
62. Graffiti artists *smear* a wall *(location)* with paint *(instrument)*

On this second meaning, the direct object of *smear* can be, like string 61, a semantic instrument *(paint)* followed by a spatial preposition *(on)* with a spatial target *(wall, arm)*. Alternatively, it can be, like string 62, a semantic location *(wall)* and a spatial preposition (with) followed by an instrument *(paint)*.

Example 60 presents a harder case for dictionaries of English and provides a closer look into why dictionaries are incomplete resources for writers. Here, the word *smeared* frames elements that creatively combine both the first and second meanings. As a verb of motion, *smeared* in 60 takes a spatial preposition *(over)* and an instrument object *(venom)*. Like a verb of aggression, the instrument *venom* culturally connotes aggression (a first creative extension) and, in light of the spatial preposition, a pliable, smearable object (a second creative extension). Both creative extensions of *venom* in 60 are required to consolidate the meanings of motion and aggression within the single verb *smeared*. The meaning of *smeared* in this string is shaped by the words with which it co-occurs in context.

For a dictionary that seeks to keep word meanings intact and independent of the surrounding context (and so, easier to learn by a language user), the complications raised in 60 constitute a fundamental problem in need of explanation.

Although 60 may seem a mere metaphor and so an exotic and avoidable extension of language, it is not. Turner (1996) has shown how many expressions of language derive from small spatial and kinetic stories that we do not experience as artistic metaphor. Consider the following:

63. on the heels of
64. on the brink of

Example 63 is a connector in English that means one item following another in a temporal and often causal sequence, as in the strings 65 and 66:

65. On the heels of their success, they made a large investment.
66. She decided to withdraw her money on the heels of the bank fraud.

The spatial story, now compressed and hidden, is that of two walkers, or perhaps horseback riders, in single file, the one at back stepping forward into the heels of the one in front. Example 64 means facing an imminent situation, as elaborated in 67 and 68:

67. She was at the brink of disaster.
68. He was driven to the brink.

The string *on the brink* or *at the brink* indicates one's perceived entrapment in a negative situation. This meaning is also part of a compressed spatial story, of a person encountering a sharp and steep precipice that blocks further passage. Were we to make an effort to avoid all the expressions that rely on the various spatial stories that have evolved with the evolution of language, we would have to discount much of what we consider our core literal language.

Traditional dictionaries present the study of words more as a discrete art of single words than an art of continuous gradients and shadings within rhetorical scrabble. Whereas very large and comprehensive dictionaries can mention some of these shadings in the context of enumerating individual word meanings, the discussion of context shadings in dictionaries organized around the single word is necessarily superficial. This is because, outside of rhetorical scrabble playing, we never experience this continuum of shadings head-on. A standard dictionary cannot fathom all the shadings that arise when writers combine words freely within the expanse of a phrase, clause, or longer unit.

The school of cognitive linguistics (Fauconnier & Turner, 2002; Lakoff, 1987; Turner, 1996) associates the creative extension of meaning not with properties of language per se, but with deeper principles of mental projection, conceptual integration, and creative categorization, part of the rich cognitive inheritance bestowed upon the human brain some 50,000 years ago. According to this view, creatively extending the language through metaphor or conceptual blending is basic to the human perceptual and categorization processes that underlie normal everyday language.

Of most importance to the cognitive linguist about string 60 is not the irregularity of the word meanings, but the regularity of how humans in a culture classify the world around them. Although string 60 may seem unpredictable as a string of colliding word meaning, it becomes perfectly predictable once we understand that it relies on a cultural metaphor that inanimate surfaces and objects are passive. When a language user classifies people as passive surfaces or objects in this way, the American listener or reader can pick up a pejorative reference. The same principle underlies the language user's ability to generate the following creative extensions, all put-downs of a rival:

69. John mowed down his rival. *(The rival as lawn)*
70. John mopped the floor with his rival. *(The rival as mop)*
71. John ate his rival for lunch. *(The rival as food)*

Cognitive linguists address the problem of language learning by shifting the seemingly limitless variety of word meaning to a surprisingly finite set of mental projection and categorization rules that govern them. The passivity of inanimate surfaces and objects is apparent when writers use them to mow, mop, or eat. Notice that the passivity diminishes somewhat when writers describe these surfaces or objects as being "dropped." We can drop something because of an active property of the object itself (e.g., *Jane dropped the slithering worm*). Thus, *John dropped his rival* carries a meaning potential that is not restricted to passivity or ineffectuality in the manner of examples 69, 70, and 71.

For the cognitive linguist, a finite set of mentalist principles of classification can explain an infinite variety of linguistic shadings. The English strings we are investigating make use of discrete word senses; but only as they figure into continuous experiences designed for audiences. Although we find support for our efforts from cognitive linguists, our priorities and focus are not the same as theirs. Cognitive linguists start with the phenomenon of language and move from there into considerations of the mind and brain's ability to create conceptual blends, a creative mechanism out of which many cognitive feats of language and thought, including rhetorical scrabble, emanate. Our focus, rather, is on the pairings between English strings and primings that skilled speakers and writers must acquire in order to control the experience of audiences through the language. Dictionaries reflect the science of lexicography, a rendering of discrete senses. The English strings we are studying are the province of a formal speaker or writer's sense of words, an art where senses mix and stabilize into longer strings depicting a continuum of experience for the audience.

Jumpstarts Interpretation Downstream

When a dictionary writer writes a lexical entry, the entry generalizes across the roles of writer and reader. When the writer plays rhetorical scrabble, the writer must assume a role that is different from the reader's. The writer primes or jumpstarts interpretations and readers complete them.

The various strings we review in this book prime, or jumpstart, the reader's deep comprehension and must not be confused with deep understanding itself.

Our remarkable ability to understand texts relies on processes that extend and elaborate English strings. These processes work in background to link English strings to the thick and situated understandings that readers arrive at based on the content, context, culture, and the unique history of experience they bring to language.

We take for granted but have little to say about the deep cognition taking English strings to downstream interpretations (but see Fauconnier & Turner, 2002, for proposals of this deep cognition). Our focus is on the English strings themselves that live upstream, which cue and control the initial phases of interpretation and tend to be robust enough to survive with some general intactness across context and reader variation downstream. On their own, English strings have very shallow meanings, inadequate and incomplete compared to what we experience as deep situated interpretation. Yet without a writer offering some shallow water to invite readers into the pool, readers wouldn't find the deep water they are ultimately looking for.

When we focus on English strings, our vantage is very close to the text, too close for normal comfortable reading for content meaning. As a painting studied for its fine strokes, a text studied for its patterning of surface strings is studied up close, eyeball to canvass, for the fine units of rhetoric that compose the overall effect. When readers step back from the page to take in the overall effect, they can no longer see the small individual strokes that cause the writing to work its magic. Conversely, when we read for the fine units of language and how they coax our understanding toward certain directions and away from others, we are, for the moment at least, surrendering our larger content interests and studying the writer's craft itself. We are no longer reading as a normal reader viewing from the balcony who wants only to enjoy the writer's magic. We are reading as a writer, as someone who is trying to step backstage behind the magic trick to learn how to make the illusion on our own.

To read as a writer is to study how writers use the surface text to prime the reader, to get the reader launched into interpretation. Novice writers with a less comfortable feel for words write from an idea of where they want the reader to end up. However, they often do not understand how to control the surface text where their readers must begin.

For a good illustration of the difference, on the one hand, between the primings triggered to get the reader to begin and, on the other, the deep comprehension downstream where the reader settles, consider the construction of dramatic irony and the unreliable narrator. The unreliable narrator tells a story from the vantage of an innocent or rube, knowing less than the author and reader know. Through the sophisticated vehicle of the unreliable narrator, a fiction writer can arouse the reader's emotion while keeping the language descriptive. Herman Melville's novel *Benito Cereno* (1856) relies on an unreliable narrator. Benito Cereno is captain of a slave ship and Captain Delano is a recent visitor on the ship. Unbeknownst to Delano, the slaves had earlier revolted and are now in command of the ship, holding Cereno as their secret captive. At various times, Cereno is trying to signal to Delano the situation of his captivity but Delano misses the signals and the narrator shares Delano's innocence. The following passage depicts one of Cereno's efforts to signal distress—a cough and a stagger—and the unreliable narrator's (and Delano's) misreading of the situation.

> But, seized by his cough, the Spaniard staggered, with both hands to his face, on the point of falling. Captain Delano would have supported him, but the servant was more alert, who, with one hand sustaining his master, with the other applied the cordial. Don Benito, restored, the black withdrew his support, slipping aside a little, but dutifully remaining within call of another whisper.*

Students to whom we have given this passage elaborate it with a great many negative-affect strings that we discuss next. They report on Cereno's signals of distress and their own frustration with Delano and the narrator for missing the signals. Yet, Melville's actual text contains none of these negative affect strings. Rather, Melville reports physical motion *(staggered, falling, slipping aside, remaining within)* rather than distress. He expects his reader to feel the distress of the literary situation, although the text depicting the situation remains descriptive, free of affect. Perhaps the most striking examples of putting details before the readers' mind's eye in order to spark emotional responses arise in melodrama. Take Harriet Beecher Stowe's *Uncle Tom's Cabin.* In antebellum America, average Americans living in the North ignored many abolitionists' overtly angry speeches against slavery. It took Stowe's fictional account, described in melodramatic details that readers could vicariously experience, to move them to anger.

Tied to Social Practices

Dictionaries are easy to distinguish from cultural anthropologies. The meaning of words is one thing. The practices within the culture are another. When we speak of English strings and their priming properties for audiences, the distinction between words and cultures begin to blur. English strings are not isolated units divorced from cultural understanding. Their formation and occurrence depends as much on social practice as on the English language proper. We have catalogued English strings by making a systematic study of strings and priming actions within texts across many genres—from imaginative fiction and creative nonfiction on the one hand to histories, memoirs, business reports, computer manuals, and marketing brochures on the other. Different texts reflect social practices and in identifying strings of American English, we are identifying the small and often unnoticed ways in which many of our larger social practices assert, and insert, themselves even in some of the smallest units of our language practice.

---

* See the references for quick Internet access to this passage.

Although social practices reflect regularities in the culture, we should be careful not to generalize too extensively from traces of social practice found in the language to the culture at large. Some (Wierzbicka, 1992) have proposed a uniform set of primitives underlying language not only within but also across cultures. In a discussion of how remnants of Thai culture lurk in the bowels of the Thai language, Vongvipanond (1994) concluded that the priority of the Thai people is harmony and personal well-being, based in part on the evidence that the Thai words for "success," "ambition," "achievement," and the like are compounds only having recently entered the language. This inference may have merit, yet we urge caution in making overarching generalizations about any culture from one specific set of practices or another, as if there were but one American culture or even one American English reflected in practice. We reject the idea that the practices underlying the strings we describe function monolithically for every language user. At the same time, we should keep in mind that these practices, as practices, are to a large extent social and shared, part of the equipment of schooled speakers and writers who have learned to pin down reliable experience for other minds in linear streams of language.

Although we don't pursue it further in this book, a useful underlying theory of what we mean by social practice owes to a current view in anthropological linguistics (Foley, 1997) that culture manifests within communities of practice. Rhetorical scrabble playing, tying strings of words at the micro-level of language to worlds of audience experience, develops within such communities of practice. Writers develop control of English strings mindful of other writers' language, purposes, texts, and contexts. Rhetorical scrabble, no less than conventional scrabble, is a social game, dependent on the time one spends listening to language and looking at texts from the fluid roles of listener, speaker, reader, and writer. Writers within a community of practice do not consciously share goals to acquire control over the priming functions of English strings. This learning takes place incidentally, through the feedback of teachers, editors, and peers, who constantly feed us signals when the language experiences we had planned for them do not match the experiences they report having. (Kaufer & Carley, 1993; Geisler, 1994; Bazerman & Russell, 2002)

Reflects Writer's Intentions When Intentions Match Language Convention

The English strings we set out to catalog advance the speaker or writer's rhetorical purposes and intentions. This is especially true when the speaker or writer is able to control words exactly and precisely to the specifications of prior intentions. However, writers and speakers also learn a great deal about the language and their intentions in it when they find themselves missing the mark and priming what they have not intended. They may misspeak. Even more interesting, speakers and writers may have uninformed intentions because of their limited knowledge of the language. Novice writers can associate strings of English with meanings (and so primings) that are flat-out mistaken.

For example, student writers often mistake *very* for a descriptor rather than an intensifier. Such students think, mistakenly, they are more descriptive when they call a movie they found enjoyable *very* enjoyable. These students are uninformed because *very* adds to the intensity of their expression rather than to the specificity of any alleged description. Some student writers use *relatively* to convey uncertainty or qualification (e.g., *the house was relatively big*) when relatively conventionally means comparison (e.g., the *house was big, relatively speaking, to a hut)*. The lesson of Humpty-Dumpty applies here; to be effective, a writer's intentions must abide by the meanings of the words chosen. When we can assume this condition holds, it is fair to say that priming actions with English strings can be associated with a speaker or writer's intentions and purposes. We should however bear in mind, from the examples of *very* and *relatively,* that this condition does not always hold. The writer's individualistic intentions may be uninformed about the social norms underlying how the strings of English prime audiences.

THE LIMITS ON STRINGS SELECTED: WHAT WE CAN'T LEARN ABOUT AUDIENCE PRIMING FROM OUR STUDY

In selecting strings for our catalog, we were aware from the start that the very properties we were seeking for our priming catalog also brought limits. We can understand these limits by examining the discrepancy between the strings we selected and the awareness a fully intelligent human being brings to matters of language and audience. What do we, as intelligent humans, know about the impact of words on audiences that the lifeless strings in our catalog cannot know? To answer this question is to understand the limits of our investigation into rhetorical priming.

No Memory or Vision Beyond Adjacency Relations

When we play rhetorical scrabble in our own practice, we have no trouble integrating our current string of words with others strings in nonadjacent units of text to build cumulative experiences. In his 1981 novel, *Prisoner without a Name, Cell without a Number,* Jacobo Timerman (cited in Hale, 1999) alternates between an anonymous first person *my* and *I* and third person *he* to create a prison mood of anonymity and monotony.

> My entire forehead is pressed against the steel and the cold makes my head ache… He is doing the same… I step back and wait… He is doing the same. (p. 34)

Timerman composed these pronouns to have a cumulative effect on the reader, an effect requiring the reader to maintain a memory of each pronoun mentioned. Timerman had a long-range plan for the experiences he wanted to create and made sure local strings conformed to the plan. Sentence planning of this sort relies on dependencies, echoes, and parallelisms between nonadjacent parts of the same sentence. Consider:

72. John wanted to give his heart to Mary and Bill, to Sue.

The ending string *Bill, to Sue* echoes and compresses the form of the earlier part of the sentence. One can produce the final run of words only with a memory of the earlier run still echoing in the reader's working memory. Our method of compiling English strings does not capture dependencies or echoes between or within sentences. We compiled and classified English strings as independent entities, with no built-in memories for other strings.

No Insight Into Unique Content Words

We categorize English strings according to the type of audience experience they prime, not according to the unique meanings of unique words. If priming were to change with every nuanced change of meaning, it's not clear that speakers and writers would ever be able to control language as an instrument of audience experience. To build our catalog of priming strings, we found ourselves having to abstract from and leave behind the unique meanings of unique words. This abstractive process poses no real limitation for function words (e.g., *just, even, so far, all together, still, finally*) and regular and deictic pronouns *(us, you, I, now, here)*, which rely from the start on the priming of the referential context more than on semantic content. However, referential terms like *dog* and *cat*, which have different referents, collapse in our categorization of audience priming into a generic string class of sense object. From the point of view of audience priming, that is, we assume the following strings are indistinguishable:

73. Sue reached out to her dog.
74. Sue reached out to her cat.

Both strings create the experience of a person involved in spatial extension *(reach out to)* toward a sense object. Although *dog* and *cat* have different meanings, they belong in our catalog to the same categorized string of audience experience. We believe this reduction of unique meanings into equivalent priming categories is justified only insofar as one can make a case that strings with different "content" (e.g., *screaming terror, wretched pain*) can nonetheless create a comparable audience experience (like negative affect).

We collapse meaning differences across classes of verbs as well as nouns. Compare the following strings:

75. John ran to Bill. *(motion)*
76. John ran away from Bill. *(motion)*

These examples have different meanings and support different inferences. An inference of string 75 is that John will be spatially nearer to Bill than before. An inference of string 76 is that John will be spatially farther away from Bill than before. This contrast owes to the different senses of the verb phrase (*ran to* vs. *ran away from*) across these strings. Nonetheless, our catalog of strings misses these sense differences. From the standpoint of our catalog, strings 75 and 76 convey the same impression—motion in a space. In the course of compiling English strings, we determined that our catalog could only capture differences in sense that, in our view, mattered to differences in audience priming.

We relied, in other words, on the intuition that differences in meaning are often insufficient to overthrow differences in the priming action taken. This means that whereas strings 75 and 76 are indistinguishable for the purposes of priming action, both had to be distinguished from the following string:

77. John ran the company into the ground *(negative affect)*

because the sense of *run into the ground,* which writers seldom use to convey literal motion, marks a priming shift from *run to* or *run from.*

Following Aristotle, who cautioned rhetorical theorists not to collapse rhetoric into subject matter and content, we made sure not to bind ourselves to marking every difference in content meaning as a difference in rhetorical priming. Learners are made when they explore the nuances of content meaning. Schooled speakers and writers are made when they recognize how to transform the medium of linear language and text, across content, into an instrument for priming audience experience.

Advantages accrue when one can categorize strings into priming classes that abstract over unique meanings. However, we should not lose sight of the losses as well. Our catalog cannot address the contribution that the unique meaning, sound, and rhythm of most content words can have on audience priming. To the extent that priming actions legitimately rely on a distinctive sense, sound, and meter, our catalog misses them.

To summarize, we have reviewed two important limitations of the string catalog we present next. First, English strings cannot capture cumulative experiences, and especially those that rely on nonadjacent dependencies. Second, as we code them, English strings cannot see into the semantic distinctiveness of most content words and their unique senses. Rather, we classify words and strings into more general categories of priming experience. To the extent that readers build experiences from unique content words and the properties of such words (sense, sound, rhythm), however, our catalog is limited.

Strings Initiate but Do Not Complete Audience Experience

For the purposes of our investigation, the primings we assign to English strings are based on the intuitions of our research group and the generations of classroom students who served as actual readers and judges of our intuitions about priming audience. Furthermore, and the important point we wish to make here, they are intuitions about how strings of English initiate audience experience. They are not intuitions about the theories of interpretation required to clinch or complete that experience. The difference between initiating (priming) interpretation and completing an interpretation (hermeneutics) is fundamental for our research.

As language users, we have a large base of implicit agreement about how words prime experience. We have no such base of implicit agreement when it comes to interpretative theories that complete the circuit of what words mean in any culturally situated language context. We are focused only on the micro-level of priming experience and do not try to account for finished interpretation in context.

Take two strings such as *do not* and *deny that*. Both of these strings prime the audience to hear a denial or disclaimer of some implied assertion. Should a speaker put these strings together to create the string *do not deny that,* listeners will integrate the denials to understand that the speaker is making a positive acknowledgment. They may further tie the acknowledgment, in context, to more significant contextual inferences, such as the speaker making a major concession or offering an olive branch of some shared agreement in the heat of a political debate. Our theory of isolated strings as primers of audience experience does not address the audience's ability to integrate the experience primed for them into clinching and confirmed interpretations.

If not through theories of interpretation, what evidence do we have to confirm our assignment of primings to English strings? Although laboratory testing of our theory is important, we do not at this juncture have laboratory data of this kind to report. As we will see below, most of our confirming evidence deals with how well our priming categories separate texts of different kinds. Because we have no conclusive results with actual readers, we are hesitant to associate our catalog with a truly behavioral model of writers or readers. The disciplinary methods we incorporated to generate our catalog are closer to traditional methods of rhetoric and discourse analysis than they are to laboratory science. As we will see below, our use of computer-aided coding techniques did not change this fact. It merely allowed us to keep consistent track of a database of language samples far larger than that explored by most rhetoricians and discourse analysts.

3

Methods for Selecting and Cataloging Strings

Once we understood we were interested in English strings as instruments for priming audience experience, we charted out a research strategy to harvest and classify such strings. We knew that it was an impossible task to seek an exhaustive collection of strings. Because of the combinatory possibilities of multiword strings, one can never enumerate all possible strings of English in the same way one can conceivably enumerate all individual words. Our aim, rather, was to sample a wide range of English speech and texts in order to get a representative understanding of the range and diversity of priming actions that English makes available at the grain size of strings.

We recognized early on that we could not harvest a collection of strings through reading and note taking alone. We would require automated methods for assistance with our string gathering. The approach we finally settled on was that of an expert system, where we used technology to harvest, rather than replace or mimic, what a culturally-in-the-know human writer or reader knows about priming actions. Rather than make the computer smart (Manning & Schutze, 2001) about English strings, we would create an environment that would allow us to encode our knowledge about priming strings with an automated string-matcher. We could then use our string-matcher on new texts to test our prior codings for accuracy and completeness. When we discovered our string-matcher making incorrect (i.e., ambiguous, misclassified, or incomplete) matches on the new texts, we would use this information to elaborate the strings our string matcher could recognize. By repeating a cycle of coding strings on training texts and then testing and elaborating strings based on how well they explained priming actions on new texts, we were able to grow our catalog of priming strings systematically and consistently.

To meet our objectives, we wrote special string-recognition software to allow us to identify, tag, and store strings of English. The software consisted of a string matcher and visualizer. The string matcher could match any literal string of English of any length. For efficiency of coding, the software allowed us to run the string-matcher on up to 500 texts at a time and over any number of user-defined categories of different strings. When the string matcher found a matching string in any of the target texts, it tagged it by name and color. The visualizer made it relatively easy for the research team to study the performance of the string-matcher and to improve it rapidly based on errors in its performance. The visualizer made it possible to build a very large and consistently classified inventory of priming strings in a relatively short amount of time.

Where did we find the speech and texts to look for priming strings? We started by seeding our environment with strings we had previously categorized when we analyzed the clauses of the Lincoln/Douglas debates (Kaufer & Butler, 1996). We began with argument texts because we had discovered in the 1996 research that argument is a highly composite form, one that includes a rich array of priming strings, associated with description, narrative, exposition, reporting, quotation, dialog, and conversational interaction. We also began identifying and isolating priming strings associated with specific genres, such as written journals, profiles, scenic fieldguides, historical narratives, exposition, popular explanation, instructions, and argument. We thought of our search and identification of micro-units of rhetoric within these genres within a framework we called *representational composition* (Kaufer and Butler, 2000). The name representational composition stemmed from our effort to reconcile what has historically been viewed as competing approaches to language: rhetorical and representational approaches. In the history of philosophical and rhetorical approaches to language, the comon place has been to regard representational and rhetorical theories of language as competitors more than allies (Yovel, 2002), one standing for truth, correspondence, and poetic in the western tradition, the other for effectiveness and community-building, in the positive sense of rhetoric; and individual opportunism and audience manipulation in the negative sense.

Through a theory of representational composing, we sought to ally representational and rhetorical uses of language by postulating that rhetorical effectiveness follows at least in part from representational effectiveness. That is to say, culturally skilled speakers and writers are effective with audiences because they can compress into linear speech and text worlds of represented experience they want their audiences to associate with the here and now. Not least important, culturally skilled speakers and writers can compose worlds of experience in speech and on paper. They can do this *because* they can *see* and *control* the micro-level priming cues required to move audiences from words to effective experience.

From the evidence of strings within written genres, we next turned our attention to three "seed" text collections. The first was a 120 text digital archive of creative fiction and nonfiction taught in a creative writing course on voice. These texts ranged from deep introspective pieces, to character-based stories, to texts with a more narrative plot. They also included essays of reminiscence, reflection, and social criticism. We took a second digital archive from a course on information systems. This database consisted of 45 electronic documents associated with a software engineering project to build a new online registration system for a university client. The database included a wide range of information documents; proposals to the client, software design specifications, meeting minutes within the design team, meeting minutes between the design team and the client team, software documentation, focus group reports, public relation announcements, and feature interviews. We had multiple instances of each of these document types and we split each into training texts and test texts just as we had done with creative fiction and nonfiction. We repeated the iterative process of testing, improvement, testing, and improvement until we had captured categories of priming strings that seemed pertinent to this universe of information documents.

We took a third archive from a miscellany available from the Internet. These archives include the Federalist papers, the Presidential Inaugurals, the journals of Lewis and Clark, song lyrics from rapsters and rockers, the clips of various syndicated newspaper columnists, the Web-page welcomes of 30 university presidents, the collected fables of Aesop and the Brother's Grimm, the writings of Malcolm X, the 100 great speeches of the 20th century, 10 years of newspaper reporting on the Exxon Valdez disaster, and movie reviews. We sampled 200 texts from this miscellany and made sure that we had multiple instances of each type of writing so that each type could be divided into training and test runs as we cycled through test and improvement cycles. We made other codings by sampling specific periodicals over an extended period. On a weekly basis over a three-year period, for example, we coded priming strings from the *New Yorker* magazine and from the editorials, features, and news pages of *The New York Times*. To capture data from speech, we coded for 2 to 4 hours every week the priming strings heard over radio stations focused on news, talk, or sports.

Although we could not visually inspect every one of the strings that our string-matcher matched, the visualization environment allowed us to visually inspect many of the matches made during test and improvement cycles. To further assure close monitoring of the performance of our string-matcher, we built into the matcher a "collision detector" that would warn us if we assigned the same string to multiple categories. This was invaluable for finding ambiguities in the string data. It was even more important for debugging inconsistencies in our thinking about the categorization of strings. By having the string-matcher "complain" to us when it found one and the same string multiply classified across our catalog of strings, we were forced to visually inspect and test the priming potencies of strings at a more frequent rate than we would have used with a more forgiving string matcher. When the string-matcher complained, it would force us to hold a discussion about the best categorization of the string. This check slowed down our categorization of strings but it also provided an invaluable quality control step in our coding.

Once we had our coding categories in place, we finally turned to an online dictionary of English, segmented into the most frequent 25,000 words, most frequent 50,000 words, and most frequent 100,000 words. While we wanted a catalog of English that accounted for multi-word strings, the possibility remained that we were missing important categories because we had not taken a selective inventory of English at the grain of single words. We made a visual audit of the 50,000 most frequent words of English for all 26 letters of the alphabet. We found many single words that we had not coded, which was not surprising. We took as a milestone of "completeness" of our coding categories the criteria that would be satisfied when all the single words we had failed to code had a home within our existing multi-word categories. After three years of investigatory work, we reached that milestone.

Let's take a closer look at how, prior to our single word audit, we categorized multi-word strings. Let us assume that, as close readers, we read a newspaper editorial that contained the English string *smeared the politician* as a verb phrase. As close readers, we formed the qualitative generalization that the string *smeared the politician* affords the idea of negative affect. We then input into our catalog of strings many variations and generalizations of this string (e.g., *smeared him, smeared them, smeared them),* all coded as priming negative affect. By running these variant strings on new texts, we could discover the limits of our initial coding assumptions. Our software might, for example, incorrectly label the string *smeared himself with paint* as a negative affect. The software made it easy for us to discover the mistake and to code the longer string *smeared him with paint* as a motion. Over 3 years, we continued this process of adding, testing, and differentiating categorizations of strings of English over thousands of texts. We continued the categorization building, testing, and differentiating process until we had over 150 categories (e.g., negative affect, motion) that seemed robust and stable and that could differentiate, in principle, millions of strings.

As our coding of strings evolved, we were able to derive formal decision criteria for classifying strings into one of 18 overall dimensions. Although our category system eventually expanded into over 160 distinct classes, each string class fell into one or another of the 18 overall dimensions.

We assigned each of the actual strings we coded to one and only one class. As already discussed, this was a methodological assumption we made to guarantee a high level of quality control in our classification of strings. We made unique class assignments to strings we felt could be disambiguated through lengthening. Even long strings often can be disambiguated when additional words are added. For example, the six-word string *on one hand there was a* can't be disambiguated until the seventh word *(freckle, reason):*

78. On one hand there was a freckle
    (spatial extension with a human hand)
79. On one hand there was a reason
    (logical entry into an argument)

Similarly, the string *reminds [one]* is ambiguous between a retrospective thinking back or resemblance. However, these codings are at least partly disambiguated depending on whether the string is followed by an *of* or *that*. This is because *of* increases the likelihood of object memory whereas *that* increases the probability of remembering a situation in time past.

80. That couch reminds me of a train berth.
    (reminder as object resemblance)
81. That couch reminds me that I promised myself to buy a new one.
    (reminder as memory of a past situation)

These are only probabilities, however, as *of* allows some continuing strings that can recall a past situation as well. This is especially true in the continuation, *of a time when,* which behaves more like the *that* than the *of* continuation.

82. The couch reminds me of a time when I promised to buy myself a new one.

The string *rooted in* we found to be ambiguous because we could find extensions that primed different experiences for a listener or reader.

83. Rooted in the idea
    (abstract thought)
84. Rooted in the soil
    (spatial extension)

The phrase *"leads to a"* is another ambiguous string, a launching point for a diverse array of primings. The writer venturing with this string can pursue continuations that still leave open the possibility of expressing internal thought, establishing relations with the reader, or providing external descriptions:

85. Their discussion often *leads to a* great many insights.
    (inner thought)
86. A downturn in the economy sometimes *leads to a* depression.
    (relational information for the reader)
87. The stream *leads to a* mountain path.
    (description)

If one looks up *lead* in a good dictionary, one will find some 15 different senses. It is doubtful that, as language users, we systematically cycle through these various meanings when we propose *lead* in a sentence part. Writers targeting the audience's experience seem to seek out composing parts that avoid the myopia of single word look-ahead. What's more likely is that we learn *lead* within complex string combinations that allow us to take audiences wherever we want to take them.

Ambiguous strings carry multiple possible primings that can be disambiguated through lengthening. In contrast to ambiguous strings, resonant (or overlapping) strings carry multiple primings that lengthening cannot help disambiguate. Take a string like *walked slowly*. The string simultaneously primes the experience of a past event and a motion. Lengthening the string will do nothing to isolate one or the other priming. As a result, we did not classify this string as ambiguous. We rather thought of it as accommodating overlaps of priming that we associated with resonance. We still coded resonant strings uniquely (e.g., we coded the string *walked slowly* as a past event rather than a motion, although it always signals both), but we also used additional pragmatic assumptions to classify resonant strings. We assumed that the ideal rhetorical scrabble player wants, as much as possible, to diversify his or her stock of priming actions. We thus coded resonant strings in a manner consistent with assuring the writer's greatest diversity of priming. The *-ed* ending allows *walked* to prime past action and to participate in a writer's narrative storytelling (e.g., *John walked his dog*). Were we to code *walk + ed* as a motion, we would be depriving the rhetorical scrabble player of a narrative element involving the verb *walk*. Additionally, other forms of that verb *(walk, walks, walking)* already capture motion. Consequently, coding the resonant *walked* as past action rather than motion obeys our diversity principle. It allows the rhetorical scrabble player, we reasoned, the most diversity of priming action with the verb *walk*. We used similar pragmatic applications of the diversity principle to assign a single coding to all resonant or inherently multifunctional strings.

Besides the diversity principle, we also appealed to a pragmatic principle of "conservative coding" to code resonant strings. According to the principle of conservative coding, one should assign a coding that makes the fewest assumptions about the surrounding context. Consider the following:

88. She trembled at the sight of him.
    (trembled = fear; negative affect; motion)
89. The mountain trembled just before erupting.
    (trembled = motion)

In both strings 88 and 89, the verb *trembled* implies motion. In string 88, it also implies negative affect and fear. Because the motion coding is accurate in both contexts and the negative affect coding misclassifies string 89, we chose the motion coding for tremble as the most conservative and so the preferred coding.

Once we decided to start harvesting strings of English to capture a speaker or writer's priming knowledge, how did we decide when to stop? We answered this question by keeping in mind our goals. Our aim was not to build an exhaustive set of English strings, an impossible task. Our aim was to seek a catalog of strings reflective of the diversity competent language users rely on to prime audiences. For us, conceptual comprehensiveness, the capacity to capture a stable and robust conceptual hierarchy of audience priming actions, was more important (and more feasible) than claims of completeness. We also knew to stop when our categories for strings began to stabilize. Early in the process, we changed our major classifications regularly, as the strings we built from training texts did not fare well when applied to new texts. Over time, a span of three years, the need to revise classifications slowed considerably and even when we did see reason to revise our classifications, the revisions began to affect only where best to assign strings within minor categories of difference. Testing our codings on new texts and text collections no longer challenged our major hierarchies.

As we built our string catalog with the help of our string matcher, we kept records of three types of information that helped us continue to debug, improve, and grow the catalog:

- String omissions (what priming strings does the string matcher miss?)
- String ambiguities (what priming strings could be disambiguated in their audience function through lengthening?)
- String Misclassifications (what priming strings have been assigned to the wrong category or even the wrong hierarchy?).

We enlisted our students for help as well in providing us with feedback to these questions. From prior research (Kaufer & Butler, 2000), we had isolated priming strings in eight writing assignments (self-portrait, observer portrait, scenic writing, narrative history, exposition, popular explanation, instruction, and argument) that we had assigned in a graduate course taught every year. Students in the course (an average of 15 per course for 3 years) used the visualization and string-matcher environment as a way of understanding and tracking the priming effects they created for readers in each of their writing assignments. As part of the course requirement, students maintained semester-long logs, keeping track of string and category omissions, ambiguities, and misclassifications in the performance of the string-matcher. In their semester logs, each student was responsible for finding 100 strings that constituted omissions (priming strings that our string-matcher missed), 25 category ambiguities (strings with multiple primings that could be disambiguated by lengthening), and 25 category misclassifications (priming strings that seemed to belong to category A even though the string matcher had assigned it to category B).

For educational purposes, we found this assignment invaluable for helping students notice and study the language of their own writing — and to our satisfaction, students did too. For research purposes, the student logs provided invaluable feedback that helped us improve and enlarge the string catalog further. The student logs contained 15 (students) x 150 (visual observations) x 3 (years) = 2250 visual inspections of our catalog of strings as priming actions. These systematic inspections were the formal tip of an informal iceberg of corrective and elaborative information students provided about the string-matcher and its catalog of strings. In retrospect, we found it very important to have communities of users outside the research team providing regular feedback on the strings we were cataloging. What started as an effort to build a "closed" coding system came to strike us as a social organic system for helping a language community share and make visible in discussion its own tacit assumption about how the English language primes experience of listeners and readers. In the next section, we discuss in more detail this transition in our thinking from our catalog as a closed coding system of strings to a more open-ended community discussion of language practices.

At the end of every semester, we studied student logs and verified each of the entries. We changed the catalog when we were able to verify the student input that asked for change. Because of the student input, we filled in category omissions as warranted and eliminated ambiguities that we could eliminate. We also used the principle of diversity and conservative coding (principles we taught students) to classify resonant or multifunctional strings in the most consistent manner possible. For example, we had originally coded *fair* as a positive standard, based on seeing it in string 90:

90. Mitch was a decent and fair person.
(fair = positive standard)

One student, using our string-matcher on texts she wrote for the class and read on the Internet, came across *fair* in different strings with different senses.

91. Mitch freckled because he was a fair person.
(fair = sense property; light-skinned)
92. Loving to show her dogs, she has always been a fair going person.
(fair = event)

The student recognized that categorizing *fair* as priming a positive standard in strings 91 and 92, as the string matcher had originally done, was an ambiguous classification. In response to the student's feedback, we assigned the word *fair* in string 90 across multiple lengthened phrases that preserved the positive standard priming—such as *acted fairly* and *tried to be fair*. We further lengthened occurrences of *fair* that isolated the priming of a property of skin: *fair skin* or *fair skinned*. Finally, we created more strings to capture the event sense of *fair,* such as *went to the fair,* or *fair at the park.*

OUR CATALOG AS A CODING SCHEME VS. AN ORGANIC SOCIAL SYSTEM

We began our research with the idea of our catalog offering a fixed and scientifically reliable coding scheme for the priming potencies of English strings. Further into our research, we came to think of our catalog as a living social archive of linguistic priming knowledge whose benefits were better realized as knowledge to be externalized and discussed rather than knowledge on which to reach complete scientific consensus. We believe that both views of our catalog have merit and that these views are complementary rather than incompatible.

Coding schemes represent public and scientific bases of knowledge. They seek to adhere to the standards of intersubjective reliability and validity, meaning that different people independently classify the same string into the same priming category and that their agreement is descriptive of the actual phenomenon being coded. By thinking of our catalog as a coding scheme relating English strings and priming properties, we have been usefully constrained by the goal to make our association of English strings and priming potencies as objective a basis of knowledge as we can. This has caused us to prefer codings that an average reader could confirm on a quick "second-take" rather than codings that require detailed context-specific interpretations to understand or to agree with. With respect to making coding conservative, we didn't mind if we made classifications that coded less information than what a human reader would take from the text. However, we did very much mind if we made a coding that took more from a string than a human reader would normally infer. We had tried to err in the preferred, conservative direction by making sure our strings captured conventional gestures on the surface of language rather than deep interpretations. If we think back to the Benito Cereno passage and study the primings that our strings do and don't pick up, one will get a better appreciation of the conservatism of our coding.

In addition to an interest in the most conservative codings, the constraint of thinking of our catalog as an objective coding catalog influenced us to aim for the more robust codings, those codings holding over the most frequent contexts of use. Consult back to our earlier discussion of *trembled* as a motion verb, which is a more robust priming classification than negative affect.

In line with our thinking about our catalog as a coding scheme, we have addressed the question of internal validity. Do our classifications of strings and their priming of audience make separations of text that human classifiers would make at the whole text level? In a test of our strings on the 15 genres of the Brown (Kucera and Francis, 1979), and Freiderg-Brown Corpus (Hundt, Sand, Siemud, 1999), Collins (2001: 2003) found that our strings successfully distinguish fiction and nonfiction genres as well as genres that are more narrative-based (histories, memoirs, mysteries) from those that are more information-based (academic, religious, government documents). In Part III of this book, we overview some of the many applications to which we have put our catalog. These applications have served as a further check on internal validity.

In contrast to internal validity, external or ecological validity means that human readers, untutored in our catalog or its categories, can reproduce our priming categories when they report the experience of their reading. On this exceedingly high standard, should our catalog report a text priming experiential categories like motion and negativity, a reader, going over the same text, should also report the experience of motion and negativity when they report on their reading. Although we have done some pilot work to indicate that average readers who know nothing about our priming categories can detect some of our categories without prompting or training (e.g., first person, motion, and narrative), we suspect that this does not apply to all our categories. This suspicion has helped us understand the limits of our catalog as an objective coding scheme.

We came to understand that some of the priming categories in our catalog become visible only when a reader is trained to look at language with a high meta-awareness about function. As mentioned above, this meta-awareness is a deeply honed tool-of-the-trade of lexicographers who must write dictionary entries that discriminate the fine points of individual words from every other in the language. It does not seem to be a discrimination knowledge required of the ordinary reader reading for basic content and comprehension (Channel, 2000). For example, the English string *anytime soon* only occurs to prime a denial (e.g., *I won't be here anytime soon)*. Yet this recognition is not immediately apparent to the average reader encountering these two words alone. It only becomes apparent when one begins to reflect on the various distributions of *anytime soon* across various contexts of words, messages, and situations. We thus came to recognize that, however useful it was to think of our catalog as a scientific coding scheme matching the judgments of actual writers and readers, we also came to understand that we were also cataloging a more elusive meta-awareness of language that speakers and writers tap into but seldom bring to surface articulation, much less public discussion. The knowledge our catalog extracts seems outside the explicit awareness of most language users. Nonetheless, it does externalize much implicit knowledge that makes our rhetorical control of language explainable. In this way, we saw our catalog as an externalized design space of tacit knowledge underlying a largely invisible social system of language use.

4

The Catalog Hierarchy

In this brief chapter, we take a bird's eye view of the top-level hierarchy of our catalog. Our catalog consists of the following hierarchies, moving in descending order from high-level concepts to literal strings of English: *clusters, families, dimensions,* and *string classes.* In various cases, we have grouped dimensions within families and (more commonly) have grouped classes within dimensions. These groupings are made to ease the reader's path through our catalog and are not an essential part of the official catalog per se. When we present our catalog next, we number string classes under each controlling dimension.

In this chapter, we overview the major clusters of our catalog. In subsequent chapters, we break down clusters into families, dimensions, and finally classes of actual strings.

THREE PERSPECTIVES OF CLASSIFICATION: INTERNAL, RELATIONAL AND EXTERNAL

We classify English strings into three clusters: internal, relational, and external perspectives.

Cluster 1: Internal Perspectives

Internal perspectives indicate the stings of English that prime audiences to engage the interior mind of the speaker or writer or a character the speaker or writer references. Strings priming an internal perspective include first person, expressive, affective, subjective, and time-projected thinking. Communications primed from these strings strike audiences as personalized and disclosing.

Personal disclosure describes, perhaps, our earliest experiences with writing, revealing to readers a rich and diverse warehouse of thoughts that reflect the unique perspective of the individual self: personal cognitions, subjective estimates of confidence, diffidence, neutrality, intensity, expectancy, contingency, affect, retrospection, and anticipation.

Interior thought can pop up in inexperienced writing even when the writer tries to suppress subjectivity. Ask anyone poised with a camera to take a photograph of a chair and the result will be a picture of a chair. Ask an inexperienced writer poised with a pen to describe a chair and one is likely to get strings like:

93. I see a chair that…
94. The chair in front of me looks like a…
95. The chair has an interesting shape…

Unlike the photograph, words that tumble from our minds without forethought tend to reveal our inner mind at work. Among all media of representation, speech and texts most effortlessly plop the reader in the midst of the communicator's thought. In film, it takes special production techniques, like voice-overs, to let the audience overhear a cinematic character's silent thought. With texts in particular, the impression of silent thought comes early. Children can keep personal diaries before they can keep time. Getting children writers to write from inside their own head is no trick. Getting them to see beyond their spontaneous thought is the harder challenge. In one preliminary study (Collins, Kaufer, Neuwirth, Hajduk, & Palmquist 2002), we found inexperienced writers overtly exhibit their inner thinking in their writing significantly more than do expert writers, even when given the same writing task.

The tense-aspect system of language adds a rich dimension to interior writing. It unmoors the writer's thought from a static present and frees it to project backward and forward in time. With the tense-aspect system, writers can express not only what they, their narrators, or characters think now. They can portray what such individuals, from an anchored point in time, have thought or will think. Speech and texts can accomplish these shifts in time with incredible efficiency. In addition to tense and aspect, many content ideas encode time-shifting. A rich example is the concept of *conspiracy*. "The gang was to make off with the loot when the clock struck one." In this sentence, we meet a cabal of persons planning the future, under cover, from the vantage of the past. The sentence portrays a conspiracy because of a future projected from a past vantage point (*was to* + *verb*). Conspiracies are hard to prove in the physical world but easy to concoct as objects of thought because of the fluid ability of language concepts to distribute a communicator's thinking across multiple horizons of time.

Cluster 2: Relational Perspectives

A speaker or writer's art at priming audiences draws from a second cluster of priming strings, what we call *relational perspectives*. English strings emanating from this perspective rely on two distinct senses of relation. The first sense involves connecting audiences to the representations within the language. These connecting strings evoke shared reasoning, social ties, and directed activity with respect to audiences. The second sense involves navigating audiences through the linear medium of language. These navigational strings aid audiences as they make their way from beginning to end in speech and from left to right in text.*

Cluster 3: External Perspectives

A writer's priming art draws from a third cluster, what we call *external perspectives*. Strings drawn from this cluster convey a world outside of mind and witnessable through the public senses. Through these externalized or descriptive strings, writers engage readers in scenic and temporal depictions. Descriptive strings allow listeners and readers to experience situations and worlds within the text, situations displaced in time and space from the immediacy of the audience's context.

---

* A theoretical footnote is in order here, especially when we talk about cues to readers in texts, implying as we may seem to be that every text presupposes an empirical reader wading through. Many documents, including much of our greatest literature, was composed for an actual readership no longer alive. Theoretical issues are thus raised about the extent to which we can talk about texts as leading a live reader when the text is hundreds or thousands of years old. Our approach to texts may be justly criticized for finessing these issues raised by old texts.

Certainly, there is an argument to be made that both individual interpretation and interpretations pooled across a population change over time. We do not read English texts of earlier decades and centuries with the same contextual and cultural implications as we read contemporary texts. The strings we report are based on contemporary English only and do not take into account the changes of English from the time we use it to Chaucer's time. (Foucault, 1977; Ong, 1975). That said, the strings we report on are deeply embedded in the rhetorical substrate of the English language and much of this substrate is surprisingly resistant to processes of historical language change. For example, we have found that the substrate our catalog research has brought to the surface is surprisingly more resistant to historical change than neologisms, proper names, and the various references of context and culture that inform downstream interpretations. Thus, for example, while strings we codes are restricted to contemporary English and ignored the English of Shakespeare's time, the context of Elizabethan London, and the Globe Theatre, the strings of *contemporary English* from the rhetorical substrate we have extracted in our catalog still do a respectable job sorting Shakespearean genres. Positive and negative affect terms of English (e.g., *good, just*) that were true for Shakespeare remain true for us. Fundamental ways of portraying rhetorical action from internal, relational, and external perspectives appear to have remained intact from the beginnings of English. Our categorization of rhetorical action from everyday strings of English seems somewhat resistant to historical change than parts of language requiring deep context and cultural reference. This, of course, is not to deny that we could do better analyzing old texts if we built representational dictionaries closer to the temporal and cultural time they appeared. But it is to suggest that the layer of language we are trying to capture, the rhetorical substrate, remains more stable across aspects of language change than other language variables.

Experienced writers understand, and control putting a single visual concept-image *(chair)* before the mind of a reader and also dropping off a more extended and scene-involving word picture *(green and white lawn chair, its cushions shabby and torn from too much horseplay at the beach)*. The writer can also create images of spatial intervals, describing a chair that is *facing,* or *abutting,* or *standing next to* a sofa. The writer can depict motion, making a character *run, glide,* or *snort* and extending motion into intervals of space as well *(running all the way home)*. The description in these cases is scenic, the camera of the writer's inner eye sampling a space without interruption. Description, moreover, can cut across scenic boundaries, suggesting a dissolve between scenes and the feeling that time has passed between the end of one scene and the start of another. When the cuts are fast and the scenes mark fleeting events in a temporal stream, the audience can feel a fast-paced narrative montage (e.g., Caesar *came, saw, and conquered)*. The simplest narratives are scene-less events that chain together the start and surcease of action along a single plot line. Temporal descriptions can also include the shifts between events (e.g., the *next time, the following week, they finally arrived)*. When these shifts cover intervals of time that are longer than eyewitnessed time, audiences feel the displacement of time as well as space. That's why *drifting across the ocean* suggests the elapse of time in a way that *drifting across the kitchen floor* cannot. Finally, temporal descriptions can include intervals of time *(for ten years, during the cold war)*. These intervals can repeat and, when they do, they become cycling intervals *(every week, most Tuesdays, each morning)* that can indicate ritualistic as well as recurring events.

5

The Hierarchy in Relation to Previous Scholarship

In the present chapter, we tie the top-level clusters just overviewed to previous scholarship in rhetoric and applied linguistics. As our research lies at the interface of these two disciplines, it is useful to single out work from both to better frame our work.

We offer I. A. Richards and Michael Halliday as important intellectual touch stones for our work. Rhetoricians who wish to locate our work will see interesting convergences with Richards, a rhetorician especially interested in looking toward applied linguistics. Applied linguists will see interesting convergences with Halliday, who is an applied linguist looking, to some extent, toward language as micro-rhetoric.

From Richards, we take assumptions about the mental versus descriptive poles of language that have provided a basis for distinguishing internal and external perspectives as top-level clusters. From Halliday, we add the idea of a relational cluster of priming action, priming ties that bind the language user and audience to a world of social reasoning, social ties, directed activities, and cues for navigating the linear stream of language. Let us briefly consider in more detail each theorist's influence on our approach.

I. A. RICHARDS

A hallmark of our division of top-level clusters is the divide between internal and external perspectives in English priming strings. The famous 20th century rhetorician, I. A. Richards (papers edited in Berthoff 1991, pp.194-196) understood the importance of this divide in the English language. He noted that the English word *sense* derives from two semantic roots, each bound to the separation of inner thought and outer sense. One root, associating *sense* with interior thought, derives from the Latin *sentia* (to think). English words that have derived from this "interior thought" string are *sentence* (middle English for "well-held opinion"), *sense* as approbation (That makes *sense!*) and *sense* as two or more minds in agreement *(consensus).* A second root, associating *sense* with outward description, derives from the Latin *sensus* (the senses). English words derived from this root are the basic sense verbs: *hearing, tasting, touching,* and *smelling,* with *seeing* occupying dual residence as part of interior thought and exterior description.

Richards understood that the fundamental division between *sentia* and *sensus:*

> comes from an opposition as deep and important as that between "outside" and "inside." This is the division between what we see, hear, touch, taste, and smell—the outer world, in short—and what we somehow find going on in our minds when we note how we are thinking, feeling, hoping, fearing, willing, and desiring—the inner world of our experience…these two are the first and the chief branches or stems through which later branches are organized. (Bertoff 1991, p.194).

In previous work (Kaufer & Butler, 2000), we independently found Richard's original insight fundamental. Nothing changes the textual experience more dramatically than shifts in the dominant string cluster—either the outer world or the writer's mind—from which language represents experience. The development of rounded characters in nonfiction and fiction depends upon the tight oscillation of strings from both of these clusters. According to Ralph Fletcher (1992, p.68), for example, a writer's ability to develop character depends on creating an oscillation of the character's inner and outer life for the reader. The character writer creates a constant shifting back and forth between a character's self-definition from the inside out; and the character's behavior, which only an external observer looking at the character from the outside in can confirm.

An abrupt shift from an outer to an inner perspective can take place with a small flip of a *sensus* string into a *sentia* string. Note the flip at work when we add *I think* to turn string 96 into 97.

96. The cat was on the mat. It wasn't on the rug because the dog was there.
    (observation of cat's whereabouts followed by an inference to explain one possible reason for its current location)
97. I think the cat was on the mat. It wasn't on the rug because the dog was there.
    (argument for cat's whereabouts followed by support for the argument)

Example 96 establishes the truth of the cat's whereabouts and relies on the follow-up sentence to explain one reason why the truth might hold. The addition of *I think* in 97 is enough to turn the string inward, referencing the speaker's subjectivity and making the cat's whereabouts no longer the launching premise of a narrative but rather an unknown to which the remaining discourse must return.

Richards understood the powerful divide between language turned outward and inward. We have benefited from this understanding by separating internal and external perspectives as top-level clusters in a theory of priming strings of English. A limitation of Richards' *sentio/sensus* distinction is to fail to feature a perspective in which the language user relates to the audience, or, more generally, one mind relates to another. Where Richards is silent, Halliday is informative.

MICHAEL HALLIDAY

Halliday (1994; Halliday & Matthiessen, 1999) has been the founder of systemic-functional grammar. This approach to language construes language as a system of wordings through which language users, not unlike rhetorical scrabble players, make interlocking decisions. Every language choice is a choice at simultaneous and interactive realms of activity. Halliday proposes three simultaneous and interactive realms of language choice, which he describes by the term *metafunctions*. He calls his three metafunctions *ideational, interpersonal,* and *textual.* He further describes three systems (transitivity, mood, and theme) that serve each meta function respectively as the speaker or writer's thought turns into expression.

In Halliday's systemic-functional grammar, once a speaker starts to speak (or a writer to write), the metafunctions become active and the language user confronts further choices down the line within each metafunction. The subsystems serving each higher metafunction become active to determine the arrangement of words, the syntax, of each sentence.

For example, once a speaker wants to make a reference (e.g., a cat), the speaker invokes the ideational metafunction. This metafunction involves cascading choices within the transitivity system of English grammar. The speaker who says "a cat" uses the transitivity system to then establish the semantic-syntactic role of "a cat" — as agent, object, or beneficiary of an active verb (e.g., *the cat walks)* or property of an individual animal (e.g., *Felix is a cat).* According to Halliday, the transitivity system supplies English with the resources to depict concept reference and experience. More specifically, the ideational metafunction governs the depiction of people, actions, events, and thoughts.

The speaker's choice-set also involves assuming relational roles with the listener or reader. Halliday referred to these interpersonal roles as the interpersonal metafunction. This metafunction triggers cascading choices within what Halliday calls the *mood system* of English. The mood system supplies English with its richest source for enacting role relationships with a listener or reader. The mood system, for example, controls whether a sentence is declarative *(the cat went)*, interrogative *(Did the cat leave?)*, or imperative *(Move the cat!)* and each of these choices structures a different relationship with the listener.

When the speaker's linguistic choice-set involves guiding the listener through the linear processing of the message, a third metafunction becomes active, what Halliday calls the *textual metafunction*. This metafunction compels cascading choices down through what Halliday calls the thematic system of English. The *thematic system* furnishes speakers or writers with signals about prominent or nonprominent slots within a clause. The thematic system accounts for the audience's associating the most new and prominent information in an English sentence with information displaced to the end of the main clause. Thus, the thematic system accounts for a speaker's, wishing to stress the current whereabouts of the cat, to say:

98. The cat, tired, went home.

rather than:

99. The cat, having gone home, was tired.

Halliday described each of the three metafunctions and the various systems of grammar serving as distinct. Yet all three metafunctions and their underlying systems interact like gears in a Swiss watch. Speakers and writers activate all three metafunctions at once when they produce discourse.

We have only scratched the surface of Halliday's systemic-functional theory and do not pretend to have given it the justice of a thorough exposition. We have said enough, however, to indicate how Halliday provided us with the impetus for a third dimension relating representations to readers. This third category, the *relational perspective,* is one we adopt as a third cluster in our top-level hierarchy of priming categories.

Let us now turn to some contrasts between Halliday and our own priming approach to language. Halliday intends his system as a grammar. Although we acknowledge that all priming elements within English fall within a full or partial grammatical description, for us the speaker or writer's art at priming calls on grammar only as a loose constraint rather than a monolithic regulatory guide (Hopper & Traugott, 1993). Recall our earlier point that priming strings can fall either within or across conventional syntactic boundaries.*

Our purpose is not to critique Halliday. Quite the contrary. If one's goal is to

---

* An anonymous reviewer of an earlier version of this manuscript, an expert in ESL, made the point that grammar being a rather late constraint in the writers' design of texts may apply to native speakers rather than non-native ones. The reviewer points out that with many nonnative speakers grammatical structure may well start as an initial frame for mapping meaning and intention. The reviewer also notes, credibly, that Halliday intends his own framework to feature meaning over grammatical structure, at least for native speakers. We thus may be overstating the difference between Halliday's approach and our rhetorical approach on the priority of intentions over grammar.

acquire a comprehensive understanding of the grammatical structures of English language representations and if one believes in the comprehensiveness of grammar as theoretical construct underlying experiential priming, then Halliday's approach would be harder to distinguish from our own. However, if the goal, as is ours, is to develop an account of a speaker or writer's priming of audience, and if one sees grammar as a constraint more than the guiding force of representation, as we do, then our way of thinking about English priming maintains an important difference in emphasis from Halliday's.

Furthermore, from our point of view Halliday's system fails to capture Richards' all-important distinction between internal (sentio) and external (sensus) experience.

Figure 5.1 below traces the genesis of our current catalog from the intellectual perspectives of Michael Reddy, Richards, and Halliday. We start from the insight of Michael Reddy (1979) that language is not a simple container of meaning (the conduit metaphor). From Richards, we take the importance of the sensus and sentio distinction in language. From Halliday, where language structures a relationship with the online listener or reader, we take the importance of a relational element to language.

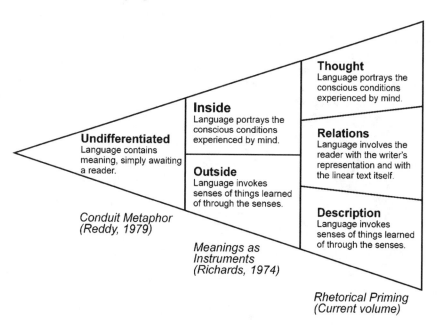

Figure 5.1: Comparison of language differentiation concept in three schemata

II

Results:
The Catalog in Depth

In this part of the book, we describe in detail the full hierarchy of our catalog of priming strings. From the top-level clusters, we turn our attention to the finer granularity of families, dimensions, and finally classes of strings. From the three major clusters of strings we have already overviewed, our catalog expands into six families, eighteen dimensions, and over 100 classes of strings. For each string class, our aim has been to include enough examples to help readers get a conceptual feel for the distinctness of each class.

The following chapter considers English strings from the first cluster, of internal perspectives, and the various families, dimensions, and specific string classes that constitute this cluster.

6

Cluster 1:
Internal Perspectives

Language, more than visual media, make the interior of minds directly accessible to readers. Write the sentence:

100. John thought that the world was round.

and the content *thought the world was round* depicts priming actions from internal perspectives. Journals, diaries, and memoirs are distinctive because of the relatively high proportion of internal perspective words they contain relative to other features. Engineering reports and scenic fieldguides are distinctive for their relatively low proportion of internal thinking references relative to other features.

In this chapter, we cover families, dimensions, and finally, specific classes of English strings depicting internal perspectives. The internal perspectives we tend to think of most involve the present and often first-person cognitions of individual minds. These strings also involve private feelings and affect. They further involve temporal projection. Our memories and anticipations are, after all, just thoughts. We start with first-person cognitions first. We then turn to affect and temporal projections.

FAMILY 1. INTERIOR THINKING
(EXPOSING AUDIENCES TO MINDS)

Dimension 1: First Person

Class 1: The Grammatical First Person The strings stereotypically associated with a mind on the page involve first-person (typically singular) self-reference, the speaker or writer's use of *I, me, my,* or *mine.* Self-referential pronouns individuate a point of view from all the mentalities and objects outside of it. Although a writer may establish point of view in the absence of first person or self-referential pronouns, self-referential pronouns, singular or plural, are sufficient to indicate that a message has a point of view.

Nonetheless, first person pronouns are not by themselves sufficient to establish a point of view that is personal or subjective. Impersonal and intersubjective technical reports can contain first person. A scientist or engineer can refer to him or herself *(I* or *my* or *we)* only to indicate that his or her individual consciousness is present. Consider the following:

101. I often use facts about Einstein's laws in my work.

Writers can make first person self-reference without being visibly idiosyncratic, subjective, personal, or controversial. Moreover, even when writers never use it explicitly, the first person is arguably implicit in all writing. In her 1979 book *White Album,* Joan Didion observed that, from the start, "writing is the act of saying I, of imposing oneself upon other people."

Some style manuals admonish writers never to use the singular first person *I.* This admonishment is an example of prescriptive grammar with little descriptive foundation. Unless a writer makes a conscious practice to follow the prescription, or a publisher expressly forbids it, the first person singular pronoun is, we have found, ubiquitous across all types of writing. With external pressure, writers can avoid it, but to do so can cause its own awkwardness and infelicity. Compare the colloquial 102 against the more awkward 103:

102. I believe it's the right thing to do.
103. The present writer believes it's the right thing to do.

First person singular pronouns, in summary, individuate a mind without specifying it or imbuing it with historical particularity. For further specification and historical particularization of a self, other words must be recruited — sometimes with the self-referential pronoun, sometimes not — to particularize and specify an historical self. We now turn to various string classes furnishing such recruitments.

Class 2: Self-Disclosure One of the surest ways English particularizes a first person consciousness is to frame it within a simple past or future. The result is a first person consciousness that self-discloses.

104. I went to the store daily.
     (simple past retrospective)
105. I'll go to the store daily.
     (future resolve)

The past tense *went* signals an individual that has historicized him- or herself. The writer of 104 offers individuation as a way of particularization, framing a unique life from a reflective vantage. The future *I'll go* (105) signals a resolve for future action. In contrast to a past or future that provides a particularizing historical frame, the present generic (106) dampens the effect of particularization by moving from a unique mental act (e.g., retrospection or resolve) to a ritual that implicates the actor without revealing his or her inner mind.

> 106. I go to the store daily.
>   *(present generic)*

The present generic *go* signals a routine or habit in which the writer participates. Example 106 provides a survey response to help a questioner understand classifications (e.g., shoppers), but not the expression of a unique historicized self.

Class 3: Autobiographical Reference Speakers and writers achieve autobiographical particularization when their first person utterance resonates with a sense of historical continuity reflective of historical identity. We may think of the historical particularization of first person as autobiographical when it is accompanied with a more habitual and continuous past verb phrase *(I would often)*, a temporally displaced past reference *(I used to)*, a more time-bound specific action *(I used the Kodak flashbulb)*, or a time-bound recurring reference *(during World War II, I used to go...)*.

Autobiographical strings combine self-referential pronouns and the perfect aspect *(have, had)* with past phrases like *used to*, or with continuous temporal adverbs like *always*.

> 107. I used to go to the story daily
>   *(I don't anymore. The practice is over.)*
> 108. I had *(always)* gone to the story daily.
>   *(I don't anymore...something happened to change that practice but that event is not specified. Compare with string 109).*
> 109. Before Jake died, I had *(always)* gone to the store daily.
>   *(I don't anymore...Jake's death put an end to that).*
> 110. I have *(always)* gone to the story daily.
>   *(still do)*

These various strings prime the impression of a speaker or writer tapping from autobiographical memory. A major difference across strings 107-110 as autobiographical reports is that the writer of 110, relying on the present perfect *have*, recalls a phase of life that continues through the present.

Refashioning simple self-reference into the particularity of an individual life can also be achieved when self-referential pronouns are combined with the future tense. In this case, an historical life is not recalled but anticipated and personally willed. Consider by way of contrast:

111. I see you all the time.
    (present generalization)
112. I'll *(get to)* see you all the time.
    (future contraction; expression of desire; autobiographical)
113. I will *(get to)* see you all the time.
    (future; expression of desire; autobiographical)
114. I will *(tend to)* see you all the time.
    (generalization of the present-in-future)

In 111, a present tense self-reference inhibits the perception of a subjective or historical self. The writer comments about bumping into the reader with a high frequency of occurrence while making no subjective commentary about this happenstance. In 112 and 113, the writer relies on the future to convey the private volition of a historical self. Note that in 114, a string that can overlap in surface form with 112 and 113, the writer projects a present generalization into the future. The present generic *"tend to"* reduces the personal and willful sense of *will* into an impersonal statistical regularity. The effect of 114 for the reader thus reproduces the effect of 111 but with future projection. Although a complex array of impressions, all of these various strings illustrate how tense specification can combine with self-reference to root particular, historical, and autobiographical selves on the page.

Dimension 2: Inner Thinking

Speakers and writers of English have more than tense as a resource with which to portray private and historical selves. They can also portray their inner mind through a dimension of strings we call *inner thinking*. The strings associated with this dimension form a variety of specific string classes: namely private thinking verbs, disclosures, evidentials, expectancies, and contingencies. We review each of these string classes next.

Private Thought and Subjective Disclosure

Class 1: Private Thinking   Writers convey inner thinking through private-cognition or thinking verbs (e.g., *contemplate, decide, discover),* with or without an accompanying first person or temporal framing.

115. John contemplates leaving home.
116. Mary decides to find her mother.
117. Jill discovers she has lost her watch.

Of interest about these strings is that while we have all recognized ourselves in the act of contemplating, deciding, or discovering, we have never actually witnessed a contemplation, a decision, or a discovery (as direct objects of perception). The science of psychology may be uncomfortable about making assertive claims about our minds, but the English language is not. The strings just mentioned, unremarkable English, are direct and unqualified reports about that which we have no direct access — the inner minds of distinct and particular human agents.

Recall that we had cited string 106 to clarify how one can use first person and present tense without particularizing oneself or revealing one's mind. What we learn from strings 115-117 is that with a specific subject, private-thinking verbs reveal the particularization of mind, no matter what other factors apply, including present tense. John's contemplation (and Mary's decision and Jill's discovery) are not only individuating but also distinctive and historically particular to the individual. No one can share the private thoughts of another, but through thinking strings, speakers and writers make the act and often outcome of private thought visible to audiences.

Some further samples of private-thinking strings in our catalog, drawn from the letters F through I, are: *ferreting out, figure out, figure on, fill her in, found it out, flirt with the idea, flummoxed, forget, form an opinion, found it out, get a fix on, get a grasp of, get a handle on, getting a grasp of the idea, give the idea time to sink in, guess, had been curious about, had been focusing on, heeded, imagine, and in quest of.* Note that we have drawn widely across tenses and expression length because tense families and expression length don't matter to the capacity of these expressions to prime action from an internal perspective.

Class 2: Disclosures   Disclosures are the spoken or written simulation of private thought presented to an audience as part of an unofficial leaking. When speakers and writers use disclosure strings, they suggest they are making public inner thinking that remains the property of the discloser and was not designed at its core to be public information. This is in stark contrast, as we will see, with strings in the relational cluster (reasoning, shared social ties, directed activities) that seek to convey information designated from the start to be social and shared. Disclosures can take the form of verbs of speaking *(confessed, acknowledged)* and often participate in verbal formulas, such as *personally, frankly, tellingly, telltale,* and *in all candor.*

A class related to disclosures already discussed is self-disclosures, disclosures from the first person. By contrast, third person disclosures cite another person's disclosing behavior. Compare the following strings:

118. John confessed to murder.
     (referencing a disclosure without making one)
119. Frankly, Lester doesn't know what he's doing.
     (self-disclosing)

120. To be candid, we can't make the deadline.
    (self-disclosing)
121. I say to you, sincerely, I am sorry.
    (self-disclosing)

Whether issued from first or third person, the felt effect of a disclosure is the leaking of private information, with a whiff of personal risk to the discloser. Texts that make first-person disclosures form the basis of so-called "personal" writing. Writing teachers (Bleich, 1998; Elbow, 1991) have long advocated assignments calling for disclosure as ways of helping students come to grips with authenticity and ownership over their writing. As Ann Gere (2002) recently observed, personal writing favors disclosure and revelation over withholding. However, as Gere noted, full revelation does not automatically make a text more positively impactful on readers. In research we have conducted comparing students and experts in professional settings, we have found that expert writers purposefully withhold disclosure in comparison to novices on the same task, who disclosed their private thought significantly more often (Collins, Kaufer Neuwirth, & Palmquist 2002). In certain professional genres (e.g., software documentation), experience seems to teach that the "professional voice" requires withholding self and remaining within an inherited professional persona.

Nonetheless, it is too simple to imagine that all professional writing withholds subjectivity whereas personal writing reveals it. All writing, personal or professional, is a balance of disclosing and withholding and writing differs only according to where it places the boundaries. The following strings, often overlapping with denials and disclaimers (discussed later on), signal information withheld, but only as a way to set limits on one's willingness to disclose.

122. This is all I will say on that subject.
123. I can't say this in a family publication.
124. The details are too intimate for me to render here.
125. I'm sure you get the basic idea.
    (implication: so no further detail is needed)

As illustrated in this example, such strategic withholdings continue to function as disclosures. However, they indicate principled limits on what the writer has and will disclose.

Gere saw a speaker or writer's limits on disclosure as serving aesthetic, ethical, and political-deliberative ends. They serve aesthetic functions because no writer, no matter how forthcoming, can disclose everything. Keeping the reader moving along always requires pruning, which explains such strings as:

126. I won't bore you with all that happened.
    (I want to keep you awake)

127. To make a long story short...
   (I want my story contained within your attention span)
128. I could go on but it would be too painful.
   (I can indicate my pain just as forcefully by leaving it to your imagination than by dictating every specific to you)

Examples 126 and 127 indicate limits on disclosure from the reader and story perspectives respectively. Example 128 telegraphs personal suffering as a reason for withholding a narrative. The writer arguably heightens emotional intensity by suggesting that what is revealed is but the tip of an iceberg of what is not. The effect is to hint at an overwhelming emotion the reader is mostly spared.

Limits on disclosure also serve ethical functions, as Gere noted, when to disclose fully would break promises, violate confidences, and flout another's rights. We frequently find examples of this kind in the discussion of legal and medical privacy rights.

129. I have sworn not to give further details.
130. The rest violates confidences and I can't get into that.
131. In the interests of protecting her medical privacy, this is all I will say about her condition.

Finally, as Gere indicated, limits on disclosure serve political-deliberative correctives when a reader would mistake a speaker or writer's discourse with being more forthcoming, forthright, or complete than is actually the case. Such strings are often used to jolt the reader that what has been covered has only scratched the surface:

132. I have covered much. But I have only scratched the surface.
133. I have given an overview of X. I have left out many important details that deserve attention in their own right. But that's another paper.
134. *(After 375 pages of describing herself as an Indian woman in Guatemala, the author startles the reader with)* I'm still keeping my Indian identity a secret.
   (From Rigoberta Menchu's autobiography, cited in Gere, pp. 27-8).

Examples 132-134 are authorial conventions for telegraphing to the reader limits on disclosure.

Should, of course, the speaker or writer withhold what the audience deems essential to know, the writer's admission of limits on disclosure may cause a negative audience reaction:

135. I have only scratched the surface.
   (audience reaction: You have failed, dear writer, to be substantive)

136. I have left out many important details.
     (audience reaction: You have failed, dear writer, to be informative)
137. I'm keeping my Indian identity a secret.
     (audience reaction: not a happy outcome, dear writer, when I was looking for you to share your secrets of identity).

The adverb *just,* an adverb we will be referencing throughout, contributes to strings of disclosure. *Just* adds a sense of the writer's feel of timeliness or vividness about a disclosure. Compare how strings 139 and 141 add timbres of subjectively felt timeliness or vividness to strings 138 and 140 respectively:

138. I can see it now.
     (a disclosure)
139. I can just see it now.
     (adding immediacy to the disclosure)
140. I can imagine what he must have said.
     (a disclosure)
141. I can just imagine what he must have said.
     (adding subjective vividness to the disclosure)

Other examples of disclosure strings from our catalog include*: may I be blunt, candidly, sincerely, respectfully, personally I feel, out of my mind, I must fess up to, let me speak my mind, let me say it straight.* A surprising disclosure string we found was *let on that.* Let is an extremely versatile word of English but the *let on that* construction seems mainly restricted to a verb of disclosure. Compare the following forms:

142. Please let me go.
     (request for permission and direct address)
143. He let on that he was unhappy
     (report of personal disclosure)

Speakers and writers can indicate to a reader the confidence they hold in the ideas presented, and discourse analysts call these indications evidentials. Johnstone (2001, p. 240) defined evidentials as "any grammatical or lexical strategy for indicating how the information expressed in an utterance was acquired or how certain it is." Evidentials combine with disclosures to indicate the degree of subjective confidence toward the truth of an expression. The following two classes of the inner-thinking dimension deal with the evidentials of confidence and uncertainty.

Evidential Stances: Projecting Confidence and Uncertainty

Class 3: Confidence   When the mind of the speaker or writer evaluating seems certain and unshakeable, the speaker or writer primes audiences to recognize confidence in the message. To appreciate what confidence adds to an English string, let us first consider some strings where confidence is absent or at least unmarked:

144. This was a victory.
     (past indicative)
145. You are the right choice.
     (present indicative)
146. You will go.
     (future indicative, directive, predictive)

Now consider the effect of adding confidence markers, such as *hands-down, it is clear,* and *absolutely.*

147. This was a hands-down victory.
148. It is clear that you are the right choice.
149. You absolutely will go.

Other confidence strings involve emphatic phrases starting with *flat out and had better and had best: flat out false, flat out right, for all the world like, for certain, for sure, foregone conclusion, guarantee of, had best, had better get that, had better take, handily, hands down.*

Confidence is the unmarked subjective attitude behind a speaker or writer's assertions. The lexical markers that denote a speaker or writer's confident attitude about an utterance also denote the truth of the utterance as an assertion.

150. The cat is on the mat.
     (unmarked assertion with the speaker's confidence also unmarked)
151. The truth is, the cat is on the mat.
     ("the truth is"—marks both the assertive status of the statement and the speaker's confidence in the statement's truth)

In the presence of the second person you, confidence can overlap with insistence. Confidence stresses the strength of belief, whereas the second person stresses the interpersonal force and insistent pressure one can exert through a confident expression.

152. You had better believe it will rain today.
     (confidence, insistence)

When conjoined with mental states of knowing, the versatile *just* contributes to confidence strings. When writers are intense about their degree of knowing, they appear even more confident. Compare the strings here:

153. I knew it.
     (confident and satisfied)
154. I just knew it.
     (more confident and more satisfied)

Notice how *just,* as an intensifier, strengthens the confidence of knowledge asserted. Notice also that it strengthens the degree of internal satisfaction implied from that knowing.

Another sense of the adverbial *just,* (sense 19 of CCD) also participates in confidence strings. This sense, part of the string just about, is more confident and less qualified than the qualifier *almost,* as evidenced in the following:

155. I eat almost everything.
     (if you make me think, I maybe can come up with what I won't eat ... but I'm not inviting you to)
156. I eat just about anything.
     (I can't imagine what I don't eat)
157. Almost everyone we invited came.
     (except Sally)
158. Just about everyone we invited came.
     (I can't think who didn't come)

In string 155, the writer indicates confidence about what she does and does not eat. The word *almost* supplies a restrictive qualification. "I eat almost everything except spinach." In string 156, with *just about,* the writer indicates confidence about what she does eat and seems hazy about what she does not. The *just about* creates a hedge rather than a precise qualification. Consequently, it sounds imprecise and somewhat misleading to write, "I eat just about everything, except (definitely not) spinach."

Some thinking verbs that imply the truth of their complement clauses, what linguists call *factive verbs,* like *know that, recognize that,* or *understand that* overlap with confidence. This is because writers select these verbs only when they assume the situations involved are true states of affairs:

159. I know that the world is round.
     (implies confidence that the world is round).
160. I recognize that I must go.
     (implies with confidence an obligation to go).
161. I understand what I must do.
     (implies confidence that there is an obligation to do a particular action).

The *that*-complement turns out to be an important contributor to this effect. When writers follow the verb *know*, for example, with a *to* or *how*, they declare their competence more than their confidence:

162. I know that the box is upstairs.
     (confidence where the box is)
163. I know how to find the box.
     (competence to retrieve the box; confidence in this competence a strong implication)
164. I know to go upstairs for the box.
     (competence to retrieve the box; confidence in this competence a weaker implication)

The use of situational *it* conveys factual occurrence, and so, like the factive *that*, can indicate revelatory confidence in the existence of an event (e.g., *it's a boy! It's a rainbow! It's a hurricane!*). Similarly, the existential *there* can convey existential confidence of a similar kind, meaning that an entity in a pre-designated class actually exists (e.g., *there's an apartment down the street you can afford*). Other confidence strings stress a firm mind, free of doubt, or qualification—such as *proof, knowledge, certainty, rightness, proved, purely, right as rain, say categorically, simple truth, simple truths, sure, obvious, patently,* and *simply*.

Class 4: Uncertainty   A confident mind is conveyed by strings that communicate a plain, simple, and undivided truth. The uncertain mind, in stark contrast, is chronically measured *(allegedly, to the best of my knowledge)*, qualified *(nearly, almost, just about somewhat)*, divided *(divided about, ambivalent, torn between, doubtful about, dubious, am of two minds)*, or conflicted *(waffling, baffled)*. Watch how the *simply* of a confident mind is washed over with doubt when under the control of a contingent *whether*.

165. John thought he could simply go.
     (John is confident he can go)
166. John thought (about) whether he could simply go.
     (John ponders the consequences of confidently going)

Modals of contingency like *may* and *can* overlap with the contingency and hedging associated with uncertainty: *may appear, can conceivably, may perhaps, can possibly, may seem*. Other contributors to uncertainty are thinking words whose meaning overlaps with the uncertainty of knowledge *(conjecture, speculate, guess, estimate)* or decision-making *(bewilderment, vacillation, waffle)*. A common source of uncertainty is the direct denial of certainty—*not certain that..., not convinced, not definite, it's not clear*. Uncertainty overlaps with spatial location in the English word, *whereabouts* (e.g., "I wish I knew her whereabouts"), a favorite of the criminalist:

167. The police are still looking for the killer's whereabouts.
     (a spatial location they can't specify)

Against the confidence of strings 144 through 154, compare the tentativeness of the following strings:

168. This was arguably a victory.
     (I know some see it as a loss)
169. Perhaps you are the right choice.
     (You may be the wrong one)
170. You might want to go.
     (You might not)

Uncertainty is cued by the English indefinite pronouns *some* and *any*.

171. Someone was here to see you.
     (I don't know her name)
172. Let me see if I have any change
     (I don't know how much, so I'll look)

When an indefinite, indicating uncertainty, combines with a conventional cue for specificity, the combination can lead to a blended effect that is not part of either input cue (see Fauconnier and Turner, 2002). For example, the most frequent time-shifting preposition is *at*. When we want an audience to move mentally to a specific time frame other than the present, *at* is English's most serviceable and pinpoint confident preposition about destination.

173. I'll be there at 5 o'clock.
174. We met at 9 sharp last Tuesday.

When we want the audience to time travel, but are uncertain about the destination, we must avoid *at* or at the very least qualify it:

175. I'll be there sometime around 5 o'clock.
     (at avoided)
176. I'll be there anytime from 2 to 5.
     (at avoided)
177. I'll be there at approximately 5 o'clock.
     (at qualified)

The string, *at any* + *time,* blending the *at* of specific time reference and uncertainty, comes to mean not a time reference at all, but a projected window priming a sense of immediacy, suspense, uncertainty, and anxiety.

178. She should be hearing about the promotion at any time now.
(so she is excited)
179. The soldier may be called up for duty at any moment now.
(so his family is on pins and needles)

What initially seems in the input string *at* to be a time reference becomes, with uncertainty, a projection of future anticipation or apprehension.

There is sometimes a fine line between confidence and uncertainty, depending on whether the string contains other markers of reliable or unreliable evidence. Reliability and unreliability sometimes blend, as in the remarkable string, *sure seems:*

180. This lock sure seemed in good shape.
(uttered after the lock is found broken; indicates an impression that seemed confident and reliable though it retains the status of an impression)

The English words *appear* and *appearance* both indicate masks that cloak reality. Words like *evident* and *apparent,* in contrast, indicate the revelation of the real. Compare the different associations produced by these words in the context of priming confidence or its absence.

181. John wants to be an accountant.
(direct assertion)
182. John appears to want to be an accountant.
(hedge on the assertion; signs point to John's aspirations but these signs could be incorrect; hint of uncertainty)
183. John apparently/evidently wants to be an account.
(reliable shared evidence that John wants to be an accountant; hint of confidence backing the assertion)
184. It appears that John wants to be an account.
(embedding John's desire within a personal impression that weakens confidence, adds uncertainty about John's aspiration)
185. It is apparent/evident that John wants to be an accountant.
(grounding John's desire within visible circumstantial evidence that strengthens confidence, subtracts uncertainty about John's aspiration)

The writer can convey uncertainty not only in meaning conveyed but also in speech act force. The adverb *just* modifies the speech act itself by hedging the force through which it is made. Compare the following:

186. I suggest that…
(please hear my suggestion)

187. I just suggest that... .
    (it's only a suggestion, not a command, so there's no harm listening)
188. I think that... .
    (please hear what I think)
189. I just think that... .
    (it's only a thought, not a conviction, so there's no harm listening)

The writer employs *just* in these strings to weaken the force through which the information is presented or the goals for presenting it.

Emotive and Temporal Force: Intensity and Immediacy

The string classes below prime the speaker or writer's forcefulness of expression, marking the forcefulness of emotion (intensity) or of temporal recency (immediacy).

Class 5: Intensity As one string class marking audience experience, intensity shares with confidence the felt-presence of a mind that is decisive. When intensity blends with confidence (e.g., *absolutely, certainly*), one produces a kind of emphatic that Hyland (2000) called *boosters*. However, unlike evidentials conveying confidence, English strings conveying intensity underscore the writer's emotion more than the assurance of truth. Intensity ranges across positive and negative affect (discussed next). The writer capturing intensity in tone can be intensely negative or intensely positive. Writers produce intensity with words, like *very, incredibly, worst, astonishing, shocking,* along with the overused *really* and *actually,* which refer to existence but which writers use to signal different shades of intensity. As an intensifier, *actually* seems to convey a slight exceeding of expectation and the call of duty, whereas *really* emphasizes sincerity and conviction:

190. I actually visited him.
    (I visited him and that was beyond the reasonable call of duty)
191. I really like him.
    (I like him and I mean it)

The exclamation point (!) also contributes intensity from the English punctuation system (Nunberg, 1990), as do some uses of typology. Consider in the following strings how the inclusion of intensity words adds to the perceived tone:

192. This was an incredibly great victory.
    (more than great)
193. The committee picked the worst stinking choice.
    (worse than worse)

194. I find it astonishing that you would go.
(more than unexpected)
195. We are finally going!
(more than an event; an event too long delayed)

One characteristic feature of intensity is the speaker or writing priming a sense of strong but nonspecific feeling. Some examples are, *torrid, totally, completely, under a compulsion to, under the sun, unprecedented, urge, vehement about, very special, wait for no one, well I'll be a, well I'll be damned, went all out, went ape over, went at it hammer and tongs, went at it tooth and nail.*

Some intensity words overlap with content, depending on syntactic context and placement. As an adjective following a stative verb *(is, was)* or a verb of resemblance *(looks), pretty* indicates attractive, a positive feeling toward a female's appearance (e.g., *Mary is/looks pretty).* As an adverb modifying an adjective, *pretty* serves as an intensifier, strengthening a negative judgment or weakening a positive one.

196. His condition is pretty bad.
(= really bad; pretty intensifying the negative)
197. Her first try was pretty good.
(= not quite good; pretty weakening the positive)

Writers skilled in the priming art find countless opportunities for punning based on the variation of part of speech and priming potencies. One of us overhead the following punning on *pretty* in an actual conversation:

Michael: "I just took my young nieces to the zoo. That was pretty exhausting."
Jonathan: "Michael, there's nothing pretty about that!"

Michael's intonation indicated he wanted to use *pretty* as an intensifying adverb to strengthen the sense of his own exhaustiveness. Jonathan saw an opportunity to echo Michael's use of *pretty* within a pirouette of meaning that reverted to the descriptive adjective denying the positive.

We should not be surprised to find the flexible *just* adding to intensity strings. Compare:

198. Just look!
(pay attention to nothing else except looking)
199. Just think of that!
(clear your mind of everything else but that thought)
200. It's just stupid!
(there is nothing else to call it)

In examples of this kind, the adverbial *just* sets the stage for the words or phrases following it (e.g., *look, think, stupid).*

Class 6: Immediacy Immediacy in a string conveys the inside experience of an event happening now or within the window of now. For the speaker or writer, strings conveying immediacy rely heavily on the word now, the emphatic *right* (e.g., *right here, right now, right over, right up),* a short interval boxing in the now of speaking *(today)* or a longer time frame kept current through a demonstrative pronoun *(this month, these weeks).* Also apt for conveying immediacy are verbs considered important enough to mark milestones *(accomplish, achieve, announce).* Some further examples of strings priming immediacy: *starting today, effective today, as of this day, right now, had just been, still sees her, even as we speak, currently has, right here, right this moment, right this month, now accomplished, now announce, now at hand, now hear this.*

Immediacy is not only the inside experience of time, but the feel of ongoing and direct relevance, even when it comes from a time interval that started a long way back. The string *ever since* provides a connective tissue that retains the immediacy of a past event. To appreciate better the workings of *ever since,* consider the lone work of *since,* a conjunction that typically signals a time shift:

201. Since his immature days, he's learned a great deal about himself.
(Time shift from his immature days)

Coupled with *ever,* in *ever since,* one is able to sharpen the feel of immediate relevance for a time interval still going on.

202. Ever since his immature days, he's learned a great deal about himself.
(What started in his immature days is evident in him today)

The demonstrative *this* functions as a marker of felt immediacy and relevance of a past state, especially when expressing time (e.g., *at this point, at this time).* Note how *this,* in comparison to *that,* plops the speaker and audience into time past as if the past were unfolding now.

203. At this point, I was helpless.
(= experiencing my past helplessness like it is just happening)
204. At that point, I was helpless.
(= experiencing my past helplessness from the psychological distance of a truly past event)

Like *this, just* is a workhorse in English for bringing immediacy to the listener or reader.

205. They are just coming.
(The event is happening as I speak)

The felt immediacy of something's happening often blends with a confirmation and confidence that it has happened. With this in mind, consider how the writer of 205 not only expresses when the event will be happening *(right now)*, but also confidently confirms that it has started happening.

Immediacy figures into many other English strings, but often in a subordinate role to storytelling (see the analysis of the storyteller's *just then* later).

Subjective Expectancies: Perceiving From the Inside

Subjective expectancies prime audiences to recognize the internal assessment of contingencies, the interior experience of time, or the interior perception of objects or events.

Class 7: The Perception of Contingency Contingency strings indicate perceived but often nonspecific dependencies between events. When contingency within a string arose from the indefiniteness of time past (e.g., *could have happened)* or time future *(e.g., might yet happen)*, we classified the string as belonging to another category of inner thinking discussed later, namely temporal projection. We restricted the present class of contingency strings to those indicating possibilities defined by logic and hypothetical thinking rather than through projected time travel, forward or back. Consequently, contingencies in our catalog are composed of strings like *as if, whether, provided that, if only, only with, might have, would have, it all depends, lest, can't help it if, fluke,* and the adventitious use of *just* in such phrases as, *he just happened to bump into her.* Here are some other strings priming contingency.

206. it depends
207. if you are willing
208. happened upon
209. he might have got lost if you hadn't helped.
210. he can't help it if he is poor.

A seldom-noticed workhorse for contingency in English is the word *without,* which signals necessary conditions for executing contracts of permission and consent.

211. Without their permission, she can't go to the prom.
     (conditional on permission)
212. Without a scholarship, he can't go to college.
     (conditional on a scholarship)
213. Without her apologizing, they will never get back together
     (conditional on an apology)

Strings of contingency combine *with* or *without* with second person interactivity when the speaker or writer needs to make the audience an agent of the condition.

214. With your permission, I'd like to leave
     (contingency + interactivity)
215. I can't do this without your consent.
     (contingency + interactivity)

Yet another word introducing contingency is the verb *have,* which writers package variously to indicate contingent possession or ownership. Compare:

216. I own a doll.
     (possession, ownership)
217. I have a doll
     (possession, implied ownership)
218. I own a mess.
     (not a string we've found)
219. I have a mess on my hands.
     (contingent possession, I didn't ask for it)
220. We have a two-hour delay.
     (contingent hardship; very common usage to express contingent problem conditions in traffic and police reporting).

Thoughts that form the basis of logical contingency are frequently also the object of uncertainty and displacement in time. For this reason, stings of logical contingency commonly overlap with strings of uncertainty and temporal projection, which we examine later on.

Class 8: The Subjective Feel of Time's Passing   The subjective feel of time indicates time that is experienced as shorter than or longer than the objective elapse of clock time. Strings from this class often use the prepositions *in* and *within* and especially the adverbs *only* and *just* (e.g., *in only six months, within just six short years*). These strings sometimes use accelerative and comparative adverbs like *slower (slower than molasses)* and *faster (faster than you can spit).* They rely on temporal adverbs like *before (before they knew it)* and on psychological and negative standard adjectives indicating the feeling of too much time passing with too little action *(protracted, prolonged, overlong, boring, procrastinating, overdue)* or too little adaptation to the present *(anachronism, too little too late).*

Six adverbs that are very important string-builders for temporal subjectivity are *ever, enough, finally, still, already,* and *yet. Ever* is interesting because its best-known cultural stereotype sets it within the proverbial happy ending *ever after.* Within this stereotype, *ever's* direct opposite is *never.* Consider:

221. They lived happily ever after.
     (a future of uninterrupted bliss)
222. They lived happily never after that.
     (a future of uninterrupted misery)

The subjective temporality of *as ever* and *as ever before*, meaning maintaining constancy from what came before, also seems to make it the diametrical opposite of *never as* and *never as before,* the latter meaning breaking precedent from what came before.

223. He was handsome as ever.
    (handsome then; handsome now)
224. He was never as handsome.
    (more handsome now than then)
225. The president is as fit as ever.
    (subjective time+ update; now is just as good as then)
226. The president is fit as never before.
    (subjective time + update; now is better than then)

However, these stereotypical uses seem to misrepresent the preponderance of uses with *ever.* This is because many strings with *ever* do not rely on its stereotypical opposition to *never.* Indeed, many uses of *ever* make it a virtual synonym with never! This is especially true when ever is preceded by a modal verb *(would, could, should)* or followed by a finite verb to mean something like *never before* or *never after,* indicating an unparalleled break from the past that does not repeat into the future.

227. It's as much money as I should ever need.
    (never after will I want for money)
228. It could be the best day I ever had.
    (contingency + never before have I had a day so good)
229. This is the biggest pumpkin I ever saw.
    (never before have I experienced a pumpkin this big)
230. It was the only love she has ever known.
    (projecting back from living memory (has) + up to this point in her life, she has had but one love.)

The writer can produce a voice of poignancy and nostalgia when *ever* is used in an omniscient narration, often to isolate a happy moment from a span of other, presumed less happy, moments over a lifespan. This voice can be retrospective when combined with a past *would* or *had (would ever, had ever)* or a confident all-knowing and so oracular predictor of the future, when combined with future *will (will ever):*

231. It was the only love she would ever know.
232. It was the only love she had ever known.
    (poignancy through retrospection. The "would ever" or "had ever" projects backward from the end of her life to her isolated love. The point of view of the obituary writer)

233. It was the only love she will ever know.
(poignancy through oracular decree. The "will ever" projects from the moment of her love ahead to the end of her life).

When speakers and writers adopt retrospective *(would never)* and oracular *(will never)* negativity, it is interesting to contrast the negativity of these subjective forms with the negativity of simple denials *(did not, never did)*. The negativity of the retrospective voice seems the most sympathetic, the voice of, say, a biographer writing about a flawed human being from the evidence of the subject's life. The oracular voice in the negative seems the most harsh and dismissive, often used to pronounce summative judgments. The voice of simple denial seems somewhere in between. Contrast the following examples:

234. He was never to amount to anything.
(retrospective dismissal, least prejudicial because of its evidentiary feel of judging the subject from the record of a life lived)
235. He will never amount to anything.
(oracular dismissal, prejudicial negative affect because of its summative feel)
236. He never amounted to anything.
(simple denial; declarative negative fact now recorded and so less dismissive than oracular "will never amount to")

Like *ever, enough* is regimented to subjective perception (e.g., *enough rope, enough money)* and often to the subjective perception of time, typically with a negative cast *(not enough hours in the day; not enough time to think).*

237. The speech was long enough for me to fall asleep.
(too long)

English signals a speaker's impatience with the elapse of time through strings with the temporal adverbs, *finally** and *still.*

238. I am still waiting in the doctor's office.
(I am impatient to do so)
239. I finally got out of the doctor's office.
(I was impatient while there and relieved now to be out)

As a string priming the subjective perception of time, *finally* signals the writer's relief at finishing a period of trial or impatience. *Still,* by contrast, is only appropriate when the time interval remains ongoing. One can use subjective

---

* *Finally* also functions as metadiscourse indicating a speaker or writer's final point. This is discussed in a later chapter.

finally only when one is relieved about surviving a trial. However, one can use *still* to indicate intervals one would never like to leave:

240. We are still in love.
     (positive affect)
241. We still have our health.
     (positive affect)

Still runs the gamut when it comes to good or bad feeling about experiencing an interval of time. *Finally* focuses on the speaker or writer's involved feeling of relief from escaping or overcoming a bad situation.

242. We still are happy.
     (holding on to a positive affect)
243. We still are miserable.
     (holding on to a negative affect)
244. We finally are happy.
     (relief from moving beyond the condition of no happiness)
245. We finally are miserable.
     (awkwardness indicates that finally favors reversals only for the better)

Already indicates a belief that the audience has been waiting for an event to be completed, that it is now complete, and that the audience has yet to be told.

246. Mom, I've already got a job!
     (appropriate if mom has been tracking my getting a job, I have a job, and no one has told her)

To understand the subjective-temporal timbre of *already,* consider its objective counterpart, which is *has since been. Has since been* anchors the event completed to an objective past event without regard for the audience's prior expectation. By contrast, *already* anchors the event to the audience's expectation that the event should have been initiated prior to speaking. Assume that a company has been taken over and the CEO recently sacked. When speakers or writers want to anchor the firing to the objective event of the takeover and pay no mind to the audience's subjective expectations, they will use *has since been* to reference the past of the firing. Should they address the audience's prior expectation of the firing, they will use *already.*

247. He has since been fired.
     (Since anchored to the past takeover of the company; no accommodation to the audience's expectations about the event)

248. He has already been fired.

249. *(Already anchored to the audience's subjective expectation that the CEO's sacking was only a matter of time)*

Both *still* and *already* function in strings that update audiences and we discuss their role as updates in a later chapter.

Yet, oriented to the subjective future, signifies the anticipation of something happening that has not happened, often preceded by a perfect aspect *(have)*. The effect is to provide continuity from past to present and, when followed by an infinitival *to + verb* construction, the effect further binds the present to the future.

250. Mary has yet to go.

(The "has yet to" signals the writer's judgment that the over-time interval involving Mary both exists and is not completed.)

As a string-ending (and typically sentence ending) word, often with a negative of denial earlier in the string, yet can be an emphatic, indicating a strong prediction, and implied imperative that an open interval of time is soon to close.

251. John hasn't taken out the garbage yet.

(yet = emphatic that he most certainly will even if I have to stand behind him every step of the way)

Some strings of subjective time are ambiguous between the subjective perception of time intervals and more descriptive portrayals. These stings, like all ambiguous strings we came across for our catalog, disambiguate only with lengthening. One example is the string *by the time*. The subjective version of this string signals a time interval outliving its usefulness. *By the time* in this sense roughly means *too late*. The descriptive version of *by the time* indicates a time interval in the future in which the speaker and hearer will stage a rendezvous: Contrast the following examples:

252. By the time we get it fixed, it will be time to replace it.

(subjective, it will take too long to get it fixed)

253. I will have it for you by the time you get back from shopping.

(descriptive, shifting time reference to a period in the future)

A similar ambiguity between subjective and descriptive indicators of temporal intervals arises with the string *every time* and the idiom, *everytime (everywhere) I/you… look/turn:*

254. Every time I look, I see your room is a mess.

(subjective impression of time = you leave your room a mess too often)

255. Every time we went out, we had a good time.

(descriptive repeated occurrence)

As these examples indicate, words that record the subjective perception of time often overlap with a narrator's time shifts within a story frame. We revisit these more objective narrative time shifts when we consider time-shifts within narrative situations in a later chapter.

The adverbial *just* adds its mark to subjective time perception, particularly either in conjunction with the adverb *when* (e.g., *just when*) or when following a verb (e.g., *came in just*). In both cases, *just* adds a tinge of immediacy to the audience experience, making time-spans feel shorter. Consider the following:

256. He came just when I called him.
     (I felt no lag; he's that reliable)
257. He came in just a few minutes.
     (quicker than I thought)

Class 9: The Subjective Perception of Objects or Events   We typically see objects in the world from the vantage of our prior expectations. When our actual perception overturns our prior expectations, speakers and writers can mark the event through wording choice. English regularly marks this subverting of expectation with string-builders that vary on the formula *just/only/even + an + object*.

258. It was just a shadow.
     (I was fearing a ghost!).
259. It was only a dream.
     (I thought it was real).
260. He didn't even recognize his mother.
     (I thought he would be able to).

The expression *only/just + a* indicates how the observed properties of an object or event cause surprise by making the actual a poor and dim substitute for what had been expected. By contrast, the expression *even + a* works in both directions of surprise—that is, either by showing how a hard-to-meet expectation was surprisingly easily met or an easy-to-meet expectation was surprisingly hard to meet:

261. The suitcase looks light but even a weightlifter can't lift it.
     (= a low expectation that the actual surprisingly can't meet)
262. The material looks hard but even a dummy can get through it.
     (= a high expectation that the actual surprisingly can)

In either direction, the expression *even + a* precedes a noun stereotype (e.g., *weightlifter, dummy*) that the speaker employs to culturally frame a mismatch between the expected and observed.

The word *all,* often used as a quantifier of generalization, can also indicate a subjective effort to lower expectations about personal gain, ambition, or capacity. Contrast a generalization sense of *all* from the subjective use, where *all* mimics a subjectively perceived *only:*

263. All men are mortal.
     (quantifier of generalization)
264. All I want is to make a decent living.
     (subjective lowering of event expectation)
265. All I could do was stare at the walls all day along.
     (subjective lowering of capacity)

Strings priming subjective perception blend with storytelling or narrative strings, where a narrator, as a plot device, reports on unexpected perceptions (e.g., *the ghost, alas, was only a wind in the bushes).* Strings of subjective perception also overlap with relational strings, like instructions and assurance, where offering the audience reassurance, and so moving the audience from the anxious and the unknown to the familiar is the goal:

266. You can ignore these menus for now. They are just for advanced users.
267. You aren't hurt. It's only a small cut.

We saw that the word *enough* can indicate the subjective perception of time. At its most basic, however, *enough* indicates the subjective perception of any continuous quantity and, in particular, the subjective perception of whether that quantity is in sufficient supply. *Enough* as a quantity term of subjective perception frequently combines with negative affect. This combination is pronounced when it is perceived that some subjectively defined prior expectation of sufficiency is not met or overly exceeded. There is either a negative undersupply or a negative oversupply:

268. There are not enough teachers for the students.
     (enough + negative affect because of undersupply)
269. Enough already.
     (enough + negative affect because of oversupply)
270. Enough is enough.
     (enough + negative affect because of oversupply)

Not all oversupply is negative however, and when an oversupply is positive English relies on the string *more than enough* to create an audience sense of positive surplus:

271. We have more than enough for everyone.
     (enough + positive affect because of oversupply)

For many content words, a reliable test for their subjective standing is their capacity to oscillate between positive and negative polarities (see below). A case in point is the word *cheap:*

272. The suit could be had for a cheap price.
     (cheap = positive evaluation)
273. The restaurant servings were cheap.
     (cheap = negative evaluation)

The judgment of cheapness is a subjective judgment. It is its fundamental subjectivity that helps explain its easy participation in positive or negative judgments.

Affect and Evaluation (Positive and Negative Polarities)

We now examine how inner thinking strings can convey affect. The impression of strings of this type is minds that feel as well as think. Speakers and writers prime affect in their audiences by using emotionally loaded words, positive or negative. This is hardly news to students of language. Less well documented is that the polarity between positive and negative language seems a fundamental one in the pragmatic foundations of language. Textual genres differ in their tendencies toward affective language. More specifically, strings bringing out overt signals of affect underlie crucial differences between fiction and nonfiction texts. In an unpublished study of the Brown corpus containing 378 randomly chosen nonfiction texts and 122 random fiction texts, we found that affect terms (positive and negative) are used, with statistical confidence, more frequently in the surface language of nonfiction than in fiction. Writers of nonfiction, from simple news to argument, are more interested in referencing and commenting on the world than in fashioning it artistically. Consequently, they are inclined to bring affect into the surface text. By contrast, as we saw with the Melville example, writers of imaginative literature understand that emotions too overtly gestured in the surface language can inhibit audiences from elaborating their own emotional response to the situations of the text. They thus would prefer to fashion a world within cool descriptive detail and leave it to the reader to judge it joyful or dreary.

Strings conveying affect fall into two dimensions: thinking positive and thinking negative. While a surprising number of words live on both sides of this polarity (e.g., *cheap),* many remain on one side or the other.

Dimension 3: Think Positive

Think positive covers a large class of "feel good" words and phrases that signal positive feeling. Some obvious single-word examples are: *commendable, loving, succulent, fantastic, delightful.* These are but a tiny sampling of thousands of individual words and multi-word strings employing positive affect. Although it seems commonsensical that positive words should remain positive, common-sense does not always pertain. If ever there was a standard for positive affect in English, it should be the word *good*. However, when used with the indefinite article (viz., *a good*) to describe distance, time, money or some other countable unit, *good* functions as a subjective intensifier to describe quantities that exceed expectations:

274. We walked a good five miles.
    (more than we thought)
275. He'll have to pay a good thousand bucks.
    (more than he wanted)
276. I've been waiting a good hour.
    (more than I should have)
277. Despite these and other unexpected instabilities in affect terms, they often are stable as single words.
    (not just well-customized, but well-customized in the best way a boat can be)
278. The award had to be just so wonderful for her.
    (not just wonderful but wonderful in the best way an award can be)

Lakoff and Johnson (1980) noted that American speakers map spatial adverbs like "up" and "down" into positive and negative construals:

279. The stock market went up.
    (good news)
280. The stock market went down
    (bad news)

Speakers and writers with sensitivity to priming audiences know tacitly that physical descriptions of some body parts in motion add attitude while descriptions of other body parts in motion do not:

281. He held his head up.
    (he was proud)
282. He hung his head down.
    (he was dejected)
283. He moved his feet up
    (motion without attitude)
284. He moved his feet down.
    (motion without attitude)

As with all the words and strings discussed in this book, think positive strings are greatly affected by the larger strings in which they appear. In a study we conducted using 20 vintage cigarette ads of the 1940s and 20 from the 1950s (Wooden, J. A., DeVore, J., Graef, C., & Westman, L., 1998) we found a statistically significant effect for the "feel good" positive language of the 1950s ads. In the 1940s sample we studied, the ads invoke the tension of wartime in America. Here is one example of a typical 1940s ad:

> "All America's living at split-second time today... from the bombardier at his bombsight to the men who make the bombs like Jerry Lorigan below. You...and you...and everybody!" "He's a Bombardier. He's the business man of this B-17E bomber crew." His office is the "greenhouse" of transparent plastic in the nose of the ship. And he works there on split-second time. But when those "office hours" are over—well, just look below and watch him *enjoying* a Camel—the *favorite* cigarette on land, sea, and in the air."

Note the sparseness of positive affect in this passage—there are but two occurrences of positive language (e.g., *enjoying* and *favorite),* that we have placed in italics. Using this same italicizing to indicate positive feeling, let us contrast the 1940s ad with the more ample strings of positive language in a vintage ad of the 1950s.

> "Your voice *of wisdom* says SMOKE KENT!" "With your very first carton of KENTs, you will discover the *cleanest-tasting, freshest* cigarette flavor you have ever known. One that stays *clean and fresh-tasting,* no matter how much you smoke. There's a *sound scientific reason* why. You draw KENT's *rich* tobacco through KENT's *famous* Micronite Filter. This filter is made of a material scientists developed for places where filters have to work. It's the *finest* material known for filtering smoke."

The stringing of positive language affords an upbeat tone for the 1950s ads that is not evident in the language of the 1940s ad. We return to this archive in the final section of this book, when we discuss data applications of our theory of rhetorical strings as priming instruments.

Dimension 4: Think Negative

Negative affect strings evoke distress in the mind of the writer, narrator, or a character referenced. Like positive affect terms, such as *good,* negative affect terms exhibit wide variability and instabilities at the grain size of a single word. For example, a common negative affect term is the adverb *too,* meaning *more than desirable.* The negative affect meaning is often associated with quantity words, like many or much: *too many, too much.*

285. I had too much to eat.
286. We had too many chores to do.

However, this string is ambiguous, as *too* also functions as an intensifier, meaning a confident, insistent, and echoing *also:*

287. You can go.
     (I want you to come, with no background implication)
288. You too can go.
     (I want you to come, with the background implication that you didn't expect you could)
289. I like that candidate.
290. I like her too!
     (echoic reinforcement)

Despite this instability at the grain of a single word, negative affect like positive affect, strings are nonetheless frequently stable—even at the grain of a word. Consider the following samples: *enemy, bribery, disaster, plague, scourge, famine, rivalry, and theft.* Many negative affect strings can be built on a common header word of negative affect that causes contiguous words downstream to inherit the negative affect. An example is the negative term *loss,* which generates the following negative affect strings: *losing face, losing ground, losing heart, losing her cool, losing his cool, losing out on, losing out to, losing sleep over, losing touch with, losing track of, loss, loss of, loss of face, loss of heart, loss of property.*

Negative affect strings are rife in argument writing, which often seeks to raise dissatisfaction, discontent, or anger in the reader. When studying the strings students wrote in a writing class where we taught a variety of textual genres (journal, profile, fieldguide, narrative history, information, instruction, and argument), we found that the argument texts were statistically distinguishable from all other genres by virtue of their high occurrence of negative affect strings. This is because arguments are the genre of discontent. Some of the arguments our students wrote contained the following negative affect strings:

291. The decision not to raise the pay of the workers is a scourge.
292. Soft money in campaigns is nothing less than theft.

We saw earlier that a sense of *just* can reassure a reader that a task is more manageable than a reader fears. In a different sense (CCD, sense 7), *just* contributes to a negative affect by indicating that a supposed remedy only makes things worse:

293. Calling his mother just made him depressed.
294. Scratching the wound just made it worse.

Affect strings, positive or negative, are freely combinable with one another. Indeed, we commonly find positive and negative affect strings juxtaposed in the same English sentence.

295. Jill's studious dedication *(positive)* to being a floozy *(negative)*...
296. The maniac *(negative)* brought a curious tenderness *(positive)* to dining.
297. Jack was plagued *(negative)* by good fortune *(positive)*.
298. We must seek justice *(positive)* against oppression *(negative)*.

Such juxtapositions lay the groundwork for the writer's creation of subtle shadings of mood and feelings. With some words, like *swear,* positive polarities can shift abruptly into negative ones simply with a shift in the preposition following it:

299. John swore by Mary
   (= positive affect: Mary is the recipient of loyal feeling)
300. John swore at Mary
   (= negative affect: Mary is the recipient of wrath)

Furthermore, some strings act as reversals or mitigators of affect. They precede affect strings to turn a positive affect into a negative one and vice-versa. One of English's key reversal words undercutting the positive with the negative is *scant.* Watch how scant reverses the polarity of a positive standard string — like *progress* — and turns it into a placeholder of failure.

301. She has made great progress in her studies
   (progress = positive polarity; great = intensifies the positive)
302. She has made scant progress in her studies.
   (progress = positive polarity; scant = reverses the positive)

Although there could well be one, we found no corresponding reversal word (like *scant)* that reverses negative into positive. Rather, English seems to offer speakers and writers only positive mitigators, like *amusing,* and neutral reversers, like *ostensible:*

303. It was a real failure.
   (failure = negative polarity; real intensifies the negative)
304. It was an ostensible failure.
   (failure = negative polarity; ostensible subjectifies and so lightens the negative experience; maybe a failure from some points of view but certainly not from all points of view, especially my own)
305. It was an amusing failure
   (failure = negative polarity; amusing mitigates the experience; maybe a failure from some perspectives but still across many or even all perspectives, there is room for some humor to seep through)

FAMILY 2. PROJECTING AHEAD OR BACK (EXPOSING AUDIENCES TO CONSIDERATIONS OF PAST AND FUTURE)

With few exceptions, such as autobiography and particularizing a historical self, the strings of inner thought we have so far considered do not require one or another tense or aspect marking. First person, states of inner mind, and states of affect, as we have mainly discussed them, have been largely unconcerned with tense and, in all cases, have not required audiences to time-travel back or ahead in time to feel the priming of the relevant string.

We now turn to a family of inner thinking strings that are centrally marked for tense and aspect and, specifically, for priming audiences to travel mentally forward or backward in time. Human beings have the unique ability to think about the future or the past from the horizon of the present. Only the present contains situations, descriptions, and live readers. The past resides only in memories and retrospections; the future, only in projections, conjectures, prophesies speculations, and imaginings.

Just as positive and negative are overwhelmingly the dominant binary values for cataloging affect strings, ahead and back (in time) are the dominant binary values for cataloging the family of strings dealing with thinking that carries future or past implications. We thus break our discussion of this family into two dominant dimensions: thinking ahead and thinking back.

One way to understand the very complex tense aspect system of English is to understand it as a language providing scores of shadings about how human beings are able to think about the past, present, and future from the vantage of the past, present, and future. In our archive, we enumerate 15 classes of English strings that project thinking forward in time, indicating anticipation, and 30 classes of English strings that project thinking backward, which indicates retrospection. This enumeration barely does justice to the fact that many strings in English *(was to have come and arrived by tomorrow)* blend past, present, and future in one integrated sweep of language. For ease of exposition, we do not split hairs and we keep our discussion at the dimension level (think ahead and think back), distinguishing considerations of the past from considerations of the future.

Dimension 5: Think Ahead (Anticipation)

Speakers and writers prime an audience's anticipation of what is to come when they can compose an event (typically a finite verb) that has potential for actuality. English strings that commonly do this work form around the infinitive *to + verb* (e.g., *Mary wanted to go to the party*) and around special project-ahead verbs, such as *projecting, planning, portending, premonition, speculating, prophesizing, forecasting, predicting, and preparing.* The future can blend with positive affect, as in *proactive* or negative affect, such as *preemptive* and *foreboding.*

Think ahead strings reference an uncertain and contingent future. There is for this reason an invariable resonance between thinking ahead, contingency, and uncertainty. All three audience experiences make use of the future contingency auxiliaries *can, could, may,* and *might.* In various cases, the same think-ahead string will also prime contingency and uncertainty, with these latter audience functions separating out only according to whether the future event is a logical probability rather than a definite reality (a mark of contingency), or the fact that one may have no certainty about its becoming a reality (a mark of uncertainty).

306. This research may lead to some progress in curing the common cold.
*(may lead to = temporal contingency insofar as the reader focuses on
the probability, not actuality, of the future event;
may lead to = logical contingency insofar as the reader focuses on the
future event having only a probable, not deterministic, status;
may lead to = epistemic uncertainty insofar as the reader focuses on
the writer's subjective state of not knowing whether the event will
be actualized)*

Using the verb *come* as an example, let us consider some of the various strings that thinking ahead includes:

307. may come
(the verb has yet to actualize)
308. may be coming
(not yet actualized)
309. may have to come
(not yet actualized)
310. in order to come
(not yet actualized)
311. about to come
(not yet actualized)
312. is about to be coming
(not yet actualized)
313. will be coming
(not yet actualized)

These strings indicate a potential arrival following a path to actuality. They differ in the decisiveness with which the writer estimates the prospects of actuality. The modal *may* (strings 307–309) signals less confidence in the arrival than the expectant *(about to)* and *will* form in 311 through 313. Notice also blends between thinking ahead and affect. Verb strings like *look forward to* and *looking with (great) anticipation to* indicate not only a way of looking to the future, but also through a lens of hope and optimism. Verb strings like *brace for, steel themselves for, anxious for,* and *foreboding* combine thinking ahead and negative affect.

The English preposition of most general utility to the writer projecting ahead is *to*. This preposition consistently projects ahead in the combination *in order to*. It also projects ahead with a good deal of reliability in the simple infinitival *to* + *verb*. This is particularly true when there is a present tense verb of thinking or affect preceding the preposition:

314. She knows to go.
     (think + project ahead)
315. Jim wants to go.
     (thinking positive + project ahead)

Interesting cases arise when the verb of thinking preceding the forward projection is past or future:

316. She decided to go.
     (project ahead from past reference point)
317. Jim will want to go.
     (project ahead from future reference point)

The following is a fascinating forward projection that we humans seem to handle effortlessly without a second thought.

318. He was surprised to learn that the game was canceled.
     (surprised = past; to learn = project ahead; was canceled = past)

The phrase *surprised to learn* at first defies logic because the *to* (as forward projection) seems to imply that the surprise initiated a plan to learn. Yet the deeper semantics are quite otherwise, suggesting that the surprise is part of the content learned rather than the catalyst for learning. In this context, the *surprise to* construction seems an imperfect substitute for the more precise *surprised when*, *surprised as a result of*, or *surprised because*. Compare:

319. He was surprised when he learned that the game was cancelled.
     (surprised when vs. surprised to; time shift vs. future projection)
320. He was surprised as a result of learning that the game was cancelled.
     (surprised as a result vs. surprised to; result vs. future projection)
321. He was surprised because he learned that the game was cancelled.
     (surprised because vs. surprised to; cause vs. future projection)

All three of these last sentences appear to capture the semantics of a learning that leads to surprise better than 318. So why have the *surprised to learn* construction at all if it captures only imprecisely what other strings capture more so?

The answer seems to be that *surprised to learn* requires a different semantic analysis, one restricted to curiosity events/verbs (e.g., *learn, discover, find out, inquire*) and the learning events (e.g., *confirmation, rejection, surprise, bafflement*) that result and cause repetitive ripples into the indefinite future. In this analysis, *surprised to learn* implies a past event spawning curiosities that continue to flow forward as a self-replenishing stream. The person who is *surprised when learning, surprised as a result of learning,* or *surprised because of learning* is a learner to be sure. Yet, only the person who is *surprised to learn* primes the additional idea of a learner who knows to replenish self-learning as an ongoing and self-renewing project. One who can be *surprised to learn* suggests not only past learning, but more important, a penchant for turning incidental accidents of learning into anticipated and controlled learning projects.

We take the time to invest in this fine-grained analysis to illustrate how reflecting on English strings can often lead to deep insights about language and its hidden assumptions. Yet deep hermeneutics are not required to become adept at rhetorical scrabble. As we argued earlier, our production know-how seems considerably more lightweight than our capacity for hermeneutic depth. Although there are deep semantic analyses at play in completing our interpretation of strings that project ahead in time, these dynamics are less an issue when it comes to the priming necessary to induce audiences to start the journey.

The adverbial *just* (CCD, sense 9) used with uncertainty modals like *might* or *may,* calls attention to the increasing odds of what had been understood to be a low probability event.

322. His graduation from college just might happen.
   (He's been flunking but his latest report card is decent)
323. She just might get a job.
   (She has recently enrolled for vocational training)

As we already observed, think ahead strings often overlap with uncertainty only because the future is unknown. This may explain, in part, why the modals *may* and *could* show such a flexible range between future possibility (e.g., *it may/could happen*) and subjective uncertainty (e.g., *but it may or could not, I'm not sure*).

Despite the basic rules relating the future to uncertainty, we have found some English strings, such as *(only) a matter time,* that confidently tie together future projection and certainty:

324. I know he will get well. It's only a matter of time.
   (only a matter of time = getting well is assured)

There are industries that earn high fees by helping customers associate the future with certainty and security. These industries rhetorically encase their language with as many ways they can think of to bind the future to confidence, security, and prosperity. Such industries rely on predictable string builders, like *optimistic.* More impressively, these industries have managed to keep *pessimistic* a strategic term for optimistic future prospects: Compare the following strings:

325. Projections for future stocks are optimistic.
(bullish outlook; stock values will go up; better buy now)
326. Projections for future stocks are pessimistic.
(bearish outlook; stock values will go down; better keep a long-term outlook or sell)

Industries that sell the future have kept terms like *optimistic* and even *pessimistic* useful terms for strategic action. Consider that when *optimism or pessimism* is preceded by the negative affect *too,* the negativity impugns the investment strategy and the need to change it rather than the actual future (which in the investment industry must remain a future of open promise for the growth of wealth). Consider the following:

327. Projections for future stocks seem *(too)* optimistic.
(= not all that optimistic; we need some pessimism to balance the picture and our investment strategy should reflect this)
328. Projections for future stocks seem *(too)* pessimistic.
(= not all that pessimistic; we need some optimism to balance the picture and our investment strategy should reflect this)

Dimension 6: Think Back (Retrospection)

Think-back strings indicate a mind recalling an event from memory. Such strings are signaled with verbs indicating memory retrieval: *recall, recount, remember, think back on, look back on, realize afterwards, hark back, recollect, rehash, reminisce, and view in retrospect.* The verbal auxiliaries, *have* and *was,* serve many of these think-back strings as well. Consider the following think-back strings with auxiliaries, each string using an arrival (and the verb *come)* as the event reported in retrospect:

329. has been coming
(the moment has reached actualization; not finished)
330. may have been coming
(the moment was in process and has passed. ...if it arrived; all this is a matter of some uncertainty)
331. should have come
(the moment was expected, maybe insisted on, and has passed... if it arrived)
332. would [often] come
(the moment repeated and all recurrences have passed)
333. was to come
(the moment was expected and has passed. ...if it arrived)

334. was to have come

(the moment was expected to have been completed by now and has passed. ...if it arrived)

335. was to be coming

(the moment was in process and expected and probably passed. ...if it arrived)

In each of these strings, the speaker or writer reflects on an event whose moment has passed. The strings differ in the level of the speaker or writer's certainty whether the moment ever arrived. The modals *(may, should)* in 330, 331 suggest uncertainty and insistence along with occurrence. The future-in-past string, *was to,* (333–335) conveys a prior expectation of occurrence.

Strings priming thinking back are distinct from simple references to the past, which we discuss in a later chapter. To appreciate the difference between retrospecting on the past and merely referencing it, imagine a person who is interviewing for a job as a teacher of French. The interviewer asks the candidate whether he or she is qualified to teach French. Now imagine the candidate responds in one of the following two ways:

336. I lived in Paris.

(a simple reference to an event that is past)

337. I have lived in Paris

(a retrospection from living memory on the past)

Either response may be helpful to the candidate, but they are not equally effective responses. String 336 is a simple reference to the past, mentioning an event that happened and is now over. The response will permit the interviewer the inference that the candidate speaks French. Still, this is an inference the interviewer must make. String 336, employing the perfect aspect, retrospects on the past and brings to the fore a living memory, relevant to the current context. Rather than mention an event that is over, the emphasis of past reference (336), think-back strings recall living memories that remain current.

The currency of living memory in think-back strings explains why the depiction of retrospection figures so importantly in the tool-kit of the narrative history writer. The writer of narrative history must restore a world on the page that feels displaced from the current reading context (Chafe, 1994) and yet vivid enough to make the reader feel as if that world happened only yesterday. The balance of displacement and immediacy are the priming effects that narrative history writing must accomplish. We have studied how students create this balance in oral histories they write by interviewing their parents and grandparents (Kaufer and Butler, 2000). Our experience suggests that student and professional writers achieve displacement through a combination of think-back strings and the selection of nouns *(hoola-hoops, Philco radios, singer sewing machines, horse and buggies, vinyl record-players)* and event descriptions *(paying a nickel for bus fare)* that strike the contemporary reader as dated.

338. I still remember swinging in my bright orange hoola hoop as Elvis Presley sang on the Philco. I had just broken up with Sam.
    (Interpretation of priming action in this sentence: Balancing displacement and immediacy in narrative history writing. Macro goal is to bring a world to the page that is no more with the vividness as if it were still here today. Displacement is achieved from think back strings [I remember] and the selection of out-of-date nouns — hoola hoop, Elvis Presley, and Philco. Immediacy is achieved from the vividness of description, the specificity of the noun, and the adverb "just")

These anachronistic, literally "out of their time" words, create a displaced reader effect. Writers must do historical research to find them and to fix their reference in time past.

We further found that writers achieve their immediacy in two ways. First, as one might expect, they couch these terms of immediacy *(right here, right now, today, this month)* in time past (Grant said to his troops, "Now go.") Second, they describe characters projecting their idea of time past and future from an anchor point in the past.

339. My grandfather feared he would never survive the bunker he occupied in France in 1942.
    (achieving immediacy of a displaced world by having a character of that world project his or her living memory of time future.)
340. By 1946, my grandfather missed the days when he could see an airplane overhead and make a wish for good luck.
    (achieving immediacy of a displaced world by having a character from that world project his or her living memory of time past.)

A common word for forming thinking-back strings is the habitual-past *would.*

341. Lincoln would often study by candlelight.
    (Abe's youthful habits)
342. John would come every Tuesday.
    (John's weekly ritual)

Although the auxiliary *would* typically references a habitual past, with thinking verbs such as *like* and *prefer,* it references thinking ahead, the future.

343. He would like a front row seat.
    (for the upcoming concert)
344. I would prefer a shorter haircut.
    (by the time I leave the barber chair)

The future-directed *would* is less frequent than the past-directed *would.* This may have something to do with the fact that the future would can also rely on the explicit marker *will.* Consider the contrasts between *would* and *will* in the following sentences:

345. Bill will want to go.
     (simple/nonhabitual; when he hears we are going to the ballgame.
     ...future based on a one-shot prediction of what Bill will want)
346. Bill would want to go.
     (habitual sense; when he hears we are going to the ballgame because
     he loves baseball)

We need to appeal to context to separate the differences in priming between *will* and *would.* Example 345 expresses the simple future, true in a context when a desire will form in the future. Bill does not yet know about the game. When he finds out about it, he will want to go. Simple futures of this type make one-time predictions about Bill without revealing any regularity in Bill's over time. A speaker is most likely to utter or write string 345 in a context where he or she does not know Bill personally but assumes that males like baseball. Example 346 is different. Here, *would* tells us more about Bill's habit of mind than a one-shot prediction framed from stereotypical desire. *Would,* unlike *will,* retains a sense of personal history with Bill. With certain verbs of inner thought *(prefer, want)* that look to the future, habitual *would* strengthens the base of historical acquaintance from which a person's future action is predicted.

These observations help us appreciate the overlap between habitual *would* and precedent strings (e.g., *the founding fathers would often endorse the pursuit of liberty).* Precedent strings, part of the relational cluster, link current shared ideas to their historical antecedents. The habitual *would,* part of a thinking-back string, can participate in this precedent effect as well. Compare:

347. The United States will never agree to socialized medicine.
     (thinking ahead /future prediction)
348. The United States would never agree to socialized medicine
     (thinking back /public precedent)

String 347 is a statement of public resolve, with a weight on the future. String 348 ties the weight of that resolve to America's historical past. String 348 is the language of a determined office-holder; string 348, the language of the historian equipped with a vast knowledge of previous cases.

Speakers and writers can retrospect on specific historical scenes, broken down into motions. Let us examine how a writer depicts motion retrospectively through the string: *would* + *be* and [the progressive marker]—ing.

349. Sam would get up at this time.
     (habitual past; no progressive marker)
350. Sam would be getting up at this time.
     (progressive as imaged sequence)
351. Sam would just be getting up.
     (progressive as imaged sequence; just implies start of sequence)
352. Sam would now be getting up.
     (progressive as imaged sequence; now implies start of sequence)

Example 349 shows the role of the progressive by illustrating a nonprogressive *(get up)*. The simple progressive 350 invites us to imagine a sequence of motion without directing us to any particular segment within the sequence. We are invited to imagine the overlap between the writer's reference time and any phase of Sam's getting up. Examples 351 and 352 show how the adverbials *just* and *now* can both index the start of this sequence. These strings leave no doubt that the time of writing coincided with Sam's first stirrings in mornings past.

The strings *would (just) now* and *just then* contribute to the priming of thinking back. *Would + verb* and *would (just) now + verb* both emphasize the immediacy of a habitual past. *Would + verb* does this directly (string 353). *Would (just) now* goes further. The *(just) now* string with retrospection adds immediacy to the past and so reduces the felt distance between the present of thinking back and the past being recovered. The string *would (just) now* focuses our attention on the image of an action starting up (string 354) and so animates the past.

353. Sam would get up at 5 everyday.
     (emphasizes the immediacy of Sam's habitual past; get up = verb)
354. Sam would just now be getting up.
     (emphasizes an image of Sam's starting to get up, by habit, on a particular day. The habit feels so close, we see the past as if it's happening right now)

The string *just then* adds immediacy to the displaced then of the past. Compare 355 and 356.

355. Then, there was a knock at the door.
     (then emphasizes the displacement of time past when the door knocked)
356. Just then, there was a knock at the door.
     (just then emphasizes the immediacy of the door knocking)

Storytellers wanting to keep readers on the edge of their seat rely on the felt imminence of *just then* primings. The adverbial holds the action and suspense from the character's point of view. The storytelling remains retrospective, a look back to the past; yet the adverbial permits the audience to feel the story as a character experiences it, looking vulnerably into a contingent future, anxious and unknowing about what will happen next.

The English word *once* is a rich contributor to the displacement and immediacy associated with retrospective storytelling. The string *once upon a time* has been conventionalized (especially in children stories) to transport the listener or reader back in time when a story begins. However, this is only the tip of the iceberg of how *once* contributes to audience time travel within English strings. Coupled with the simple past, *once* invokes a shift to time past without necessarily indicating a sustained retrospection (e.g., *Mary once lost her keys in the sofa)*. Coupled with the present tense (e.g., *arrives)* and spatial adverbs (e.g., *inside), once* primes a notion of immediacy arcing toward the future as well as the past (e.g., *once she arrives, please take her coat; once inside, you will need to take your shoes off)*. Coupled with the indefinite pronoun and a time interval (e.g., a day, a month, a year), once primes a sense of event recurrence across any horizon of time (e.g., *She went/goes/will go to the club once a month)*. Thus, although *once* is a contributor to think-back strings, it also primes considerations of time beyond retrospective thought.

In the thinking strings thus far surveyed in this chapter, the speaker or writer assumes an audience who is offstage and unacknowledged. The audience is primed to peek into the speaker or writer's mind and the speaker or writer is not looking back. The speaker or writer has only a "field of dreams" regard for the audience — build "an engaging subjectivity" and audiences will come. In the next two chapters, we look at strings that assume a more interested and interactive online audience.

7

Cluster 2:
Relational Perspectives,
Part I

In this and the next chapter, we turn from strings that fashion thinking as an individual enterprise and toward strings that refashion it into a social and largely cooperative one. We also move from strings that hold the audience at arm's length in the role of unacknowledged eavesdropper and toward strings that acknowledge and even address an audience as an interactive presence. More specifically, the strings we review fall under a second major cluster, strings implementing a relational perspective, or relational strings for short.

The relational cluster contains two major families of strings, each family large and diverse enough to require a chapter of its own. The first family of relational strings relates audiences to representations encoded within the language. This family is active when speakers and writers engage their audiences in mutual reasoning, in sharing premises and values of the larger culture, and in directing activities with audiences. In each case with this family of strings, the speaker or writer helps organize and focus the attention of audiences on the interactive world represented in the utterance or text.

The second family of relational strings helps audiences accommodate the fact that language is a linear medium that can cause audiences deprived of linear cues to bog down. Strings within this family are active when speakers and writers anticipate audiences to need navigational help through the linear stream of words. Such strings help audiences get their bearings as interactive partners, to help them locate the most important or weighted information in the stream of words, and to clarify their linear progress through the linear stream when the stream muddies. We now turn to each of these families of relational strings and the dimensions and string classes that constitute them.

FAMILY 3. CONNECTING AUDIENCES TO REPRESENTATIONS WITHIN THE LANGUAGE

Let us now examine a family of relational strings whose common function is to relate audiences to the representations within the language. Before proceeding further, let us take a closer look at how in this context we define *representations within the language*. We find it useful to follow Lev Manovich (2001), who observed that the notion of representation is best understood not as one categorical idea but as a web of contrastive ideas, with each idea of representation contrasting in different ways from some notion of unmediated or naïve realism.

To take Manovich's proposal seriously is to ask not what one thing representation is, but rather to look into the specific contrasts with naïve realism one is trying to push under the umbrella of representation. One of the definitional contrasts Manovich cited that we find applicable to the scope of Family 3 strings is the following:

Defining Representation in Contrast With Durable Knowledge

Contrasts with durable information, likening representation to immersion and directed action within the world of linear language rather than long-term changes in the audience's knowledge. (pp. 16-17)

Strings within family 3 trade on this understanding of representation as contrastive with durable knowledge surviving outside the flux of language. With Family 3 strings, we focus on how strings of language expedite the organization and management of the audience's mobile and fleeting attention in constructed worlds of language.

Family 3 strings themselves divide into various dimensions, each depending upon the implicit organizing frame within which an audience's attention is organized and managed. One dimension of strings, what we call *reasoning,* involves strings that organize and manage the audience's online attention within a path of reasoning. A second dimension, what we call *sharing social ties,* organizes and manages the audience's attention around common histories, standards, and values that create solidarity. A third dimension of strings, what we called *directed activity,* organizes and manages the audience's attention around local spatial tasks and actions in the audience's immediate environment.

Let us now review each of these dimensions on their own terms.

Dimension 7: Reasoning

Strings associated with reasoning indicate the sequenced thinking of an individual making a bid to make an audience share the sequence and so think alike. Reasoning strings are the small language actions that help constitute larger actions of assertion (avowing statements of individual thought bidding as social knowledge) and refutation (exposing putative bids of social knowledge as false-hoods). In the following sections, we discuss the various and varied string class-es that help constitute acts of asserting and refuting respectively.

Aspects of Assertion

Speakers and writers posit assertions to share thoughts with audiences they take to be shared truths and that they hope, if not expect, their audiences also to accept as true. We have isolated a wide assortment of string classes that help to develop assertions, including string classes with the following names: *assert that, reasoning forward, reasoning backward, direct reasoning, generalization, example, support, confirming another's thinking, transformation, cause, exceptions, and substitutions.*

For ease of exposition, we try to say enough about each class for the reader to follow the guiding principle defining the class, along with representative exam-ples. The reader should bear in mind that our electronic archive associates each specific string class with tens, hundreds, thousands, and sometimes hundreds of thousands of unique English strings. We try to represent the diversity of our catalog without being complete.

Class 1: Assert That   Assert-that strings posit mini-propositions of subject-predicate judgments. Along with refute-that strings, assert-that strings are unique in our catalog because they are the only string classes to include a full subject-predicate continuation. One cannot assert (or refute) something without the blueprint of a whole thought (a subject + predicate) to assert or refute. One common manifestation of assert-that strings are subjects composed of first per-son singular or plural (e.g., *I, we, our*) plus assertive verbs of information (e.g., *say, assert, declare*) across most suffix endings — *I assert that, we claim that, we are arguing that, our avowal that, I affirm that, we attest that, I claim that, we contend that, we state that, I declare that, we pronounce that, I profess that, we proclaim that, I say that, we observe that.* Assert-that strings also include other forms of declamation, preceded by verbs like *wish* (e.g., *we wish to declare),* using demonstrative pronoun subjects (e.g., *those were),* situational-pronoun subjects (e.g., *it is about),* nonagentive subjects (e.g., *the answer is),* and there-subjects (e.g., *there is the matter of).*

Punctuation can be an important consideration for determining whether a string constitutes an assert-that or not. Contrast:

357. This, I feel, is a good thing to do.
     (subjective commentary on an observation not itself asserted)
358. I feel that this is a good thing to do.
     (assertion of a subjective commentary on an observation)

Assert-that strings frequently overlap with narrative strings (discussed in a later chapter), but insofar as they do, they bind the narrative with verbs of speech and inner thought and, often, *that* complement clauses that embed the narrative within a propositional thought.

> 359. Jack went to the baseball game on Saturday.
> *(narrative report about Jack)*
> 360. To the best of my knowledge, Jack went to the baseball game on Saturday.
> *(inner thinking + narrative = assertion of narrative report)*
> 361. I know that Jack went to the baseball game on Saturday.
> *(verbs of inner thought + that = assertion of narrative report)*

Inasmuch as they are first person involved, assert-that strings can also overlap with self-disclosures and autobiographical statements. Yet, they also differ from the latter strings in predictable ways. First, in contrast to autobiographical strings, assertions rely on a sense of present-ness rather than past habit or practice. Compare:

> 362. I had often walked these streets as a child.
> *(autobiographical string)*
> 363. Let me say, I walk these streets everyday.
> *(transformation of above string into a present assertion*

Shorn of first person and the immediacy of an on-the-spot declaration, strings that convey assertions become indistinguishable with verbs of (third-party) citation: *affirm, attest, claim, avow, say.* We discuss citation later on when we examine ways that speakers and writers bring external voices into their language.

Class 2: Reasoning Forward Strings associated with reasoning can direct audiences forward or back through a reasoning chain. Forward chaining preserves an expected or natural order of how events occur in the domain of logic or experience. In logic, and often in our experience as inferencers, premises precede conclusions, causes precede effects, purposes precede actions, evidence precedes conclusions, and actions precede implications or results and consequences.

When a reasoning string preserves this expected order, we categorize it as reasoning forward. Examples of reasoning forward strings in English texts are the following: *the result is, consequently the consequence is, it comes to this, this causes, this leads to, that is the reason for thinking that, as a result, arrives at the conclusion that, thus, thusly, this allows me to say, this allows us to think, this supports the, this is support for the idea, this is why, and so, this is why I argue that, this means that, which goes to show that, then it's clear that, then it's obvious that, then you conclude, then you know, then we can conclude, then we can say, then we know that, thereby, therefore, which implies that, warranted it's, warrant that, allows one to conclude, allows us to embrace the claim, a possible inference is that, and so we can go on to claim.*

What is the common forward direction in these strings? Each moves the audience forward from an expected earlier to an expected later link in a reasoning chain.

Class 3: Reasoning Backward   Reason backward strings lead the audience backward in a reasoning chain, in reverse order from natural or expected sequencing. Such strings, in particular, take the audience from conclusions back to premises, from actions back to their purposes or reasons, from effects back to their causes, and from results, consequences, or implications back to their originating actions.

Examples of reason backward strings are the following: *is owing to, is the result of, as a result of, is the upshot of, because, for, for it was, in view of the, for being the, owing to the fact that, whereas, for after all, in light of, given that the, granted that the, seeing that, as a result of the fact, being that the, for it is because, for the reason, due to the, due to the fact that, another reason is moreover, base my opinion on, because these happen, but since, conditioned by the fact that, on the premise that, because of the premise that, conditioned on her, conditioned on his, follow from, following from, following from the claim, the foundation for this idea, this idea derives from, in consequence of, on account of, on the basis of, on the grounds that, on the strength of, one given is that.*

Each of these strings escorts audiences back from a later (in logic or experience) to an earlier link in a reasoning chain. The vast majority of these strings take audiences back in logic more than time. A case of reasoning backward in time as well as logic is the string — *must have been + [optional] verbed:*

364. Susan must have been here already, for I see she changed shoes.
     (Seeks to explain the logical best premise about the past that is consistent with the present evidence that Susan has changed her shoes)
365. David must have been called to the office.
     (Seeks to explain the logical best premise about the past that is consistent with the present evidence that David is not around)

Although *must have been* always signals reasoning backward into the past, *must be* is ambiguous between reasoning backward and insistence, depending on the continuation:

366. The phone must be my mother calling.
     (reasoning backward from the ring to the caller)
367. The phone must be answered.
     (insisting on someone acting to pick up the phone)

When Joseph Williams (2000) discussed the stylistic symptom of uncontrolled writing that he described by the name sprawl, he relies on examples that illustrate the jerkiness that comes when writers make abrupt shifts between forward-projecting and backward-projecting stings, conjoining forward and backward reasoning with no signaling of a shift in the order of progression. Here is one example of sprawl from Williams:

> The construction of the Interstate Highway System, owing to the fact that Congress, on the occasion when it originally voted funds for it, did not anticipate the rising cost of inflation, ran into serious financial problems. (p. 173)

The sentence sprawls because *owing to* is a reason backward string that asks audiences to step back in the chain of thought. *On the occasion when* is a time-shift string that projects audiences even farther back in the context of the reasoning. However, the *ran into* string suddenly jerks the audience ahead into the more recent past. If we line up all the information chunks in natural (logical, premise to conclusion, and temporally, earlier to later) order, we end up with the following:

1. Congress did not anticipate inflation with a vote for the highway.
2. Congress voted funds for the highway.
3. The highway was constructed.
   (result/cause of 2).
4. The project ran into financial problems
   (result/cause of 1 and 2).

A prescribed revision, keeping within a consistent chain of reason forward strings, would be:

368. Congress did not anticipate inflation when it voted for the highway. As a result, when the highway was constructed, the project ran into financial problems.

Note the difference between *as a result* — a string carrying the audience forward — and *as a result of* — a string taking the audience back.

369. I lost my job. As a result, I can't help you.
     (As a result...moves the reader forward in the reasoning chain; I lost my job came first; I can't help you came next.)
370. As a result of losing my job, I can't help you.
     ("As a result of"....this string moves the reader immediately backward, back to the cause....This is in contrast to simple "as a result," which moves the reader immediately forward, into the effect)

Class 4: Directing Reasoning Strings of this class summon an audience to initiate a mental process. Some examples are, *picture a, picture this, imagine this, suppose this, notice that, note that, consider this, now picture a, just picture a, imagine a, now imagine a, just imagine a, suppose a, now suppose a, just suppose a, consider a, now consider a, just consider a, imagine that you, imagine that your, imagine that we.* These strings sustain audiences down a chain of projected thought, typically using the imperative form of a thinking verb and early in a sentence or clause.

Directing an audience to construct a mental picture and insisting on the audience's taking up a course of reasoning or acting can overlap, but they need not. Compare the non-insistent directed reasoning strings 371 and 373 with the insistent strings 372 and 374, which combine directing reasoning and insisting.

371. It's a good idea to think about the environmental impact.
  (directing reasoning without insistence)
372. I insist you think about the environmental impact.
  (directing reasoning with insistence)
373. You might consider leaving your job.
  (direct reasoning without insistence)
374. You *(really)* should consider leaving your job.
  (direct reasoning with insistence)

Class 5: Insistence on Reasoning Insistence strings involve second person, often direct address (discussed later), and a modal like *should* or *must* to indicate the speaker or writer's forceful commitment that the audience embark on a certain course of reasoning (e.g., *you ought to think this over)* or action (e.g., *you should vote).* These strings tend to incorporate future obligation verbs *needs to* and *ought to.* A further requirement is a verb indicating thinking and reasoning. Examples of this string class are, *you must assess, you should judge, one must be careful to avoid rash conclusions, one needs to ascertain.*

Although insistence implies confidence and intensity over what one is insisting, it features confidence and intensity mainly as a means to pressure the audience to conform. For this reason, we classified insistence under the social interactive assumptions of the relational cluster rather than the individualist expressive assumptions of the thought cluster.

Class 6: Generalization As a class of English strings, generalization allows an audience to fill in a rule or a larger picture from previous or anticipated details. Characteristic examples of this string class are: *in general, overall, in sum, it boils down to, to generalize, viewed overall, universal, universally all, by all, of all, with all, from all, every, each and every.* These various strings reliably cue generalizations when they are followed by inference-indicating verbs such as *indicate, suggest, point to the conclusion:*

375. Every test indicates there is nothing seriously wrong.
376. All signs point to a upward turn in the market.

The universal quantifiers, *all* and *every,* recur in generalization strings. *Every,* however, more than *all* can imply the subjectively felt achievement of earning one's way, an instance at a time, to the generalization:

377. I counted all the cars in the lot.
     (generalization covering all the cars)
378. I counted every car in the lot.
     (it was quite a feat; every—generalization + intensity)

Class 7: Example   This string class supplies evidence, support, or simply concretization of a nearby generalization. Common examples of this string class are *for example, for instance, as in the case when.* There is sometimes a fine lexical line between examples, which make a generalization concrete and so supportable, and specifications, which make a generalization more informative and so aids the audience's navigation though a text. In this regard, consider the fine difference between *so as,* which cues audiences to reason backward to an originating purpose or rationale and *such as,* a string to specify a previous more general string.

379. He came so as to retrieve his money.
     (cue reasons [backward])
380. He found many diversions, such as attending concerts.
     (specification)
381. He found ways to use his money wisely, such as for example the time he invested in the local hospital.
     (specification + example-giving)

We need to discriminate strings that directly prime examples and strings that prime the audience that an example or examples (or any other experience for that matter) will be forthcoming. Such foreshadowing indicates metadiscourse about examples rather than strings from the example class per se. Contrast:

382. The civil war was a bloody battle. For example, at Gettysburg alone, 50,000 men died.
     (for example = priming an example)
383. The civil war was a bloody battle. We will have plenty of examples to show this.
     (will have plenty of = metadiscourse to aid audience navigation about what's to come)

Class 8: Support   Support strings add evidential weight to a nearby clause or sentence that makes an assertion. More precisely, they signal the communicator's belief that such weight is being added. Examples drawn from this string class are, *as evidence of this is, lends support to, is support for, is evidence of, makes a case for, support for this is.* Many support strings are implied and not overtly expressed. Audiences in these cases determine their presence in speech or text only through inference. Consider:

384. John is a rich person. As support for this, I heard he just withdrew one million from the bank.
(support cued by the string)
385. John is a rich person. I heard he just withdrew one million from the bank
(uncued support, determined solely from inference)
386. I heard John just withdrew one million from the bank. He is a rich person.
(uncued support, determined solely from inference)

Audiences can understand the second sentence in 385 as support for the first sentence and the second sentence in 386, a generalization of the first. Yet these understandings are based only on inference not on overt strings.

Class 9: Confirming Another's Thinking   Strings of this class endorse the reasoning of others. They can frequently overlap with citation strings (discussed later), especially when the third parties are also the originators of the ideas. However, they tend to be citations that are more restricted in that they are always positive and often bring confidence into the mix:

387. I agree with Smith.
(citation + confidence; Smith had the idea and he had it right)
388. I second Smith enthusiastically.
389. I follow the ideas of Jones.
390. I concur with Smith when he argued that...
391. I am on the same page with Brown.

Class 10: Comparisons   Comparisons tell audiences about the quantity of similarity or difference between two objects. Instances of this class are *more, less, fewer, than, more, much more than, much less than, far more so than that, far less than, something more than, something less than, less than, less commonly, than, far less, less often than.* The noun entities placed in comparison (e.g., *diapers, tuna fish cans*) and the attributes of comparison, sometimes preceded by the preposition *in (in absorption, in weight)* are boundless.

The expression *more than once* implies multiple recurrence, which creates an interesting overlap between comparisons and temporal recurrence:

392. Tom has made this mistake more than once.
     (comparison with a previous occasion = temporal recurrence;
     Tom keeps making this mistake)

When comparisons are made across periods of time, signaled by *last* or *next,* English allows spatial adverbs, like *above, below,* and *beyond* to complete the comparison.

393. The box office this year was well above last year's.
394. The box office next year is projected to be well below next year's.
395. The box office is well beyond last year's.

Comparisons interact with affect in different ways. *More than* intensifies a positive or negative affect.

396. Sue is more than happy.
     (intensely happy)
397. Jim is more than sad.
     (intensely sad)

Less than mitigates and even reverses a happy affect but does not provide so decisive a signal when interacting with a sad affect. Compare:

398. Jack is less than happy.
     (not at all happy, in fact sad)
399. Myrna is less than sad.
     (denies Mryna's sadness but doesn't decisively signal her being
     overjoyed either)

Comparisons are also primed with time intervals. The following are examples:

400. Kate worked for more than ten years
     (ten years=benchmark; Kate's time of employment referenced through
     comparison to it)
401. Ashley worked for less than ten months.
     (ten months=benchmark; Ashley's time of employment referenced
     through comparison to it)

Class 11: Transformations   Some verbs are especially effective at reporting transformations, namely *change, convert, evolve, morph, transform, make into,* *and turn into.*

402. The sculptor turned clay into a statue.
     (implies one-way and irreversible change)

403. The family business was converted into a multinational conglomerate.
(implies one-way and irreversible change)

While transformation often semantically implies consequential, one-way, and irreversible change, speakers and writers can use verbs of transformation creatively, to convey light-hearted, ephemeral, and reversible change.

404. Her smile slowly morphed into a frown and then back to a smile.
(transformative verb used outside conventional assumptions of transformation; information verb blended with motion)
405. With no place to sit, he quickly converted the table into a stool.
(transformative verb used outside conventional assumptions of transformation; information verb that leaves it to the reader to infer sitting on the table with the body posture of sitting on a stool)

Class 12: Causes   Cause strings are tricky to analyze because the English conjunction *because* means sufficient reason more often than it means necessary cause.

A. I didn't go because I didn't want to.
B. What's the real reason?

In our catalog, we restricted causes to a few verbs *(cause, force, compel, brought with it)* and nouns referencing effects *(effects, aftereffect)* where the sense of causation is more explicit and distinctive from reason giving.

406. John caused the accident.
407. Mary forced Sue to come with her.
408. Ula got Mary to see her point of view.
409. The bombing brought it with a host of complications.
410. The bombing effected the lives of millions.

Class 13: Exceptions   Exceptions call the audiences' attention to what does not fit a nearby or implied rule or generalization. Characteristic strings of this class include: *with the exception of, save for, only case of, no one besides, but for, rarely do, none other than, nothing to say....but good things, only once, except for, with nothing but a.* A noun can inherit an exceptional status because of unusual properties *(he's too tall for the army)* or because of the particulars of circumstances *(she was sick and so couldn't take the test)* or conditions *(bring only wine)*. Strings conveying reasoning can sometimes blend with strings conveying exceptions. This is especially true when a speaker or writer wants to express how certain thinking, good or bad, is out of the ordinary *(an exceptional idea, there is no other conclusion than, the dumbest idea I ever heard)*. Although the adjective *exceptional* specifies an out-of-norm attribute, English has all but frozen it to indicate the exceeding of a typically positive standard (e.g., *exceptional in being well* *behaved).* Although the adverb *exceptionally* adverbializes states or acts that lie outside norms, English has all but frozen it to intensify the particular act or state referenced (e.g., *is exceptionally smart, did exceptionally poorly on the test).* In these cases, exceptionality combines with different part of speech markers to indicate public standards or inner attitudes respectively. Using the adverb *only* as a marker of exceptionality, a speaker or writer can combine exceptionality and intensity to create an impression of single-minded focus.

411. John focuses on his schoolwork.
  (inner thinking)
412. John focuses only on his schoolwork.
  (inner thought + exception; his focus on school is the exception; if you approach John with another focus in mind, you won't access him = John is intensely single-minded about his schoolwork)

Class 14: Substitution Substitution strings make up only a small collection in our catalog. They are signaled by verbal phrases such as *substitute replace, and stand in for,* and prepositional phrases such as *in place of.*

413. John stood in for Mary.
414. Mary came in place of John.

None of the strings in the 14 string classes associated with assertion guarantees that an assertion in the speech act sense will be made. Each class, however, typically plays one or several supporting roles in the micro world of language when recognizably macro-level assertions emerge.

Aspects of Refutation

Refuting is the counterpart of asserting. If asserting is an individual's initiative to posit sustainable thoughts to audiences, refutations are counter-initiatives to retract or repudiate such thoughts. Our catalog distinguishes three classes of refutative strings: *refute-that, denials/disclaimers,* and *resistance.* This family of strings is all bound to negativity.

Class 15: Refute That Like assert-that strings, refute-that strings match subjects followed by predicates, the seeds of a full thought if not the whole thought itself. Unlike assert-that strings, refute-that strings introduce negativity into the linear stream of a thought (e.g., *subjects + copula verbs + negative judgment).* Common examples are, *this does not follow, it doesn't hold water, it's fallacious, it's nonsense, this is irrational, it's a small-minded point of view, she is skirting the issue, the argument begs the question.*

Refute-that strings can also consist of first person singular or plural agents (e.g., *I, we, our)* coupled with specific refutative verbs across most suffix endings (e.g., *counters, deny, counter-assert, retort, rebut, refuting, deny*), and often (but not always) followed by a *that* complement. The refuting *verb* + *tha*t string signals that the writer takes the upcoming clause as false or unappealing and invites audiences to take up the same thinking: I *counter that, we take exception to, we deny that, I object that, we reject the notion.*

Shorn of their connection to first person, *refute-that* strings can become indistinguishable with tokens of resistance or speech act citations incorporating negative speech act verbs (e.g., *denying, objecting, and taking exception*).

Strings conveying refutation in English can launch appearance-reality contrasts, well documented in argument theory (Perelman & Olbrechts-Tyteca, 1969). In these strings, reality, facts, and truth provide a confident but also sobering and overriding resistance to appearance, pseudo-facts, and falsehood.

415. but the reality is
    (where the earlier clause is implied appearance only)
416. but the fact is
    (where the earlier clause is pseudo-fact only)
417. but the truth is
    (where the earlier clause is implied falsehood only)

Each of these examples assumes an earlier text that the current text overrides. Resistance words like *ostensible* and *ostensibly* signal to audiences that they are being presented with appearance, half-truths, pseudo-fact, or falsehood that are easy to confuse with the truth. Because these words signal faulty (and so subjective) information processing, they bring together subjective perception and resistance:

418. Ostensibly, she was unhappy, but the reality/fact/truth is
    (For all the world, she looks to be unhappy but she is not.... subjective perception + resistance)

The adverbial *just* contributes to refutation (CCD, sense 13) when a speaker or writer, taking advantage of or mimicking the interactive qualities of speech, seizes the floor with impatience after (more patiently) describing an opponent's position or listening to it.

419. Just a moment! Can we really buy that?
    (the adverbial used to launch an interjection)

Just further contributes to refutation in the string, *it's just that* (CCD, sense 24) as a connector to begin a counter-attack.

420. I understand that he believes what he is saying....It's just that he
    is wrong!

Class 16: Denials and Disclaimers   Denials and disclaimers can also negate propositions but their scope is not restricted to negative propositions, as is the case with refute-that strings. Denials can negate prior propositions in the interest of conveying positive judgments:

> 421. He's not at all incompetent.
>
>   *(negation of prior assumption of incompetence; judgment of positivity and perhaps relief; not restricted to negative judgment in the manner of refute-that strings)*

Because of their implication of directly addressing — and negating — a prior assertion, denials also overlap with strings of direct address and interactivity (to be discussed).

> 422. We are not going to war.
>
>   *(denial + negative assurance about the future; interactively addressing those who counter-assert and think we ARE going to war)*
> 423. The finance bill is not a done deal.
>
>   *(denial + interactively addressing those who counter-assert and think the bill IS a done deal)*
> 424. There is no conspiracy.
>
>   *(denial + interactively addressing those who hold there IS a conspiracy)*
> 425. We have nothing to hide.
>
>   *(denial + interactively addressing those who maintain we DO have something to hide)*

Disclaimers are denials that speakers or writers issue to correct misimpressions they themselves have created, or could create, through their own words. The author acknowledges partial or full responsibility for the assertion that the disclaimer corrects. Compare the following examples:

> 426. I am not a crook.
>
>   *(a simple denial)*
> 427. I said I was desperate, but I never said I was a crook
>
>   *(denial that is also a disclaimer; my previous statement may be responsible for the misunderstanding).*

Both strings 426 and 427 report the author denying being a crook. In 428, the speaker takes responsibility for the misinference. When one disclaims, one counterasserts against some (mis)impression one has allegedly caused or some misimpression that one is likely (in the future) to cause. Disclaimers issued to preempt future harms have ethical and legal relevance in contractual language.

The food critic of the local newspaper needs the following kind of disclaimer to avoid misleading readers.

428. The restaurant gives you good value for your money. I don't mean to say it's cheap.
(without the last disclaimer, you may end up washing dishes).

Writers of corporate warranties provide disclaimers to protect the company legally.

429. If you misuse your portable CD player, by, for example, dropping it or using another company's batteries, the company will not replace it.
(easy to understand but a potentially rude disclaimer in its directness).

This disclaimer is honest but also confrontational. More typical corporate disclaimers suppress the second person marker — you — indicative of threats and confrontation and focus on the positive coverage of a warranty. Compare, for example, string 430.

430. The warranty covers normal wear and tear, but not mishandling or abuse.
(legalese and hard to understand. The meaning may have diffused but so too has the direct tone.)

This corporate disclaimer devotes the main clause to what the warranty positively covers. By conveniently suppressing mention of the agent (a direct *you,* referencing the reader) of mishandling and abuse, the disclaimer eliminates one overt trace of a confrontational tone.

The adverbial *just* participates in denial strings. It does so (sense 4, in CCD) in the string *just because* with a negative *not.*

431. Just because you think so doesn't mean it's true.
(I deny what you think)

The *just because* signals a reason that is unfounded and can be overturned. The adverbial *just* also fits into sarcastic denials, featuring positive affect terms.

432. Just great!
(= this is not great; denial and ironic sarcasm)
433. Just my luck.
(= I have no luck; denial and ironic sarcasm)

Ironic sarcasm is the surface affirmation of positive standards that are patently inapplicable in the context (e.g., proclaiming *a beautiful day* during a hailstorm).

The *just* in the denial heightens the intensity of the negative, ironic effect. Some denials have become sufficiently conventionalized to function transparently as confident assertions. An example is the string *I don't believe,* which primes an audience to hear a confident assertion of skepticism even if there is no previous assertion in the context to deny. It is as if the string elements *don't believe* have been fused into a new lexical item suggesting *believe strongly that not.* To be unambiguously heard as denying a previous belief and (at the same time) not making a confident assertion of skepticism, a speaker or writer must turn to strings that insulate the element of denial from the element of an unhedged confident belief, such as *it is not necessarily the case that I believe that.*

As a final observation, denials seem to be the trigger for the rhetorical figure known as paralipsis, where a speaker draws attention to an idea by pretending to overlook it:

434. I won't even mention my opponent's corruptness.

In this case, the speaker appears to reject a presupposed assertion (e.g. my opponent's corrupt isn't worth mentioning) that the speaker, in truth, rejects not at all.

Class 17: Resistance   Strings indicating resistance share negativity with refute-that strings and with denials and disclaimers. But unlike refute-that and denial strings, where the scope of the negativity includes unstated propositions or projected inferences that might arise from outside the immediate discourse, the scope of negativity within resistance strings is localized to markers that signal resistance expressly in the prior discourse. These markers include contrastives, such as *but, yet, despite, in spite of, ostensibly,* and concessives like *even though* and *granted that.* Such markers freely combine to create longer resistance strings: but be this as it may, *but despite any, even though, but in spite of.*

Resistance markers can be seeded purely through lexical content as well. Examples are *fighting, filibustering, resisting, rebutting, rejoining, conceding* and compounds like *resist the idea,* all of which we have catalogued as resistance strings. In these last cases, resistance strings function to evoke negative content without requiring the speaker or writer to subjectively align with the resistance or to be seen as resisting. This makes resistance strings good candidates for journalist functions, where a speaker or writer wishes to report on a *fight* or *filibuster* while suppressing commentary on it. The negativity involved is sealed within the message, insulating its force from the subjectivity of the messenger. By learning resistance strings apart from refute-that, denials, and negative affect strings, speakers learn how to report resistance and negativity without requiring them to subjectively identify with it.

This concludes our overview of the dimension of reasoning strings, tied to constituents of assertion and refutation. Whether helping to assert or refute a thought, reasoning strings help convey to audiences bids to promote individual thought into social thinking or to demote it from social to individual thought.

Dimension 8: Sharing Social Ties

Strings associated with this dimension help to remind audiences of the wealth of common thinking that already exists between communicators and their audiences. The ancient rhetoricians had an umbrella term for the devices of language needed to create such social ties with audiences — commonplaces. By invoking commonplaces, ancient orators could gently coax the audience to share their thought based on reminders that their thought was already well in tune with a culture to which the audience already belonged. The explicit rooting of one's thought in commonplaces was thus an orator's strategy to seek a sense of camaraderie with audiences.

Many commonplaces are well-known and resonant literary phrases. They can be found in the language of the bible (e.g., *a bird in the hand is worth two in the bush);* in proverbs (e.g., *raining cats and dogs);* in Shakespeare (e.g., *a plague on both your houses);* in phrases that derive from England's history as a nautical power (e.g., *batten down the hatches);* in expressions plucked from popular literature (e.g., *a catch 22);* and in euphemisms (e.g., asking *to be excused* to mean using the toilet). (The Phrase Finder website is a trove of such literary commonplaces: see http://phrases.shu.ac.uk.) When these culturally notable strings are short and contiguous and have stable priming effects on the experience of audiences, we have included them in our catalog. However, because of the length and relative infrequency of many of these expressions compared to the shorter, more frequent, and less culturally memorable strings that have been our focus, we have made no effort to include memorable literary expressions comprehensively.

We must further distinguish contiguous literary phrases, such as those just mentioned, which we sometimes do include in our catalog, with the classic rhetorical figures (Quinn, 1993) of speech and thought, which we did not, and more importantly, could not in principle include in our catalog.

There are two reasons for this in principle conclusion. The first reason is that figures of speech and thought more often than not violate assumptions of contiguity. The figure of chiasmus, for example, requires an ordering of pairs (a−b ... b−a) in which the pairs are not strictly contiguous (compare Cicero's, "Renown for conquest, and in council skilled" where the chiasmatic pair "renown" and "skilled" are nonadjacent. The second, more important, reason is that figures commonly function not as literal surface tokens of language but as a generative system covering infinitudes of potential expression. For example, the figure of assonance is defined by repeating a sound across an extended expression. Yet the actual expression that derives from this formal definition is open-ended and, for all intents and purposes, unbounded as surface expression. The brilliant assonance of the biblical *Thy kingdom come, thy will be done* is underdetermined from the formal definition of assonance. The mechanisms underlying figurative effects exceed in complexity the simple game of rhetorical scrabble that underlay our selection and cataloging of rhetorically relevant English strings. Consequently, our dimension of shared social ties does not focus on figures and tropes, as important as figures and tropes can be to a rhetorical interest in commonplace language. We rather found ourselves focusing on the shorter, less visible, and less complex strings through which speakers and writers remind audiences of the context and culture they share.

We now turn to the various strings classes we came to associate with the dimension of sharing social ties. These string classes are easier to follow when we put them into natural groupings, which we call: sharing premises, inclusiveness, like-mindedness, and acts of assuring.

Sharing Premises

A key aspect of sharing social ties is sharing premises. Sharing premises breaks down into various string classes, including classes invoking shared history or precedent, common authorities, prior knowledge, and received points of view.

Class 1: Precedents Speakers and writers share premises by sharing with their audiences stories about their collective past and how a shared past has helped bequeath a shared present. These stories of collective history are accomplished in part through precedent strings. Precedent strings depict the decisions and actions of longstanding authorities, traditions, and collectives (e.g., *the founding fathers)* that audiences know and respect. Linguistically speaking, precedent strings feature the present perfect aspect *(have, has, has been)*. The effect conveyed is a continuous, unbroken, line from past *(previous, long ago)* to near present *(recently)* to the present situation *(at this moment, now, currently)*. The perfect aspect nourishes the feel of ideas in circulation for a long time that occupied social agents *then* and that, in an unbroken line, occupy them *still* and (importantly) *now*. Look at the following precedent strings:

435. Previous efforts have…
    (I root my thinking in previous work)
436. Previous writers…
    (I am not the first)
437. long ago established…
    (I am working from a longstanding tradition)
438. Jones has argued that…
    (I may not agree with Jones, but I need him to advance my case)
439. was long supposed to have…
    (I am writing out of a tradition with authorities and expectations)
440. recently there has been…
    (a shift showing how I've kept up with trends)

441. Some have argued…
(I probably disagree with some, but their arguments are relevant to mine)
442. Others have argued…
(I probably disagree with others, but their arguments are relevant to mine)
443. I agree with Jones when he said…
(Jones confirms my own thinking, even as I confirm his)
444. Recent work has shown…
(I root my thinking in this work)

The *long supposed to have* string (439) suggests dogmatic ideas holding sway for an extended period, but now discredited. The near present (440) indicates a momentum shift in thinking or interest about the ideas under discussion. The strings with which the speaker or writer cite other agents (441, 442) reveals some of the natural overlap between precedent strings and citation strings. The citation of the agent in third person subject position [Jones] (438) is often a sign that the writer will not entrust to Jones the complete story of the past or present. The same is true when the subject is an unspecified pronoun *(Some…, Others… ,* as in 441, 442). Readers experienced in the conventions of academic writing that combine precedent and citation understand that writers never stake their bets on thinking of authors they only weakly cite in the indefinite general as "some" and "others" (Geisler, 1994). By way of contrast, speakers and writers signal positive citation when they include self-reference to confirm the thinking of an outside source (443) (see confirming another's thought, previously discussed).

Precedent strings imply inclusiveness with the audience and, in some cases, explicitly signal it with an inclusive marker like our.

445. In the way of our ancestors, we respect the land.
(inclusive our + precedent marked by "ancestors")

Precedent strings also combine with strings explicitly marked for time intervals, such as:

446. In keeping with tradition, we exchange gifts during the evening.
(time interval [in keeping] + precedent marked by "tradition")
447. In the way of our ancestors, we have continued to respect the land.
(time interval [continued to] + precedent marked by "ancestors")

Under precedent strings, we also classify strings that signal rare breaks with precedent. Two common formulae for these strings: *is only + rank number + time* (e.g., is only the second time) and not since. The first formula indicates a rare break with precedent by focusing on the exceptional nature of the occurrence. The second formula indicates it by focusing on a denial of the implied recency of the last occurrence.

448. It's only the second time a President has gone to war without popular support.
(only = exceptional nature of a repeated occurrence)

449. Not since Vietnam has a President gone to war without popular support.
(not since = denying the implicit recency of the last occurrence)

Class 2: Common Authorities   Strings classified as common authority provide speakers and writers another way to share premises with audiences. These strings invoke prior persons, practices, customs, or beliefs that command widespread deference and respect. In informal conversation, the all-purpose common authority is the ubiquitous and anonymously named expert class, referenced by the indefinite plural pronoun, *they:*

Speaker 1: They've just invented a scooter that flies.
Speaker 2: What will they think of next?

In written English, writers share authorities through the reporting of the actions and decisions of an anonymous elite, usually rendered in the passive with an institutionalized verb or verb phrase. Examples are, *was voted on, has been discussed, has been agreed, has been decided, authorized by, the decision was made to, on approval of, it was concluded that, was approved, was rejected, was informed that, has been briefed as to.* The passive voice leaves the identity of these actors a secret. The institutional verbs (e.g., *agreed, decided, approved, concluded, recommended, briefed*) indicate a unified group cognition used to smooth over messy institutional processes. The combination of a unified and anonymous authority working against the audience has obvious implications for uses and abuses of power (Fairclough, 1989). In institutional contexts, language that communicates authorized action may thinly veil a presumption of power. Compare the opening of the following corporate memorandum, distributed to the rank and file:

450. The closing of X division has been authorized by the central office.
(Because you, dear reader of the rank and file, are part of the organizational hierarchy, you obviously consent to this action)

A communicator's private and tentative thought can transform itself into a dictum of institutional authority by a slight prose revision. Compare:

451. He judged /ascertained/ deemed/ found that
(Private thought with hint of common authorization)

452. It is judged /ascertained /deemed/ found that
(Common authorized with weakened sense of private judgment)

Notice how the situational *it* + *passive* can transform strings of otherwise private thinking verbs, like *judged, determined, ascertained, deemed, and found that*, into verbs of common authority: *it is ascertained, it is determined, it is recommended, it has been discovered that, it is found that, it is deemed.*

Through a slight syntactic alteration, from *know* to *know to*, a verb of public cognition, like *know*, can become a verb of collective social authority.

453. John knows the world is round.
   (Report of public cognition individuated to John)
454. Mary knows to listen before she speaks.
   (Report of public social authority individuated to Mary)

What rhetoricians since Aristotle have called rhetorical ethos, persuasion through personal credibility, credentials, and good will relies on aligning one's personal presence, beliefs, and projects with authorizing premises shared by the audience. A standard locution for summoning this ethos in the micro world of language is the *as a* + *role identity* construction, linking the speaker's role as an individual conduit of public credibility. Speakers use this construction to justify why they are worthy individual representatives of public ideals or good public dealers on matters that might ordinarily remain in the realm of the personal. Consider:

455. As a long-life member of the ACLU, I am qualified to speak on the first amendment.
   (Invoking a public role to establish individual ethos to speak)
456. As your friend, I need to tell you the truth.
   (Invoking a social role of closeness to justify the ethos to speak from the standpoint of clinical distance)

Class 3: Prior Knowledge Speakers and writers can share premises by making audiences aware of the prior knowledge they mutually share. Strings of English that routinely signal prior knowledge are: *well known, as you know, as I'm sure you know, as you know, you are familiar with, as is well known, as everyone knows, according to the old proverb, of course you know, you may recall that, the conventional wisdom is, you have probably heard/read.*

Class 4: Received Points of View Speakers and writers can share premises by signaling points of views that are themselves widely established and shared. Characterizing "conventional" or "received" points of view before elaborating one's own distinctive point of view is a common move in academic writing. Academic writers know to cite received points of view in order to open a space for one's own contribution (Kaufer and Geisler, 1989; Swales, 1990). Hyland (2001), for example, found that in academic texts, it is common for writers to anticipate "the position of an imaginary reader to suggest what any reasonable, thinking member of the community might conclude or do" (p. 558). Because this idealized insider can be an anonymous social norm, English strings that present alternative or received lines of argument can rely on the indefinite pronoun referencing a generalized addressee (e.g., *one, someone, anyone).* Furthermore, they can rely on an indefinite generalized *we* or *you.* These indefinite addressees are combined with contingency modals *(might, could)* and various verbs of thinking *(judging, deciding)* and declaiming *(asserting, refuting)* to produce a "conventional wisdom" that the academic writer seeks to trump. Some common instances of strings launching the received wisdom the academic writer will try to subvert or move beyond are the following:

457. One might assert,
458. Someone could argue,
459. Anyone could object.
460. The reader might object that.

These strings characterize actual or hypothetical received positions from which the writer withholds full empathy. Academic writers anticipate these points of view as "faulty paths" (Kaufer & Geisler, 1989; Geisler, 1994) that contrast with the thinking they go on to put forward for public confirmation.

Inclusiveness

Class 5: Inclusiveness   We treat inclusiveness both as a major grouping within the dimension of social ties and a string class of its own. Strings that prime inclusiveness invoke a group identity to which the communicator and others both belong. These others may or not include the addressed audience. When they do, the inclusiveness brings with it a sense of empathy. When they do not, the inclusiveness comes without empathy.

Inclusiveness strings incorporate first person plurals (e.g., *we, us),* which do not guarantee empathy. English also furnishes certain inclusive adverbs which, more than the isolated first person plural, help to align inclusiveness and empathy. Examples of these adverbs are, *as as all of us, we together, both of us, all of us, we both,* and verbs like *join* (e.g., *join us all in).* These various expressions strengthen the feeling that the speaker or writer is thinking about the audience as well as third parties in an effort to be inclusive.

We have found it important to distinguish inclusiveness and empathy even as we mention them together. They are not the same. Inclusiveness stands as a visible marker of language indicating the "joint-belonging" of communicator and other. Empathy tends to be a more subtle downstream effect that inclusive writers are often seeking to achieve. Inclusiveness is typically a stepping-stone to empathy with the audience, but it is no more than that. Empathy, by contrast, means that the speaker or writer has managed to court the immediate audience into a shared perspective.

As suggested already, the following are some strings of inclusiveness that make most visible the courtship of the reader:

461. us all
     (writer-reader solidarity and empathy)
462. we all
     (writer-reader solidarity and empathy)
463. inspires us all to work harder
     (writer-reader solidarity and empathy)
464. we together can do it
     (writer-reader solidarity and empathy)
465. it must involve us both
     (writer-reader solidarity and empathy)
466. we both must win or lose together
     (writer-reader solidarity and empathy)
467. "Can't we all get along?"
     (Rodney King, Los Angeles Riot, 1992)

Although these inclusiveness strings court empathy with the reader, the best-known markers of inclusiveness, especially the stand-alone first person plural pronouns (e.g., *we, us),* can project inclusiveness without empathy:

468. We will bury you.
     (inclusiveness without empathy)
469. You hate us.
     (inclusiveness without empathy)

Significantly, even the inclusiveness-strengthening adverbs *all* and *together,* cannot always guarantee empathic courtship with the reader:

470. All of us hate you.
     (no reader empathy here)
471. We voted together to oust you from power.
     (nor here!)

Kenneth Burke (1969) illustrated how inclusive language can evoke audience empathy when inclusiveness is combined with positive standards, resemblance, and autobiographical retrospection:

472. I was a farm boy myself.
     (Burke's celebrated example; spoken by a politician to constituents of farmers.)

121

The English language provides a specifically addressive *let us* construction, conveying the speaker or writer's sense of an inclusiveness that calls out to the audience for shared attention so that, perhaps, more than attention can be shared. Compare:

473. We [John and I] are going on a camping trip.
    (and you are not invited)
474. Let us go on a camping trip.
    (please come!)
475. Let us work together.
    (let's reach common ground)

When American leaders find that *us* and *us all* can't keep everyone at the table, they can always rely on *let us* to invite them back.

The lesson to be taken here is that achieving inclusiveness in language is not the same as achieving empathy. Yet, since the time of Aristotle, the foundations of a rhetorical theory undergirding language have depended on understanding the additional conditions by which inclusive language can systematically recruit the empathy of audiences.

Three such conditions seem worthy of mention. The first condition occurs when the speaker and the audience, failing to share interests, manage to share enemies. Shared enemies can cause empathy, if only the frail bond of a common foe. Consider string 476. Speakers and writers enhance solidarity, of course, when they can get audiences to associate with their *"us"* and against an opposing speaker's *"them."*

476. The terrorists are a threat to us.
    (Implicit us/them dichotomy; solidarity aligns with empathy if the addressee dislikes terrorists; probably a good bet).

In this case, inclusiveness turns into empathy only because of the extremely polarized conditions of the rhetorical situation. In a less polarized world, the inclusive us may well exclude the audience addressed:

477. The Wal-Mart next door is a threat to us.
    (written by the manager of the local K-Mart to the newspaper; inclusive us refers to K-Mart and its people and excludes readers who are happy to shop at Wal-Mart or K-Mart)

The default of the English first-person inclusive, *we, us,* is exclusive to the addressee.

Let us now consider a second condition in which bids to increase inclusiveness can result in increasing empathy. This condition arises when the writer and reader share specialized learning interests, typical of their sharing an academic or professional subspecialty. Hyland (2001) looked specifically into how sharing academic curiosities binds inclusiveness to empathy in academic texts. He compiled and studied a corpus of 240 published articles (1.4 million words) culled from ten journals across eight disciplines (philosophy, sociology, applied linguistics, physics, electrical engineering, marketing, mechanical engineering, and biology). He examined each of the articles for 10 linguistic features he believed are associated with the writer's efforts to build solidarity with readers. The features consist of inclusive pronouns, imperatives, obligation modals, indefinite pronouns, knowledge references, rhetorical questions, second-person pronouns, asides, real questions, and the construction, "it is [adjective] to do" (e.g., *it is advantageous to do this.*). Hyland found across these disciplines that academic writers seek empathy mainly through inclusive pronouns (primarily *we*). These pronouns of inclusiveness accounted for 36.5% of all the solidarity actions Hyland catalogued. Hyland suggests that the context of shared curiosity among academics within a discipline made it easier for the academic writer's inclusiveness to include rather than exclude the reader.

The third and final condition favoring an inclusiveness spilling into empathy occurs when speakers and writers can address the interests they share with audiences. This third condition harks to the Aristotelian interest in deliberative (policy) rhetoric, an interest that arises because the speaker is able to convince audiences that they are all *in this together.* Aristotle had the genius to understand that speakers and audiences have common interests in the future whether or not they have common interests in the present. Watch how the grounds for the addressee's inclusion and empathetic involvement increase with the increase in future and public scope of the subject under discussion. Compare:

478. We needed to buy a new house.
     (Culturally private action; lower likelihood that addressee is part of the inclusive we)
479. We need to build a new road system.
     (Culturally public action; higher likelihood that addressee is part of the inclusive we)

Establishing Like-Mindedness

Speakers and writers can share social ties with audiences by pointing out their like-mindedness with audiences in their values and perceptions. They establish like-mindedness with audiences, in turn, by invoking standards and values their audiences uphold and value, and by renouncing standards that they know their audiences similarly renounce. As with positive and negative affect, standards sort themselves into positive and negative binaries. Unlike affect terms, standards do not express the emotional state of a single mind. They rather invoke principles of conduct and performance defined by public criteria. As a result, standards are inherently social entities making up the stuff of social knowledge. Consider the difference between praising Mr. Jones as "tremendous" (affect) and declaring him "fair-minded" (standard). The first, a positive affect term, does not specify on its own what, if any, public criterion stands behind the praise. Nor is a public criterion required. The second, a positive standard term, specifies conviction and conduct upheld by a public criterion.

Class 6: Shared Positive Standards Let us examine for the moment positive standards. Single-word examples of this string class fill, to overflowing, the boy- and girl-scout manuals: *dependable, dutiful, truthful, honorable, ideal, justice, meritorious, worthy, and credible.* Other examples are long enough to show up only in acts of positive character, such as *hold up her end of the bargain, did right by him,* and *nursed them back to health.*

Class 7: Time as a Positive Standard Positive-standard terms are frequently culture specific. In western economies, where time is money, time is revered as a value to hoard and not squander or waste. American English fashions punctuality and timeliness specifically into positive standards, establishing public criteria when it is appropriate to earn praise for being *right on time, just in time, in the nick of time,* acting *just at the moment we have been waiting for,* exhibiting *perfect timing,* managing things *like clockwork,* and managing to arrive *not a moment too late.* Within well-known social assumptions of western capitalism, we prefer the fast turnover of exchange to the slow. Thus, *an early start* is a robust positive standard in American texts, never to be confused with one who *starts late* and brings *too little too late.* Whereas the positive benefits of time in terms of speed and timesaving has been an ideal of modernism, the positive standard of time in the sense of appropriate timing is as old as ancient rhetoric. The first known linkage, arguably, of time to positive standards is the ancient notion of *kairos,* meaning roughly to align a message with the time best suited to insure its effectiveness.

When using positive standard strings, the linking of the positive value term to the pronoun *our* binds inclusiveness directly to shared standards. Contrast the following strings with and without *our:*

480. John won his confidence.
    (Positive Standard; non inclusiveness)
481. John won our confidence.
    (Positive Standard; inclusiveness of standard cued; you and I, dear reader, already confide; we are already a team)
482. The enemy will test their courage.
    (Positive Standard; non-inclusiveness)
483. The enemy will test our courage.
    (Positive Standard; inclusiveness cued; you are I, dear reader, already share, as team-mates, a mutual understanding of our courage)

In 480 and 482, the speaker invokes *confidence* and *courage* as common positive standards, inviting value sharing with the audience. In 481 and 483, the writer goes farther. The contribution of *our* is to make the utterance about the alliance of the communicator with the audience as much as about the present matters that now require their common attention as a team.

Class 8: Shared Negative Standards   Speakers and writers share social ties with readers as much by the standards they repudiate (negative standards) as by those they embrace (positive standards). Indeed, because it is arguably a smaller feat to rally around common distastes than common tastes, speakers and writers can find it easier to win adherents by sharing their distaste. A handful of such negative standard strings are the following: *garish, questionable evidence, travesty, baseless, adversaries to liberty, poor taste, inconsistent, incoherent,* and *not user-friendly.* Speakers and audiences who agree on these negative judgments agree on standards of performance and conduct to repudiate. Whereas English is generous in expressing distaste in single words, it also offers various multi-word expressions, such as *doesn't let facts get in the way* and *misplaces their trust in.*

Positive and negative affect strings, as we discussed, can be unstable at the grain of a single word. Anyone who has suffered a *good migraine* knows that *good* need not always package delightful things. Positive and negative standard terms exhibit a similar instability at the grain of a single word. Without a context, we are willing to swear by *predictability, reliability,* and *consistency* as values to be championed. However, misfits can boast all these values. We elect politicians who are *ambitious* and *conscientious,* but the context of the words can revoke their positive value:

484. John is conscientious to have done that.
   (successful action)
485. I can't really blame Lincoln (for incompetence). He is conscientious.
   (Paraphrase of what Douglas said of Lincoln)
   (well-meaning, but incompetent and failed action)
486. John will go places because he is ambitious.
   (ambition motivates positive action)
487. John will cheat his way through because he is ambitious.
   (ambition motivates negative action)

Whether a positive or negative standard, the string *just so* emphasizes the criterion of judgment and, in some cases, pulls it out for further elaboration:

488. Mary was just so smart.
   (as smart as they come)
489. John was just so dumb he couldn't get a job.
   (as dumb as they get; elaborated by consequences for being dumb)

The expression *only just so* implies a negative standard, indicating mediocrity. Compare:

490. His test score was only just so.
     (no better than average)

Class 9: Resemblances   Speakers and writers share social ties with audiences by revealing how things look to them and assuming things will look similarly to the audience. Should a speaker say, in the context of responding to an improbable idea:

491. It's much like when my brother told me I was going to be president.

The speaker bets on creating a sense of seeing things similarly with the audience. The speaker implies a similar mind's eye toward improbability, and, by implication, a similar mind. The social ties triggered through a resemblance rely on the following background inferences: "Our like sense of resemblance, dear audience, means, by turns, our like experiences, our like take on our experiences, and so, finally, our like minds. Great minds not only think alike; they see alike." A marker of resemblance is the conjunction *as,* joined with verbs of thinking and imagining. Representative instances are: *see as, imagine it as, perceive it as, looks as if, looks like, exactly the sort of, is very much like, striking parallels with, as if he were a, acting like, identified with, comes across as, easily mistaken for, reminds me of.*

When a speaker seeks to resemble in accomplishment another person, the idea of resemblance combines with inner thinking and thinking ahead. The resulting blend is caught in the English word *emulation.* In contemporary English, *emulation* is used as a positive standard term, often meaning to try or succeed to imitate a paragon of prowess or virtue.

492. He tried to emulate the idealism of his teachers.
     (a standard approached)
493. His emulated the idealism of his teachers.
     (a standard attained)

However, another meaning of *emulation,* which most dictionaries now list as obsolete, is the meaning of the surviving adjective, *emulous,* suggesting the feelings of envy toward a rival that motivates the desire to imitate and surpass. *Emulation* in the history of English has traveled from referencing competitive inner thought to high-minded public behavior. The shifts in usage, in this case, are comprehensible because the idea of resemblance falls on both sides of the shift. The only change is whether users focus on the motives for seeking resemblance or the ends that make resemblance an object of public justification.

In addition to inner thought and standards, resemblance can productively combine with denials:

494. It's not all that different from the time I lost my watch.
(= it's like the time I. ...resemblance /denial blend)

The adverbial *just* contributes to resemblance actions (CCD, sense 18) to bring out the exactness of the similarity, as in *just like, just as, just the same as.*

Assuring

Speakers and writers assure their audiences in order to guarantee a predictable trajectory for them into the future. Predictability, as we have seen, can be a positive or negative value, and the future offered in an assurance may be beneficial or detrimental. When the assurances are beneficial, they are felt as promises. When they are harmful, they are felt as threats or confrontations. When the assurance answers someone's standing need for assurance, the assurance is felt as reassurance. When the audience has done something to earn the assurance, the assurance is felt as a reinforcement or acknowledgment. The only assurances that share social ties with readers assure beneficial outcomes. We thus restrict our focus in this section to these positive assurances. We discuss negative assurances later on when we consider threats and confrontations.

Class 10: Promising   Promises assure felt obligations to oneself or others. The promise benefits the party addressed by the promise. Perhaps because the interpersonal stakes of broken promises are high, few English strings allow a promise that omits the marker word *promise.* A promise is a two-way contract and it does little good for an audience to try to infer a promise if the speaker refrains from going on the record as having made one. Only fools and the devious try to infer promises between the lines of what they hear and read. Many English promising strings lead with the avowal, *I promise,* so that their status as promises is verbatim, on the record, and understood and accepted as such. Throughout our cataloging of English strings, the only valid strings we found that managed to promise without the word *promise* were strings of self-promising (better known as resolutions) indicating an oath to oneself to decisively separate one's future from one's past:

495. From now on, I will go to the gym each day.
496. From this day forward, I will avoid red meat.

Class 11: Reassuring   Speakers and writers reassure to relieve audiences from uncertainty and the anxiety it can produce. Reassurance strings confer confidence to an addressee in a state of uncertainty and vulnerable to the negative affect uncertainty can bring. That said, reassurances must be interactive, typically second-person directed, and cannot be achieved merely be referencing a positive and confident future that omits the prospects of the addressee.

497. Mel can count on high stock returns every year.
(confidence without implications for the addressee = not reassurance)
498. You can count on high stock returns every year.
(confiĭdence + interactive addressee = reassurance)

Other common examples of positive reassurance we have found are the following:

499. Don't worry about that.
(reassurance by denying previous implied assertion that one should be worried)
500. Some assembly is necessary but it is not hard.
(reassurance in instructions; denies counter-assertion that assembly is hard)
501. You have nothing to fear.
(reassurance and denial of reader assertion — I have a lot to fear)
502. You'll be fine.
(reassurance and denial of reader assertion — I am not fine)
503. That's no problem.
(reassurance and denial of reader assertion — I have a problem)
504. Don't take it personally.
(reassurance and denial of reader assertion — I take it personally)
505. "Things will work out for the best," his mother reassured.
(reassurance in fiction)

Examples 499 through 504 are standard reassurances in spoken as well as written English. Example 500 illustrates the ubiquity of reassurance in instructional writing. Tackling instructions, readers are often anxious as well as ignorant about the spatial task they are seeking to navigate. They need to be reassured that they can make it through. Example 505 depicts a reassurance in fiction. The mother has not only issued a reassuring statement. The narrator labels the mother's utterance as a reassurance so that there can be no doubt about her intentions.

American English supplies two senses of *just* that add color and shading to reassurance strings. The first use (CCD, sense 4), mainly in the form of *just + a* or *just + verb+ ing,* demystifies for an anxious audience a potentially unfamiliar, uncategorized threat.

506. Don't be afraid. It's just a shadow.
(just = familiarizing frame so you can categorize what you've just seen or heard and not fear it)
507. Don't worry. He's just working late.
(just = familiarizing frame so his whereabouts are not a mystery)

508. If you see a dialog box saying "command unclear," don't sweat. It's just a glitch in the program. You haven't done anything wrong.
(just = familiarizing frame so that the "noisy signals" that arise in an instructional task can be understood for what they are and not impede your progress)

The second reassuring sense of *just* (CCD, sense 5) is used to give reassurance that certain task expectations the audience is facing are smaller, more focused, and more manageable than the reader may first understand. This is the *just* found so commonly in written instructions when the scope of a tutorial task is defined:

509. While there's a lot you can work with, we'll just stay with the simplest things you need to know.
(just = focusing considerations so that you, dear reader, needn't divide your attention while you are still learning)

This second reassuring sense of just depends on a *just* + *verb* string where the verb in question (e.g., *stay with, focus)* references a task focus that the adverbial *(just)* then restricts.

Class 12: Reinforcing   If the basic directive of reassurance is "keep at it," as good things will come, then the basic message of reinforcement is "keep it up," so that good things shall continue to come. Reinforcement actions combine assurance and positive feedback. They compliment a person for correct or worthy actions and for milestones crossed.

510. You are doing very well.
511. That's exactly right.
512. That's exactly it.
513. You did it!
(assumption: it = good thing)
514. Spot on.
(British English to mean "right on target")
515. Congratulations.

As with reassuring, reinforcing is common in instructional writing. The reader is working through a task and, having reached some milestone, the writer deems the reader praiseworthy:

516. Great going! One task down. One to go.
517. You are almost done. Don't quit now.
518. The hardest part is behind you.

Class 13: Acknowledging   Acknowledgments, both as verbal actions and English strings, express debt or gratitude to others for their previous acts. Books and manuscripts have acknowledgment sections just to single out the persons who made a difference to the artifact's coming into existence. Acknowledgments characteristically blend the first person, second person, positive affect, interactivity, and direct address — all mixed in with linguistic markers of indebtedness and gratitude. Some examples:

519. I want to express my gratitude for your…
520. You were so kind to…
521. I thank you for…

Acknowledgments are common in personal letters of thanks, where the object of the acknowledgment involves positive material actions (e.g., a gift, a kind action) the reader has taken. Under the trend to "personalize" consumer relationships and to indicate "responsiveness" to customers, the corporate acknowledgment often overlaps with the metadiscourse of follow-ups (discussed later on):

522. This is to acknowledge…
    (acknowledgment/follow-up blend)
523. Thank you for letter of…
    (acknowledgment/follow-up blend)
524. I want to acknowledge your complaint of…
    (acknowledgment/follow-up blend)

When acknowledgments are fronted with a hypothetical *would be,* they can signal refusals to acknowledge and, in this case, will overlap with resistance:

525. I'll be the first to acknowledge you are right.
    (acknowledgment and assurance that you are right)
526. I'd be the first to acknowledge you are right if you had the evidence.
    (but you don't…and so I won't…refusal to acknowledge = resistance)

Dimension 9: Directing Activities

Speakers and writers use priming strings to direct audiences to take up physical and spatial action within their local environments. The audience's local environment is typically immediate to the speaker in oral contexts and displaced from the writer in texts. Strings that support the audience's directed activity are frequent and varied enough, we found, to warrant status as an independent dimension in our catalog. The dimension can be further broken down into various groupings of string classes, namely imperatives, queries, instructions, and feedback. Each grouping supports distinctive string classes of its own.

Imperatives

Imperatives command audiences to comply with a recommended action. Stings that contribute to imperatives fall into various classes, conventional imperative forms, insistence on action, and task assignments

Class 1: Conventional Imperative Forms Conventional imperatives result from a sentence or clause-initial verb stem indicating voluntary action.

527. Come now
     (imperative)
528. Hold your hands above your head.
     (imperative)

Class 2: Insistence on Action In a previous section, we considered strings that insist that an audience reason in one or another way. In this section, we examine insistence on action as a form of directing an audience's activities (e.g., *you should vote for Smith*). Consider the following strings that insist on action and their overlaps:

529. You should vote for Smith, hands down.
     (overlap with confidence)
530. Whatever you do, vote for Smith.
     (overlap with intensity)
531. You will want to vote for Smith.
     (overlap with project ahead)
532. Smith is by far the best qualified candidate.
     (Overlaps with confidence and positive standards to give a direction to the insistence)

All insistence actions overlap with intensity but not vice versa. To add insistence to intensity, the writer needs to express or imply a common norm that makes compliance imperative. Compare:

533. I had a great time.
     (Intensity; one mind retrospective)
534. You have richly earned a great time. So do it.
     (Go and have fun. I insist—still intensity, but now with the normed pressure that creates an overlap with insistence)

The failure to comply with an insistence (e.g., *you must pick up dinner*) appears more ominous than the failure to comply with a conventional request (e.g., please *pick up dinner*) or direct appeal (e.g., *please vote*). When one flat out refuses what one is insisted to do, one is likely to incur loss of face and perhaps even a confrontational follow-up (e.g., *you are stupid not to listen to me*).

American writers get much mileage for their insistences from *must, have to,* and *got to,* with *simply* and *just got to* thrown in to intensify the effect:

535. You simply must go to the store for me.
     (Simply makes "must" emphatic)
536. I absolutely insist that you leave.
     (Absolutely makes "insist" emphatic)
537. I have just got to lose weight.
     (Just makes losing weight the single focus of my resolve)
538. You have just got to try that.
     (Insistence + confrontation)

When coupled with the first person and verbs like *got to,* the adverbial *just* intensifies the resolve of the *got to,* as if to fashion it into a top priority (string 537). When coupled with the second person you, as in 538, *just,* as intensifier, overlaps with both insistence and confrontation.

People who insist can be unshakeable in their convictions. So too can those who confront the one insisting. The originating insistence can be met with an equally firm counter-insistence.

539. I am NOT going to go the game.
     (An insistent denial echoing off an earlier insistence that I go)

Strings conveying insistence impose one point of view on another. When the projection is self-directed, the insistence slips over into self-determination and resolve (e.g., *I must lose weight!*). When the insistence is directed from an external and unquestioned source, such as God or natural law, the insistent form *have to* takes on a *de re* sense, meaning inevitability and resignation (e.g., *we all have to die*). Interesting ambiguities arise with narrators who relate stories from a perspective of insistent action. We cannot always know whether the insistence reflects an impatience for change or a heightened resignation that change is all but impossible. Consider the following:

540. Flunking out of law school, Betsy still had to do something meaningful with her life.
     (the "had to" is narratively ambiguous between a story teller whose insistent voice indicates impatience with Betsy and her inability to change as a student; or one whose insistent voice indicates reflective acceptance of Betsy's circumstances)

Let us make one final observation about the relationship of insistence to the personal voice. One who insists on the action of another remains resolute in enforcing a course of action. The English word *insist* derives from the Latin *insistere,* literally to *stand in* and, by implication, to *stand firm* with respect to an interlocutor. To tag a communication as insistent is to mark for notice the subjective persistence of the communicator. Insistence marks a personal voice that continues to stand in when others would have retreated. When speakers direct audiences under an institutional frame, effacing a personal voice, the opportunity to mark personal persistence, and so the personal voice of insistence, closes. While a speaker may maintain the personal qualities of one who insists, the marking of these personal qualities wanes when the speaker has the institutionalized authority *to command,* to direct audiences under the motivation of positive affect and standards (e.g. *rally, exhort, promise)* or negative affect and standards (e.g. *warn, admonish, threaten).*

Class 3: Task Assignments   Task assignments capture top-down notification delivered by a speaker or writer with the power to set agendas, form teams, and assign roles. Interviewing young engineers moving from school to contexts of work where they acquired supervisory responsibilities, Winsor (1999) found her informants confronted with having to assign tasks to others, a managerial role they had never practiced while in school.

The actions assigned by task assignments can be collaborative, signaled by the social use of the preposition *with.* They also can involve reportative verbs associated with generic office work *(meet, confer, gather, monitor)* and by the combination of the generic present and the imperative mood (e.g., *let's meet together tomorrow).* The generic present strengthens the idea that the activities assigned are routines that remake the organization every time they are carried out. Some sample strings:

541. report to
542. meet with
543. confer with
544. gather options
545. define strategy
546. set a purpose
547. weigh options

Task assignments also rely on the English *am to* and *is to* constructions, combining insistence and confidence (about power) with future projection.

548. You are to go promptly.
549. I am to leave for Chicago immediately.
550. I'm to do nothing until further instructed.

Other kinds of task assignments take concrete noun objects and indicate a focus on specific to-dos:

551. Review the Brown memo.
 (activity + noun object)
552. Write the strategic report on snakes.
 (activity + noun object)

553. Send the draft of the report to the whole committee.
 (activity + noun object)

Instructions

Instructions direct readers to change their immediate physical environment while working through a spatial task. In this sense, instructions are like imperatives and, in particular, task assignments. However, unlike imperatives, instructions require that the action required for change be multifaceted and typically multi-stepped. The audience not only needs to be told to change the physical environment. The audience needs to be given explicit guidance how to do so. Instructions in our catalog are composed of various string classes: procedures, move-body, confirm-moves, and error-recoveries.

Class 4: Procedures   Procedures are directives within a structured task. They can retain some of the politeness markers *(please)* of requests and some of the professional distance imperatives of formal queries. The reliance on the imperative verb (e.g., *please obtain, please fold, please bend, please sign, please use)* suggests an official provider of information and an audience whose compliance is part of an institutional expectation. Procedural actions can specify multistep manual action in the manner of written instructions: *Obtain a written form at the desk, use only a number 2 pencil, do not use on, review carefully, you will want to retain a copy for your records, put your signed form in the mail.*

Although the verbs in these strings are procedurally specific, they are not manually specific. They indicate general actions, prohibitions, regulations, and cautions for the reader to take or follow. Imperative verbs mirror institutional protocols, especially ones that audiences can apply when filling out official documents and forms in a clipped or succinct command language *(put, place, take, mark, check, retain, fold).* The overall effect of the imperative, interactive, and clipped tone is to institutionalize and depersonalize the voice of command. The implied voice behind procedural actions is the authority of law and the audience fills the role of legal subject who is expected, by dint of an external authority, to comply.

Class 5: Move Body   Move body strings are typically part of multistep directives involving the hands (and sometimes feet) in specific activities. Characteristic strings within this string class are, *click on, tear along the perforation, shake well, place two drops, add until full, tap lightly, peel it off, secure the lid, remove and dispose, rip out, slather it thickly, rinse and repeat, gently insert.*

Move-body strings appear on products as well as texts. The instruction *open this end* appears directly on milk containers and *do not tear* on clothing labels. Because of their placement in products in addition to texts, move-body strings are often culturally associated with the language of labels as well as texts. In longer, more complex instructions, where the audience might be overwhelmed, speakers and writers can add reassurance (as previously discussed) to move-body strings. In these cases, they do not just tell audiences what to do but reassure them they can do it:

554. Don't worry if you get lost. All you have to do is drag the mouse back to the home icon.
     (reassurance + move body)

The adverbial *just* adds a touch of reassurance to move-body actions (CCD, part of sense 11). The adverbial indicates that an action required by the audience is simpler or less problematic than it may first seem.

555. Stir for a few minutes
     (something to do)
556. Just stir for a few minutes.
     (it's easier than you fear)
557. Lift out from the bottom.
     (something to do)
558. Just lift out from the bottom.
     (something easy to do)

Class 6: Confirm Experience   Confirm experience strings are a hallmark of written instructions. They describe what the reader will or should see or experience if the reader takes the correct actions. A characteristic marker of this string class is the future *will* or the modal *should* and the second person *(you)* along with verbs of seeing, looking, and experiencing (e.g., *find, discover, experience).* The nurse's *this will sting only a little* before administering a flu shot is a good example of confirming an experience and providing reassurance about it at the same time. In instructional writing, confirm-experience actions help readers confirm that they are taking correct actions. Some examples are:

559. After you press "search," you should see a dialogue box.
560. You will then see a menu…
     (after you do what I tell you)
561. You will be looking at a taskbar.
     (if you followed the last step correctly)
562. A window will then come into view.
     (after you take the right step)

Confirm-experience strings can give readers of written instructions the secure feel of an adaptive tutor peering over their shoulder as guide. To create this effect, writers must be able to anticipate the changes in the user's immediate environment should the user take correct or incorrect action. Because they are often composed with the assumption that the user has already acted, confirm-experience strings often refer to the users' actions in retrospect, with the retrospective marker *should have:*

> 563. Harry should have been here by now.
>   *(thinking back about Harry's past plans for now)*
> 564. You should have seen two dots cross the screen
>   (if you completed Step 1).
>   *(confirm experience + retrospection; confirming a move a user has recently completed within an instruction set)*

Class 7: Error Recovery   Error recoveries provide the information that readers require in order to backtrack should they get lost. In this sense, they function much as the "undo" menu option in a software program. They tell readers of written instructions what to do should their actions go awry and should they thus need to backtrack. Strings in this class are characterized by second person, an indication of the contingency of the reader's failure to take correct action (e.g., *if you get lost),* and the corrective steps required to move the reader back on course (e.g., *you should press the home key.)*

> 565. if you don't see it, you can always
>   *(contingency of failure + corrective action)*
> 566. if you can't find it, you might try
>   *(contingency of failure + corrective action)*
> 567. You can always return to home if you get lost.
>   *(contingency of failure + corrective action)*
> 568. if you can't locate it, why not...
>   *(contingency of failure + corrective action)*

Forms of Feedback

Feedback strings convey a writer's evaluations of ideas or performance from another, typically an outside source.

Class 8: Generic Feedback   Generic feedback is commonly marked by politeness, conveyed through a tentative inner mind *(seems, sounds, I think)* and a generic positive affect *(nice, good, okay)* to blunt the force of direct evaluation. Contingency actions appended to feedback strings are another way to mitigate the possible sound of negativity *(If you ask me...).*

569. All right.
    (feedback)
570. Seems okay.
    (feedback + positive feedback)
571. I don't think so.
    (feedback + negative feedback)
572. I think that you might want to think further about that.
    (feedback + contingency + thinking verb + negative feedback)
573. If you ask me, it sounds like a good direction.
    (feedback + contingency +resemblance+ positive feedback)

Feedback strings as listed here can be perfunctory (string 569) and can serve solely to let the reader know that the writer is paying attention. As these strings also suggest, feedback strings can also overlap with positive feedback, negative feedback, and contingency.

Class 9: Positive Feedback   When feedback blends with positive affect and acknowledgments, the result is positive feedback. Some examples are, *well it sure beats, well done, good job, a great improvement, better than I ever thought, better than I ever expected, it certainly beats, I really appreciate, my accolades to, kudos to.*

One discriminator that helped us keep positive feedback distinct from acknowledgments in our catalog is that acknowledgments, as we came to make sense of them, target persons for praise and gratitude. Positive feedback, as it evolved in our cataloging efforts, comments on products more than persons. Compare:

574. He's a winner.
    (acknowledgment in our catalog)
575. The interface is a winner.
    (positive feedback in our catalog)

Class 10: Negative Feedback   When feedback strings convey negative affect and possibly confrontation, the result is negative feedback. Examples of this string class are familiar to all used to criticism:

576. It still doesn't work when I push the menu button.
577. This is confusing to me.
578. A feature that would be helpful would let us copy in one click.
579. Can you improve this by changing the size?
    (negative feedback + interactivity)
580. What went wrong?
    (negative feedback + interactivity)
581. It gets annoying whenever the screen blinks.
582. It was frustrating to find I can't save.

8

Cluster 2:
Relational Perspectives,
Part II

Thus far, we have focused on relational strings that relate audiences to the representations depicted in language. These strings, as we have seen, help orient audiences to the speaker or writer's reasoning, allow for the sharing of social ties, or structure directed activities. In this chapter, we turn our attention to a second family of relational strings, strings that accommodate the navigational needs of audiences as they make their way through the linear medium of language.

Because of the linearity of language, competent speakers and writers make several assumptions a priori about the needs of their audiences. They assume that audiences must constantly monitor where they have been in the linear stream to determine where they have yet to arrive. Following the work of functional linguists (Firbas, 1992), we can think of the audiences' vague sense of territory-traversed in the linear stream as their sense of the familiar. We can think of the audiences' vague sense of territory-left-to-traverse as the audiences' sense of the unfamiliar. Should the audience perceive an imbalance between the familiar and unfamiliar, the linear stream of words will not support a fluid audience experience. Too little sense of the familiar can cause the audience to find the stream unnavigable; too little sense of the unfamiliar can bore the audience and make the stream too predictable to want to follow further. Speakers and writers with a competent feel for audience know to provide audiences with priming cues in the linear presentation for the following three reasons:

Orientation To orient audiences so that they know where they are and feel acknowledged as an interaction partner at relevant times as they listen or read;

139

Localization   To help audiences localize the information that carries the highest contrast with what they have already seen (i.e. is least familiar) so that these contrasts can be identified and integrated with what has come before;

Anticipation   To help audiences anticipate the unfamiliar yet to come so that they can navigate forward in the stream while minimizing the need to backtrack.

Audiences experiencing orientation problems cannot answer: where am I now? What does the writer expect of me as an interaction partner? Audiences experiencing localization problems cannot answer: where in the linear stream am I to focus my attention as an ideal interaction partner? Finally, audiences experiencing forward anticipation problems cannot answer: how am I to predict what is to come so that my movement forward requires the least backtracking? Addressing these various navigational issues is the business of strings within family 4.

FAMILY 4. NAVIGATING AUDIENCES THROUGH THE LINEAR MEDIUM OF LANGUAGE

This second family of relational strings also trades on a definition of representation (contrasted with naïve realism) provided by Manovich (2001):

Definition of Representation in Contrast With Unstructured User Activity
Contrasts with open-ended user control and action, likening representation to an audience's structured interaction and navigation through language as a linear medium. (pp. 16-17)

Strings within family 4 trade on a notion of representation that contrasts it with a user environment where there is no mediating structure regulating the user's behavior. Unlike such open and unmediated environments, where the user's actions are self-supervised. listeners and readers will fail at constructing interactive worlds from linear texts if they are not also willing to follow the navigational cues provided them. For their part, speakers and writers know that expecting audiences to perform their duties is a hit-and-miss expectation if they do not also provide navigational help when and where they anticipate audiences needing it.

In this chapter, accordingly, we examine the family of strings that seem most responsible for seeding the linear stream of language with these navigational aids. This family is broken down into a dimension that helps audiences remain oriented in the linear stream as an interactive partner (what we call the dimension of *interacting)*. It is broken down into a dimension that helps the audience localize the high-contrast information deserving of the audience's weighted attention (what we call the dimension of *notifying*). Finally, it is broken down into a dimension to help audiences anticipate what is to come in the linear stream so that it will be easier to integrate it with what has come before (what we call the dimension of *linear guidance*). The rest of this chapter details each of these dimensions within family 4.

Dimension 10: Interacting

Speakers and writers can never fully anticipate when flesh and blood audiences will lose their way in a message. To be sure, speakers and writers can try to make sure the message is neither too difficult nor too easy for the audience. They can try to convey a subject matter the audience finds interesting! Still, speakers and writers cannot cure audiences of drifting attention. The best they can do is to make sure the language they compose is constantly summoning their audiences back to attention. By regularly summoning the audience back to attention, speakers and writers can try to counteract the constant drift of attention. Calling the audience back to attention in this way plays an important role in helping audiences minimize orientation *(where am I?)* problems in the linear stream.*

Strings that summon the audience's attention appear in our catalog under the interacting dimension. What is the difference between the audience defined by the priming of directed activities (last chapter) and the audience defined by interacting (this chapter)? The audience of directed activities is a material listener or reader addressed in the world of the text. The audience of interacting is but a formal role identity the text itself constructs and that the material reader must don in order to navigate the text from left to right as the communicator has designed. Michael Warner (2002), a literary theorist on the public cultures that texts create, provided a wonderful illustration of why we must separate these two audiences. He cited a passage in Walter Lippman's *Phantom Public,* where Lippman complained about the inattentiveness of the public as a mass reader:

> We must assume as a theoretically fixed premise of popular government that normally men as members of a public will not be well informed, continuously interested, nonpartisan, creative or executive. We must assume that a public is inexpert in its curiosity, intermittent, that it discerns only gross distinction, is slow to be aroused and quickly diverted; that, since it acts by aligning itself, it personalizes whatever it considers, and is interested only when events have been melodramatized as a conflict. (cited in Warner, p. 60)

---

* These orientation problems can become resursive in the case of a text where characters are interacting and the interactive strings are providing orientation cues between characters rather than writer and reader directly. These problems go beyond the scope of our current discussion.

Warner pointed out that Lippman cannot even follow his own advice. For in carping about the inattentiveness of readers, Lippman summons an alert and on-the-ready reader (the "we" he exhorts in writing "we must") to catch his point. Warner understands that the "we" Lippman evoked with insistence in his "we must" phrase is not the actual material reader. Rather, Lippman's "we" in the "we must" phrase is the conventionalized metadiscursive linear guide any speaker or writer must furnish the material reader as an ever-present aid to call the reader back to attention.

String classes within the interactive dimension fall into three classes: (1) interaction with no implications for social ties; (2) interactions with the potential to weaken social ties, better known as threats, confrontations, and (in the electronic medium) flames; (3) interactions that solicit information from others, better known as queries. In the sections to follow, we examine each of these groupings and the various string classes that constitute them.

Classes of Interaction

Class 1: Basic Interactivity We call this string class of interactivity "basic" for two reasons. First, it is not the only string category involving interactivity with the reader. Strings of direct address, imperatives, requests, promises, threats, and denials also prime interactivity. Second, basic interactivity is the string class involving the most common marker of interactivity, namely the second person pronoun *(you)*:

> 583. As you can see...
> 584. Who cares other than you about...
> 585. Does that make you...
> 586. Whatever you want...
> 587. You bet your boots...

The addressed second person provides grounded feedback (Clark, 1996) to the audience. Strings of basic interactivity are legion in the environment of speech and in written dialog insofar as such dialog simulates unplanned speech.

> 588. you bet!!
> 589. you should speak up.
> 590. you are right about that.

Fitzmaurice (2002) studied the use of the English interactive over the history of English. She argued that second-person interactives are light discourse markers that have evolved over time from semantically more delineated epistemic stance markers and intersubjective comment clauses. For example, in her study of English *you see* in letters and dramas from 1650 to 1990, she finds usages of *you see* as an epistemic marker, as in 591, and then becoming increasingly frequent in usages such as 592 and 593:

591. You see that it hard to do.
(epistemic marker of the audience's actual cognition)
592. You see, it is hard to do.
(comment on the hearer's expected intersubjective perspective)
593. See, it is hard to do.
(comment that marks interactive nature of statement with the audience's cognition or perspective having dropped out)

Because we did not build our catalog from diachronic data of English, we did not try to capture these regularities directly. By coincidence, we did end up capturing some aspects of these regularities by discriminating what we are here calling *basic interactivity* strings with strings that have more epistemic weight attached to the interactive unit. We had our pattern matcher break up an interactive string such as *you see that* into two stings: *you* (basic interaction) + *see that* (inner thinking). Maintaining the distinctiveness of interactivity and inner thinking mirrors the visibility of epistemics in early English prior to the reduction of the epistemic you see into a contentless interactive particle. Furthermore, as we discuss more fully below, we found the need to create a separate class of interaction, *direct address,* that carried enough interactive weight to make the callback of the reader's attention seem explicitly marked (e.g., *let us, you can see that).*

Manuals and style-checkers devoted to the formal registers of written English frown upon a pervasive second person. The charge is that it can sound too much like unplanned speech. However, adopting characteristics of unplanned orality has become a widely used form of writing within the Internet culture. As Laura Gurak (2001, pp. 31-32.) noted in her book *Cyberliteracy,* "Our writing sounds ever more like speech, and lately, our speech has begun to sound clipped and sarcastic, like our e-writing."* Furthermore, the second person can involve generalized audience functions that can engage a more universal audience (Perelman & Olbrechts-Tyteca, 1969). For example, when blended with private thinking verbs, the second person (e.g., *you'd think)* can create the effect of what Adam Gopnik (cited in Hale, 1999 p. 42) called the "complicitous second person." In this form, the writer addresses a generalized other used like a Greek chorus to affirm the writer's judgments as an echo of a larger community.

594. The bill was so poorly conceived, you'd think you lived in a banana republic.

---

* Our catalog contains a string class called Oral Interactivity, which sought to capture what seemed to be simulations of speech on text. However, Internet writing seems to be blurring basic (most second-person textual) interactivity and oral interactivity to the point that the overlap has become as significant as the differences.

Class 2: Questions Besides the second person, another hallmark of interactivity is the interrogative, marked principally by the question mark *"?"* (Nunberg, 1990). In our catalog, questions are coded by a sentence initial word that begins with a question wh-word *(who, what, were, how, why)* or a *do* or *does*. It also involves the question mark punctuation.

> 595. Does your meeting start now?
> 596. What is your name?
> 597. Really?

Class 3: FAQs FAQ (Frequently Asked Question) strings are scripted answers to frequently-raised queries. These strings are used to anticipate and provide stock answers to a user community's actual questions. FAQs are linguistically distinctive because of their frequent marking for the first person and the generic modal *(do, can, should)* in continuous succession: *How do I? What happens if I try? How can I...?* These strings are frequent in instructional brochures, manuals, help systems, and Websites that require users to perform complex tasks. With or without the first person, FAQs typically involve verbs dealing with general matters of access *(find, get)* and mild distress *(have trouble)*.

> 598. Where do I get help?
> 599. How can I get a discount?
> 600. What if I have trouble with the interface?

Class 4: Direct Address Speakers and writers use direct address when they wish overtly to call back the audience to attention. Like basic interactivity, direct address often uses the second person as a marker word. Yet direct address in addition frames the second person in present active speech acts and imperatives. The present active verb (compare the verb *ask* in the following examples) helps speakers and writers seize and hold the audience's attention:

> 601. They asked you once about sailing I recall.
>   *(asked; past verb; interactivity within retrospection; slight overlap with direct address but weak; no bid on the reader's attention)*
> 602. Remember when they asked you about sailing.
>   *(asked; past verb; interactivity within retrospection; greater overlap with direct address; stronger bid on the reader's attention.)*
> 603. Remember to ask about sailing
>   *(to ask; infinitive; interactivity with present active imperative; higher overlap with direct address; stronger bid yet on the reader's attention)*
> 604. I ask you about sailing.
>   *(ask; present active; interactivity within present active speech act; highest overlap with direct address; strongest bid yet on the reader's attention)*

Direct address strings can overlap with strings that insist on action *(you must, you had better)* because a speaker or writer's insistence often involves the attention and compliance of another mind. Some examples of direct address/ insistence on action blends are the following, *You should do it, You need to go, You need to be, You must vote for Smith, I plead to you, I pledge, mark my words.*

Direct address in our catalog focuses exclusively on the speaker and audience's mutual interactivity in the linear stream of language. Insist on action, by contrast, focuses on the speaker's state of mind, to pressure the audience toward action, and the audiences' involvement with that state of mind. Consider how direct address can come unadorned with insistence.

605. This is something I think you'd like to hear.
(direct address, low insistence)

Now compare the gradient shadings in the following strings as we introduce increasing strengths of insistence into a direct address:

606. It may be time to vote for Smith.
(direct address with little insistence.)
607. You should consider voting for Smith.
(direct address with more insistence)
608. You have to vote for Smith.
(direct address with even more insistence)
609. You just must vote for Smith.
(direct address with most insistence yet)

We typically think of interactivity as a necessary feature of insistence as well as direct address. It is not a necessary feature of insistence, which is why we did not include it in the dimension of interactives. Example 610 illustrates how a writer can make insistent gestures without addressing any reader in particular.

610. It is well known that corpulent Americans need to exercise more
(insistence + common authority, from it is well known)

Furthermore, in string 611, John has an insistent thought about what Martha needed to do, although he may have never addressed Martha about it.

611. Martha needs to eat her peas.
(norm creating an insist on action string without addressing the target of the insistence)

When we previously discussed inclusiveness, we explored the gap between making gestures of inclusiveness and achieving actual empathy with the audience. There, we were describing the empathy of shared thought. There is also the lighterweight empathy of shared attention, an empathy achieved from taking into account the audience's needs when navigating the linear stream of language, which includes regularly calling the reader back to attention. Direct address invariably accommodates the empathy of shared attention. Insistence need not accommodate such empathy at all. Although neither of the following sentences signals the joint empathy of perspectives between speaker and hearer, the first at least signals the weak empathy of the direct-address and inclusive *let* while the second, based upon a non-inclusive and insistent *got to,* signals no empathy at all.

612. Let us work this out together!
(inclusiveness and intensity with a bid for empathy; noninsistent; please share my perspective — of cooperation — on this)
613. You've got to work this out yourself!
(It's my strong opinion that you are on your own; noninclusive and insistence on action with no bid for empathy)

The insistent *got to* overlaps with future projection *(John has got to sell his stock)* [page 153] and also with the child's pleading *got to,* which, with a third person subject, stresses a benefit granted to some but unjustly denied the speaker:

614. Jimmy got to go roller-blading.
(how come I can't?)

Speakers and writers who blend insistence and inclusiveness can seemingly reproduce some of the empathic bidding of English *let us* with a plaintive *we just gotta:*

615. We've just gotta work this out together!
(inclusiveness with no bid for empathy; neither of us has a current position that is worth keeping; we must both change into people who value cooperation).

A closer look at this maneuver reveals that it relies less on empathy than on the mutuality of nonempathy. Example 615 embraces a common perspective only by disregarding both. If insistent speakers are able to strike empathy with their audiences, it is because they are able to convince audiences that all parties need a good kick in the pants!

Direct address strings can also employ the noninclusive *let,* as in the mathematician's summons to the reader to start paying attention to the assumptions beginning a proof:

616. Let x equal...*

---

* We thank an anonymous reviewer for suggesting this example.

Direct address relies heavily on other nonmath related, and non-inclusive *let* constructions, such as *let me, let the,* and *let it be:*

617. Let us consider what to do
     (direct address, inclusive)
618. Let me consider what to do
     (direct address, noninclusive)
619. Let the party go on
     (direct address, noninclusive).
620. Let the record show.
     (direct address, noninclusive)
621. Let it be recorded
     (direct address, noninclusive)

Class 5: Cue [the Audience's] Curiosity   Cue curiosity strings assume a speaker and audience engaged in a dialectical enterprise where both are primed to focus on a common problem and to step together into, or further into, a shared problem space. Such strings can rely on a base of strings blending questions and sequence *(what then?)* with the first-person inclusive *we. What is our next step? What can we do at this point? What are our options?* These strings can also begin with a presubject *were,* indicating a summons to the audience to enter a joint engagement of contingent thought. Compare the different ways strings of common curiosity interact with contingency and thinking back.

622. We were to have been there at two yesterday.
     (thinking back on a earlier plan, now revised)
623. Were we to have thought about it that way, we would have failed.
     (using contingency + think back to direct the curiosity of the audience)

Cue curiosity strings typically co-occur with thinking verbs, such as *know, think, and decide* (e.g., *What do we know at this point? What are we to think and decide?).*

Interaction With the Potential to Weaken Social Ties

The interaction classes we have thus far considered play no visible role in establishing or strengthening social ties. When interactive strings do play this prosocial role, as they do in promises, reassurance, reinforcements, and acknowledgments, we cataloged the strings under the dimension of shared social ties. We found it useful, furthermore, to make the interaction dimension the home for strings whose social implications for interaction are not prosocial but antisocial, using interaction to weaken social ties. These are strings we recognize in confrontations, threats, and (when sent over electronic media) flames. Although these antisocial functions are different, as we explain next,

147

the strings that prime them are less so. Consequently, our catalog puts all three functions within one string class.

Class 6: Confrontations, Threats, and Flames   We just saw that positive assurances can prime social ties with audiences and specifically instill confidence, especially in instructional tasks when the audience may be anxious and less confident about getting through complex tasks. We also noted that assurance is not necessarily positive. It is now time to consider assurances that are not positive and used not to enforce social ties but to disrupt them.

These negative forms of assurance still supply a confidence about the future, but a confidence that is less happy and that binds confidence more to negative than to positive affect or standards.

624. You can count on your competitors being stronger this year.
(reassurance of bad news; assurance + negative affect; associated with straight-shooting, even if distasteful, confirmation)

Threats, in contrast to promising, arise when an action assured, overt or implied, is detrimental. As we saw, there is an advantage for promises to be explicit and verbatim, lest the intentions of the promise-maker be missed or misunderstood. There is a reverse advantage for threats to remain off the record and vague in terms of their consequences. The reasons for this are cultural and may have to do with the widespread social beliefs in the power of personal rehabilitation. Many of us threaten others to change their behavior with no firm intention to exact a penalty down the road and with no firm image of the penalty we would like to exact if the behavior does not change. The American making promises, beholden to the future, does not want to change it. The American making threats, not at all beholden to future punishment, does:

625. I promise you we will root out al Queda.
(promise: the future will happen, I guarantee it)
626. I'll ground you if you don't get a good report card this semester.
(threat: please guarantee me the future does not happen)

The significance of this cultural fact to English strings we studied is that writers have a much wider range when depicting threats in contrast to promises. Consider the following:

627. Students who misuse e-mail will lose their account.
(states the penalty; from a policy manual to e-mail users)
628. From now on, you need to get your homework in on time.
(opens like a promise... but recognized as a warning or threat because no positive follow through; e-mail from teacher to student)

629. You need to think further about what you are saying!
(confrontational e-mail between friends)

These strings indicate the writer's confrontational attitude, the audience's non-compliance to norms, and a challenge to the audience to change. Yet, these strings vary widely in the specification of punishment. Statement 627 goes on to specify what will befall the audience (losing one's e-mail account) for not changing behavior. However, the remaining statements omit the bad consequences befalling the person failing to comply. In American English, audiences feel the weight of a promise being made only when they understand, with legal clarity, the positive consequences assured by it. Yet, for American English, audiences feel a threat even when the consequences for noncompliance remain nonspecific and even unstated. The isolated string *or else* (e.g., *you had better do it or else!*) as a closer for threats is a conventional foreshadow of a punishment that has yet to be specified and that the speaker may prefer never to have to specify.

Confrontations and threats share wide overlap in their strings, but there are divergences as well. Confrontation strings tend to overlap with direct address strings. One cannot be confronted without having the message pushed in one's face. Confrontation always implies the second person *(you)* and often asserts it. Confronting requires (actual or virtual) spatial immediacy with the person confronted. Threats, by contrast, do not require direct address with the person threatened. In the following string, John has been threatened and is none the wiser about it.

630. I'm going to get even with John *(addressed to Mary)*.

Unlike threats, moreover, confrontations need not negatively implicate the other's future. Whereas threats involve future projection or thinking ahead, confrontations do not require projecting action into the future. Their main implication and focus can be the present (What are you doing here?), simply to detain and discomfort the one confronted.

Confrontational actions are a workhorse in the Internet phenomenon known as flaming. In 2000, QUALCOMM Incorporated of San Diego proposed incorporating a Flames Detector in their popular e-mail program, Eudora™. Knowing about our research cataloging English priming strings, the Eudora group asked us to study flaming behavior and to build a catalog of English strings indicating such behavior. We studied and classified over 1200 flaming e-mails on the Internet to create a catalog of 2.7 million strings signaling a flame (Kaufer, 2000).

We were not surprised about the large number of flaming strings that were standard confrontations, involving second-person interactivity, direct address, and negative affect.

631. You wonderful person!
(not a flame; no negative affect)

632. You rat!
    *(a flame; second person interactivity + negative affect +
    direct address)*
633. You dumb ass.
    (a flame)

What did surprise us, however, was the large number of confrontational flames that heighten the put-down by reversing the standard "sticks-and-stones" *you + negative affect* formula and expressing the negative affect before the second person:

634. I was shocked when you claimed to know something.
    (negative affect before you)
635. It is depressing to realize how badly you've screwed up.
    (compounded negative affects before you)

The effect of this reversal is to create and prolong a cloud of bad feeling before letting it blow onto the addressee. Using this reversal, the flamer has more time to singe the addressee. Even more surprising was the large number of flames that do not rely on confrontation or even commanding the attention of another addressed. Many flames get their scorch from confident and intense expression of negative affect (especially hate and prejudice) without the slightest trace of uncertainty. In a culture that upholds pluralism as a norm, it is chilling to read absolutist and confident hatred spewed against groups.

Although there is no specialized confrontational just in English, the *are + you + just going* to formulation comes close:

636. Are you just going to sit there?

In this usage *of just,* interactivity and the second person (you) combine to form a sense *of just* meaning *only.* This is not, however, the end of the story. The *just + going* anticipates, and often states, downstream a verb of "underachievement" and "nonaction" (e.g., *sit there),* indicting the confronted audience's nonaction and linking it to a disappointed expectation.

In the declarative form, an intensifying and insistent *just* combines with the second person you to create *you + just.* The *you + just* string has the force of laying the responsibility of an unhappy situation at the foot of the addressee. Because of the resonant insistence effect, the *you + just* formula tends to put the audience on full-threat alert. Contrast the strings here with and without *just.*

637. You don't get it!
    (fault may be implied but not emphatically so)
638. You just don't get it!
    (it's emphatically your fault; confronting with you + just/insistence)

Interaction to Elicit Information: Queries

Queries use interaction to elicit fixed or open-ended content from an addressee. Our catalog separates queries into two string classes: requests, when the elicitation is fixed and specific; and open queries, when the elicitation is neither fixed nor specific. We examine these classes more fully next.

Class 7: Requests   Requests seek targeted answers from the audience about a proposed action in the future, such as yes or no or a willingness to comply. This string class combines thinking ahead and interactivity under the contextual assumption that the audience will perform some action in the future if compliance is achieved. One recurring characteristic for request strings is the use of *please* or some other politeness marker to signal that compliance is voluntary and personally acknowledged. Requests are frequent in memos and workplace genres, where they sometimes overlap with task assignments:

639. Will you please give me a ring?
640. Won't you give me a ring?
641. Please give me a ring.
    (overlaps with action item; but with politeness marker)
642. Please fill out the form.
    (overlaps with action item; but with politeness marker)
643. Would it be possible for you to give me a ring?

The word *just* contributes to request strings by mitigating the force of the request (CCD, sense 11). We saw an indirect form of this mitigation at work in expressions of uncertainty when the writer lightens the pressure on the reader by seeming tentative (e.g., *I just want to say*). With request actions, the mitigating effect of the adverbial is more direct and the *just* telegraphs that the request is registered as small and modest rather than large and intrusive. Compare the following pairs of strings with and without *just.*

644. Can you move this out of the way?
    (request)
645. Can you just move this out of the way?
    (moving it is no big deal)
646. I'd like to request a glass of milk.
    (request)
647. I'd just like to request a glass of milk.
    (it's a small request)

Class 8: Open Queries   Open queries seek information that is more open-ended than requests. They solicit information with a stronger assumption of social distance between the communicator and audience, and with a stronger or weaker assumption of compliance depending on the institutional context. In formal surveys, open queries add formality and social distance to interactivity as a way of soliciting specific information from strangers who need to be counted. Open queries capture the syntax and tone of professional interrogation, the kind of language behind questionnaires and in-depth interviews sanctioned by institutional and impersonal authorities.

Distinctive of the formal survey are imperative verbs that define enough professional distance to treat the audience as an official news source *(provide; specify)*. They also often contain the politeness markers of requests *(please provide, please specify)*. Open queries, moreover, often solicit the audience for quantified answers *(how often, how long, how many, how satisfied)* measurable on numerical scales. They also rely on a question syntax that is formal and elaborated, *What do you think about...? What is your response to? How did you do this? How many times did you watch x last year? What is your exact mailing address? How long have you lived in your house? How satisfied are you with your current bank? How many times a week do you exercise? Overall, how do you feel about the president? With what frequency do you brush your teeth each day?*

Dimension 11: Notifying

Notifying, or notifications, name a dimension of strings, consisting of various classes, that help audiences localize on the information in the linear stream of highest contrast and so the information most likely to deserve the weight of their attention. In addition, notification strings can mark early signals in the linear stream that build the audience's anticipation for input to come that carries this special contrastive status. In short, notification strings mark newsworthy elements in the linear stream or mark placeholders that signal to audiences these elements are soon to appear.

Our catalog contains four general groupings of notifications, each broken into classes. First, *event-based* notifications reference the various string classes that report weighted (often the main predicate and in multi-word phrases) verbal events. Second, *concept-based* notifications refer to string classes that provide cues in the linear stream about specifications, definitions, and the sequencing of information. Third, *time-based* notifications describe string classes providing time, date, setting, and comparative information about setting. This information helps audiences sort out when the events reported happened and the significance of their happening. Finally, there are *anticipatory notifications,* which characterize strings that build early warning anticipations for an upcoming unit of information. Such strings summon the reader to be on alert for information elements soon to come that are supposedly worth waiting for.

We shall examine these four grouping of notifications and the string classes that constitute each. As a preliminary to this examination, let us note that, overall, the dimension of notifying seems most responsible for the conduit metaphor of language. That is to say, notification strings seem most responsible for bringing the impression that language artifacts are transparent containers of information. This much- and justifiably-criticized container metaphor, moreover, pervades the way audiences in the west now dominantly think and talk about oral and written language (Reddy, 1979).

The container metaphor of language has a history (Day, 2001). Developments after World War II, particularly the rise of information theory as a branch of mathematics, strengthened the idea that language contains "bits" whose work is to reduce the receiver's uncertainty about the world. For most recorded history of writing, the literate world knew texts to be the products of meaning and culture and not infrequently wisdom and knowledge. Recent developments in information theory came to identify the knowledge in digital speech and texts as discrete bits of (searchable) information. Thinking about texts as tubes of information, extractable and searchable word by word, is now so pervasive in western thinking and speech that we often forget that the container metaphor is only that, metaphor. Yet if texts sometimes feel to us like containers, it is because writers know that certain language choices, specifically notification strings, can make a linear message seem like a wailing teapot boiling over with "content."

As a final preliminary remark, let us also mention that strings associated with notification are sometimes imprecisely associated with information that is epistemically new to audiences, meaning that the notification tells audiences what they do not yet know and have come to a speech or a text to learn. This is an overstatement of the facts. The most one can say confidently about notification strings is that speakers and writers use them to signal what is most contrastive relative to other information in the linear stream and thus, by implication, what is presented as most deserving of the audience's attention.

Let us now turn to the four groupings of notification strings in more detail.

Event-based notification covers strings of English used most stereotypically to create headlines and leads of front-page stories and newscasts. They are represented by one dominant string class, consisting of main predicate verbs and verbal phrases used to report.

Class 1: Reportative Verb Phrases   The typical syntax consists of the main predicate verb or extended verb phrase. The verbs in question are not simple narrative past verbs (to be discussed later) but rather verbs and verbal phrases that function reportatively, often but not necessarily in the present tense. Consider the reportative verbs in the following strings headed by the present verbs *bites* and *evacuate.*

648. Dog bites the mail carrier.
649. Thousands evacuate in volcano eruption.

Besides its contrast with narrative past verbs, reportative verbs indicate single occurrences and in this respect contrast with verbal expressions indicating habitual or recurrent action. Parsons (1990) described the contrast as follows:

> In general, verbs can be interpreted in two or more different ways: the so-called "reportative" use, and the "habitual" or "iterative" use. These different uses appear in all tenses. 'Mary drank wine with her lunch' can be construed as reporting a specific incident that took place in the past; this is the "reportative" reading. "But it can also be construed as telling us what she habitually did during her years in the corporate world. In the past tense, a simple unmodified sentence taken out of context tends to be taken in its reportative sense, but in the present tense that same construction may almost force the habitual reading. (p. 33)

Parsons notes that single-word present-tense verbs with no further context are more likely construed as conveying a habitual more than a reportative sense. His example is:

650. Mary drinks wine with her lunch.
   (She does it everyday-habitual sense; more likely inference with no further context specified)
   (Mary is doing it as I speak—reportative sense; less likely inference with no further context specified)

Yet, when single verbs head extended verb phrases, the additional context added often serves to pin down a specific event report. Consider how a reportative inference comes to trump a habitual inference when we extend the single-word verb *drink* to a specific event reported by the verbal extension *drink in:*

651. Mary drinks in every bit of sun and sand on her last days of vacation.
   (report of what Mary is doing on her current Florida vacation—likely interpretation)
   (an habitual property of Mary when she vacations—slightly less likely, especially if Mary is known to take vacations that don't include sun and sand)

Weighting a verb with a longer continuation gives advantage to its serving a reportative function. This is true even when we move from present to past tense, the tense of narrative. Indeed, perfectly functioning past narrative verbs are commonly recruited to serve reportative functions when they head extended phrases. Let us look at an example of this recruitment in action. Watch how the narrative verb *entertained* can be recruited for reportative functions when the verb forms the head of a more complex event.

652. Sue entertained at her house at 6.
   (entertained = past narrative)

653. Sue entertained the prospect that she would never make it.
(entertained the prospect that = reportative verbal phrase)

English is rife with simple verbs that can be recruited into heading complex event structures — *carry, do, draw, drop, drag, fall, feel, get, give, go, have, jump, keep, leave, let, look, make, play, pop, put, raise, run, shake, stand, start, take, tell.* Note here the common verbs *have, give,* and *raise* become specific event reports when lengthened:

654. Let's have a try at...
(reportative verb phrase = have a try)
655. He gave a sigh of relief about...
(reportative verb phrase = gave a sigh of relief)
656. She raised a fuss about...
(reportative verb phrase = raised a fuss)

Each of these verbs and dozens like them take thousands of phrasal continuations that feature noun phrases later in the sentence (Spears, 2000). Take the reportative verb phrases *get on* and *line up*. The head verbs can be continued in any number of ways for a variety of experiences primed:

657. Sam wants to get on a diet.
(wants to get on = future projection)
658. Jill got on with her presentation.
(get on = report of continuation after implied interruption)
659. Mitch got on with Bill.
(get on = positive affect)
660. Darla has gotten on to the next project.
(get on = shift in attention and time)
661. He lined up the appointments.
(lined up the = references a general event)
662. He lined up the barber chairs one after the other.
(lined up the barber chairs = event, motion/spatial interval)

These examples illustrate how such extended verb phrases function robustly as event reports. Because of their length (two words and often three to five), reportative verb phrases can also add anticipatory weight and headline emphasis to the words that follow them. Contrast the following pairs, the first a single verb, the second a reportative verb phrase extending the verb into a reported event.

663. Let's try bridge.
(less rhetorical weight on bridge)
664. Let's have a try at bridge.
(more rhetorical weight on bridge)

665. He sighed with relief about
(less rhetorical weight on relief)
666. He heaved a sigh of relief.
(more rhetorical weight on relief)
667. She fussed about going.
(less rhetorical weight on going)
668. She raised a fuss about going.
(more rhetorical weight on going)

Concept-based notifications reference strings that identify, modify, and organize concepts in the linear stream. The specific string classes involved here are specification, definition, and sequencing.

Class 2: Specifications   Specifications are a diverse array of strings signaling concept information worthy of audience attention. Although we placed all these strings in one class, they have some different characteristics and it is useful to discuss them according to these differences. One type of specification signals a descent in the ladder of abstraction from the general to the particular. Key discriminators for these specification strings are words like *specifically* and *particularly* and extended phrases such as *in terms of, with respect to, in the sense of, in that, concerning the, insofar as she can, inasmuch as he can, characterized by, in the case of, as is provided in the,* and so on.

A second type of specification string involves the specific and non-sensory and in this way contrasts with descriptive information that is specific and sensory. Compare the following strings:

669. The medicine was vanilla flavored.
(specific and sensory description; we know the medicine has taste and we know what the taste is)
670. The medicine was flavored.
(specific and nonsensory specification; we know the medicine has taste but we don't know what it is)

Such judgments put specification on a middle footing between generalization and sensory experience. Specification particularizes attributes without filling in the sensory values that make audiences full eyewitnesses to the particularity evoked. Specification thus adds concreteness that still leaves the audience out of sensory range.

These considerations helped distinguish specifications, a form of notification and relational string, from sensory properties, a form of description and external string, discussed later. We should note, however, that these considerations, which seemed to hold pretty well in principle, often spotlighted two interesting puzzles in practice. The first puzzle is the degree to which one gains true descriptive information from the absence of properties. Say you write about the zoo's only *stripeless tiger?* Have you specified the tiger for your reader, leaving the tiger unwitnessed in the audience's mind's eye? Or have you added descriptive information that helps your reader visualize it? To distinguish strings functioning as specifiers from strings functioning as sense properties, we often had to appeal to assumptions about cultural expectation to determine where to draw the line. A flavorless drink is a way of specifying a drink. Is it also a way of describing its taste? What about an odorless gas? Does that stimulate our sense of smell?

The second puzzle is the degree to which one can specify, and so add particularity, even in the context of still very abstract information. Take a word like *multi-cultural,* which seems on its face quite abstract. Yet, it can still specify quite effectively when used to distinguish a *multi-cultural curriculum* from a traditional curriculum. Specification, we came to recognize, is not the antithesis of abstraction but the antithesis of an abstraction *that is not serving a specifying function.* This, of course, begs the question of how and under what circumstances abstractions specify. We leave it to future research to address these puzzles.

There is a third and final type of specification string specialized to product marketing. In these contexts, the markers of specification join with capacity-performance verbs like *hold up to, have up to, carry, output, put out, haul, accelerate,* and *push* and minima and maxima terms *(a maximum of, a minimum of).* Each of these specifiers provides parameters for why a buyer should be drawn to a product:

671. The computer can have up to four gigs of memory.
672. The hard drive should have up to 120 gigabytes.
673. The truck should have a minimum carry load of 2 tons.
674. The room can seat 250 people.
675. The scooter can accelerate up to 17 miles per hour.

Specification strings involving product performance often overlap with innovation strings, particularly when the specification featured coincides with a long-awaited goal of a new technology:

676. Finally, a computer that ordinary people can use!
     (specification, update, innovation)

Product and non-product types of specification strings can blend in the same word or string, such as happens with *sport, feature,* and *get a lot of mileage from.* These strings blend the features of human beings and products that make both seem attractive and worth coveting.

677. John sports/features a new suit from Armani.
678. The 2003 Honda sports/features a revamped engine.
679. John has given the office a lot of mileage.
680. The 2003 Honda gives a lot of mileage.

Class 3: Definitions   Definitions in our catalog constitute signals in the linear stream that an embedded concept is being elaborated with a definition. The members of this narrowly circumscribed string class are variations on the words *define, means,* and the noun *definition.* Definitions in this very strict sense are across the language far rarer than specifications. Examples of definitions in our catalog are:

681. Wraith is defined to be a ghostly apparition.
682. I define democracy as the freedom to vote.
683. Let us start with a definition of failure as follows:
684. Failure means that the business folded.

Class 4: Sequence   Sequence strings provide clues that the concepts in the linear stream are ordered sequentially. Strings from this class rely on marker words like *then, next, after, following that, further into, afterwards,* and numerical rank terms like *first, second, third,* and *fourth.* Whereas textual narratives follow a sequence, many narratives leave sequential terms implicit or rely on them irregularly. In the case of simple storytelling, the reader's following the plot does not require understanding, with precision, the internal scheduling of plot elements. The systematic and overt use of sequential terms is most evident in the writer's effort to capture processes with enumerable steps, in the form of procedures, regulations, or instructions.

685. First, cross your laces. Then loop one. Next, pull the second lace across the loop.

In the case of functional documents, the reader, as user, is expected to build a precise mental model of what happens when.

In a narrative, sequence words often indicate shifts in time or space:

686. The next time he did it, she left him.
    (next time = shift in time)
687. He kicked the next box that came down the assembly line.
    (next box = shift in space)

As these examples suggest, we coded isolated words like *next* as sequencers, with this categorization overridden if the sequence was part of a longer string specifying temporal *(next time)* or spatial *(next box)* transitions (see shifts in time and space in the next chapter).

When we discussed retrospective think-back strings under the internal perspective cluster, we broke down the recipe of the storyteller's *just then* into a sprinkle of a displaced past *then* and a dollop of immediacy *just.* Although *just then* and *and then* can both signify narrative sequence, *just then* exerts more force to keep the reader narratively involved. *And then* is an all-purpose sequencer with a range far beyond storytelling. *And then* is frequent in instructional sequences, sequences of nondramatized natural description, and logical inferences.

688. First you boil some water and then take two eggs.
(instructional sequence)
689. The tornado hits the ground and then blows out all the windows.
(nondramatized natural sequence)
690. We can thus conclude P, and then it further follows
(logical sequence)

Reported events have a beginning, middle, and end in time and place. Bull markets, marriages, and wars come and go even as they persist for a while. Language users perceive and talk about events and their histories and trajectories. These perceptions and talk, when reported, also have a time and place, a setting, associated with them. Furthermore, they carry a temporal significance (or lack thereof) in light of their placement with respect to the other events reported. This temporal significance to other events is keyed by words such as *dated, timely, latebreaking,* or *unprecedented.*

Class 5: Time and Date   Every event has a discrete or continuous (or both) time and date associated with it. Compare the following:

691. The circus starts Monday at 3 p.m.
(time/date = Monday at 3 p.m. presumed timely for the audience to know when lest we arrive too early or late)
692. During the circus, the elephants marched single file.
(time interval, presumed not timely for the audience to know when)
693. Years ago, I went to the circus every year.
(retrospective time shift, presumed not timely for the audience to known when)

In an invitation or announcement, the time and date of the announced events *(on Tuesday, April 3 at 3 p.m.)* are often combined with the reasons the event holds significance *(on the occasion of her 80th birthday...).* In a lunch negotiation, the time and date is a proposal rather than an event, where schedules overlap *(Are you free at...?).* The invitation blends event reporting and future projection.

Class 6: Updates   Updates signal to audiences what is new by reporting incoming information about an event that is known to be recently breaking. Updates command the audience's linear attention because of their presumed timeliness. They can be in response to an audience's interactive queries or simply borne from the presumption that audiences, like all humans, yearn to stay informed and up-to-date.

Updates draw on immediacy and significance for their priming effects. Immediacy as we saw means that what is happening is happening now. Significance means that what is happening now may remain important over the long haul. Both elements are necessary for an update. Consider two spurious effects at updating the contemporary American audience:

694. I am writing now.
(immediacy without significance; what's the point of writing this?)
695. Kennedy was assassinated in 1963.
(significance without immediacy; why tell me now?)

English update strings typically express a prior state as background and then a recently breaking change of state as foreground. To capture the prior state, update strings recruit the perfect progressive active *(has, have)* with adverbial modifiers such as *so far,* and combinations of both, *have so far, has so far, is so far.*

696. As you may know, I have so far been working on the Brown account.
(prior state priming the audience for the update)

A common string to indicate a prior state with no update is the noun phrase *the last* (elliptical for last news, last information) and a past verb of knowing such as *heard* or *knew.*

697. The last I knew...
(I can only report old news)
698. The last I heard...
(I can only report old news)

To indicate a recent change of state, update strings involve achievement verbs like *progress on* and *update* and strings indicating temporal immediacy and recency, such as *current, new, now*, and *latest.* When speakers or writers do not think they have an update for an audience, they can use *last* to indicate they are being recent with the audience without being new. *Last* provides a weak updating function, weaker than *latest.*

699. The last news coming out of Afghanistan was that a bombing attack had commenced
(= sense that audience may already share this, as news is stale; weak sense of update)
700. The latest news coming out of Afghanistan was that a bombing attack had commenced.
(= sense that audience hasn't heard this; news is fresh; stronger sense of update)

The following strings are all updates:

701. Let me tell you progress on Brown.
702. I want to update you on Brown.
703. I have the current information about Brown.
704. My next steps on Brown will be
705. I've found new ways to handle this account
706. My work on Brown is now complete.

Speakers and writers can efficiently combine the prior state and the focus of the update by mixing the present progressive with achievement verbs:

707. We have *(now)* made significant progress on the system.
708. The system has *(now)* been implemented.

English *still,* which we first saw when describing the expression of subjective time, updates an audience when the only news, contrary to expectation, is that there is no news. In other terms, *still* is felicitous only under the assumption that a change, expected to happen, has yet to. To see more clearly into this observation, consider the awkwardness of the following sentence.

709. The living room carpet still is green.
   (not a felicitous statement if the audience doesn't consider the color of the carpet significant and hasn't been expecting it to change)

In American institutions, the changes announced in an update often have official inaugurations or starting dates. American English marks the official starting date with the word *effective,* used adjectivally.

710. I am announcing my resignation, effective immediately.

English conventionally signals the act of updating through the communication verb *announced.* When speakers or writers announce something, they imply it carries the combination of significance and immediacy required for an update string. Compare the news weightiness implied by the communicative verb *announce* over the generic say.

711. John announced he was leaving the house.
   (implies that John's exiting the house is news, requiring an update; compatible with John's being a homebody or making a permanent move)
712. John said he was leaving the house.
   (implies a ritualistic occurrence; update effect much weaker)

One must have title and position to announce things. Experienced jokesters know they can draw characters with a comically inflated sense of self-importance by having these characters "announce" trivialities:

713. Mary announced to the whole family she wanted corn flakes for breakfast.

The English word urgency blends the interactivity, immediacy, and significance of updates with a negative affect.

714. It's urgent I talk to you.
(immediate, significant, interactive)
715. We need to get her to the hospital. It's urgent.
(update, negative affect)

When we discussed the subjective feel of time's passing within the internal perspective, we observed that the adverbs *finally* and *still* can indicate relief or impatience respectively. These usages can blend either with positive or negative affects. Such adverbs also make important contributions to update strings:

716. We can finally announce that the stadium is finished.
(We were impatient too but it's been worth the wait—finally as a signal of relief from impatience)
717. I am announcing that the stadium will still take a year to complete.
(We are impatient for the construction to end—still as a signal of ongoing impatience)
718. We are happy to announce that the patient is still resting comfortably.
(Still as a form of relief that a process is ongoing)

Like *still* and *finally*, the adverb *already* is a subjective time adverb that indicates the personal relevance to the audience of an event's completion. However, the major effect of *already* is updating the audience. More specifically, *already* implies that the audience has tracked an event to its completion, that the event is now completed, and that the audience has yet to be informed of its completion. The speaker, gathering all of these connections at lightning speed, issues an *already* and the audience feels the update function. To see these facts more clearly, contrast the examples here:

719. Mark sold the business.
(=statement about what Mark did with no further assumptions)
720. Mark already sold the business.
(update/subjective time = you were waiting to hear, dear audience, if and when Mark would take this action. He took it and no one has told you. I just did. = Information sharing that has updated the audience.)

Example 719 is a declarative stating that Mark sold the business. Example 720 adds additional premises to the communication context, namely that the sale of the business is something the audience was waiting to hear about, that the sale has now happened, and that the audience has yet to be told. The declarative changes the audience's state from not being told to being told.

As immediacy is a residual element of an update string and as the adverbial *just* can contribute immediacy to a string, one can make a systematic study of the contribution of *just* to update strings. Compare the following updates with *just:*

721. We were just married.
(just adds the immediacy to make this an update string)
722. It has just come to my attention that you graduated.
(just adds heightened immediacy to an already intact update string)
723. It just happened and I can't comment further.
(just adds heightened immediacy and, in this case, becomes part of the update message— "it's too soon to comment.")

Class 7: Innovations Innovations share with updates the prominence of timeliness and the presumption of immediacy with marker words such as, *newly, new, novel, recently,* and *lately.* Innovations further add to immediacy a sense of cognitive and precedent-breaking historical significance, indicated by another grouping of marker words, namely *research, discovery, innovation, creativity, cutting edge, and breakthrough:*

724. recent innovations
(immediacy + cognitive significance)
725. newly discovered
(immediacy + cognitive significance)
726. newly invented
(immediacy + cognitive significance)
727. recently discovered
(immediacy + cognitive significance)
728. recently invented
(immediacy + cognitive significance)
729. breaking new ground
(immediacy + cognitive significance)

Strings conveying scientific and technical innovation are frequently imported into the culture of advertising. Some innovation stings frequently enough hyped have become recognized buzzwords: *design, technology, cutting edge, at the forefront, push the envelope, enabling technology, breakthrough technology, a smart way to, at the forefront of, breaking new ground in, cutting edge, first of its kind, major advance in.*

The mix of innovation buzzwords and advertising can yield actions that may make audiences want to reflect:

730. Think out of the box. (cognitive deviation, being a maverick)
(Was I ever thinking in a box? Does freedom from constraint guarantee creativity?)

Innovation language is in high currency in workplaces that organize themselves around new product development. Corporations invested in yearly and seasonal new product cycles have sought to make major innovation a routine selling point. As a result, innovation strings line the annual reports, official press releases, and marketing documents of major firms.

Whereas *new* is a common marker for an innovation-based string, it also can carry a negative and sobering potential when modifying terms that are often used to expose the gimmickry of novelty—namely the terms *truth* or *reality*. *New* under the influence of these nouns assumes a nostalgic (and negative) view toward change, where a change is presumed to be superficial change for the worse:

731. The new reality/truth is that we work harder for the same pay.

As part of our study of innovation-based strings, we have analyzed corporate documents for the international multiconglomerate ABB, the company that coined the phrase "think globally, act locally." The company owns hundreds of businesses on many continents, each business with its own research and development units. Every year, the company puts out an annual report, detailing for actual and potential investors the latest in ABB research. To write the report, ABB asks the chief engineers from each local company to write a report of its latest innovations and submit the report to ABB's central headquarters in Zurich. A writing team in Zurich then takes each submission and revises it. This revision requires several iterations and is expensive and time consuming. ABB wanted to understand, systematically, what their writers do with the engineers' reports so that the engineers can submit reports that are closer to final copy. The ABB consulted with us to study the differences between what the engineers originally wrote and the revisions the corporate writers made to these originals.

What we found surprised us. We had first thought that the engineers were probably leaving out innovation actions in their writing or were burying innovation beneath impenetrable jargon. This was not the case. The engineers were as good as the corporate writers were in talking up innovation for a layperson's understanding. What they had not done, which the corporate revisers saw to do, was blend innovation with positive standards that shareholders would find essential: Compare the following:

732. Enabling technology that fully automates production is now used.
(innovation without including the positive standards that shareholders understand and are drawn to — what the engineers tend to write before it gets to the corporate writers)

733. Enabling technology that doubles profits and reduces costs by automated production is now used.
(innovation + the positive standards that shareholders understand and are drawn to — what the text looks like after the corporate writers rewrite the engineer's first copy)

Although stockholders care about technological breakthroughs, their main concern is how the technology links with the positive standards of Wall Street culture, not just the rave and applause of nerd cultures.

Class 8: Anticipatory Notification: Making the Reader Wait We now turn our attention to a class of notifiers that notify nothing by themselves except that a notification of weight is coming down the pike. These anticipatory notifications create in audiences an anticipation of what is to come.* The power of these strings to notify is thus restricted to making the audience realize they are waiting and to imply the wait is worth it.

Anticipatory notifications rely on grammatical-syntactical processes in order to make the audience priming work as it does. To see why and how, we need a brief digression into linguistic theory. In their pioneering treatment of grammaticalization, Hopper and Traugot (1993) rejected the idea of grammar as a monolith of structure holding up sentences as bones hold up a skeleton. They rather described grammar as a process that depends on the contingent practices of writers and speakers. Depending on these practices, the (syntactic) ties between words can tighten or loosen. For example, the English verb *go* indicates motion through a space. Through grammaticalization, the verb attaches to the preposition to in order to indicate a near future tense, inhibiting the tie to motion.

734. John is going home.
(go as motion verb)

735. John is going to stay in bed day.**
(go to as grammaticalized near future; no motion)

To explain anticipatory buildups, we rely on a similar image of grammar's interaction with a speaker or writer's practice. Consider the difference between strings with and without anticipatory buildups:

---

* Linguists sometimes call this creating an imminent focus in the stream of text. See Hopper, 2002.

** This example is due to Johnstone 2001, p. 240

736. He needs to do nothing.
    (no anticipatory build-up to the word "nothing")
737. What he absolutely needs to do is nothing.
    (anticipatory build up to the word "nothing")

Strings that prime audiences to wait rely on various grammaticalized syntaxes of delay that make delaying the audience strategic. Prescriptive grammarians and stylists in the plain language movement have come to regret the syntax of delay as a wordy and bloated style (see Lanham, 1999; Williams, 2000). Often it is.

We should not be willing, however, to discard a stylistic option uncritically if it can serve strategic functions. Consider the following contrasts:

738. They entered into an agreement regarding disarmament.
    (NP [agreement] + PP [regarding] + NP [disarmament]; wordy in prescriptive grammar)
739. They agreed to disarm.
    (not wordy; NP+ PP + NP reduced to finite verb + infinitive)
740. The war over the preservation of civilization is imminent.
    (NP[war] + PP[over] NP [the preservation]; wordy in prescriptive grammar)
741. War is imminent.
    (not wordy; NP + PP + NP reduced to predicate adjective)

Examples such as 738 and 740 are often cited as wordier, and so dispensable, alternatives to examples 739 and 741. However, when the speaker or writer seeks to prime the feel of a weighty topic, these extended prepositional phrase strings can contribute desirable metrical weight to the words they precede. Such weight further signals the potential of the upcoming words to function as an independent topic of discussion. For example, string 738 more than 739 signals that the disarmament agreement is a potential topic deserving of its own space of discussion. By cueing the topic potential of war in (740), the audience signals, better than 741, the tensions that explain the imminence of the situation.

What may seem like absolute "bad writing" from the vantage of prescriptive grammar may sometimes be very strategic. The syntax of delay, after all, works well when the writer has ideas truly worth waiting for or has some cultural reason for creating a delay. A common prescription in American rejection letters is that they work more effectively when they delay the bad news (Locker, 1999). Schryer (2000), however, noted that whether delay is effective or not remains very much an empirical question that needs to be tested on actual audiences. We would say much the same thing for strings in English that embody a syntax of delay. To be sure, such a syntax reflects shabby ethical behavior toward the audience when the speaker or writer's sole reason for employing is exerting naked power over the audience. However, this is not the only reason for making audiences wait and some reasons may be less than shabby.

In our catalog, we created a separate class for the various classes of strings that seem, routinely, to prime the audience to wait. Because of the interplay of syntax and rhetorical function in the creation of these anticipatory delays, we found it convenient in our catalog to associate different anticipatory-notification strings with the various grammatical units that launch them. What we present next is not a full enumeration of the grammatical units that launch anticipatory notifications. However, it a large enough sample to indicate the rich variety of syntactic starting points that launch anticipatory notifications in English.

The passive is an effective launch point for anticipating the agent of an action.

742. Mary is schooled by her parents.
    (passive creating anticipation about who schooled Mary)
743. Mary is being schooled by her parents.
    (present passive progressive creating anticipation for Mary's current teachers)

A gerund recruiting English *being* launches an anticipation for the words downstream.

744. Being the best student in the class helped her confidence.
    (Being the best student opens up a gerund subject, asking the audience to wait in anticipation for the predicate)

Auxiliary verbs (e.g., *is, was, have)* derive their name (a.k.a. helping verbs) because they precede, or help out, more substantive content verbs. Their semantic leanness makes them good candidates at creating anticipation for a more substantive verb or nominalization downstream, sometimes on behalf of a mitigating effect.

745. Her poor scores stink!
    (a harsh and quick judgment)
746. Her poor scores are certainly something to note.
    (The auxiliary—are—used to make the reader wait for the information to come; making the reader wait can also make the writer wait for a more tempered response)

Consider the anticipatory delays caused by initial *there* and *it's:*

747. There is the need for…
    (there opening; emphasizes the need by delaying it)
748. It is the last inning of a terrific ballgame!
    (it opening; emphasizes the terrific-ness of it all by delaying it)

749. It's been good to see that you are actually finding the work interesting.
(it's opening; emphasizes your interest in the work by saving it for last)

Descriptive grammarians note that these sentence openings exist. Prescriptive grammarians sometimes regret these openings as limp prose that make the audience wait too long for substance. From the standpoint of the speaker and writer's priming art, our take on these openings is that they range from successful anticipation to failed efforts (causing audience frustration) depending on the skill of the artist and the context of the performance. If one wants to give the audience the feel of an important predicate, it requires an opening drum roll. The grammaticalized openings of *there* openings and *it* and *its* openings are scrabble moves beating the drum. However, part of the speaker and writer's priming art is the savvy to know whether a drumroll or more direct statement is called for. If a drumroll is not called for, knowing how to beat the drum provides the reader little consolation.

Sentence initial *as* can prime anticipatory interest for an upcoming main clause.

750. As a way of mending fences, he decided to apologize.
("as" instigating a comment on the reason for the apology; overlaps with cue reasons)
751. As far as she should could walk, she was able to walk.
("as" instigating a specification on walking to her full capability; overlaps with specification)
752. As far as he is concerned, let's invite him.
("as" instigating a specific person reference as topic)
753. As to how it will work in the future, I have no idea.
("as" instigates a specific aspect on which the main clause comments)

A well-known way English builds an extended noun phrase is through a sentence-initial *that*.

754. That Mary can come to the party was a pleasant surprise to me.
("that" introduces an extended noun phrase creating anticipation for the predicate, was a pleasant surprise. The audience is left to anticipate the writer's response to Mary's coming rather than reading it right off the bat.)

The prepositional phrase, start with *at, in, to,* and *for* are launch points of anticipation. *At* combines with *verb + ing* to form a gerund creating anticipation for an upcoming noun phrase.

755. He's remarkable at absorbing pain.
(affords anticipation of his power not satisfied until the audience gets to pain.)

756. She will do well at reaping the full investment of house.
(affords anticipation of what she will well at under the audience gets to house; even a longer wait than above)

Sentence initial *in* combines freely with reasoning, specification, and metadiscourse strings to build the audience's anticipation for the main clause.

757. In the best way she can, she will show she is a good student.
(specification that builds anticipation)
758. In being driven, she has no equal.
(specification that builds anticipation)
759. In keeping with his faith, he attends Church weekly.
(cue reason that builds anticipation)
760. In keeping with our tradition, we attend the mosque regularly.
(inclusiveness blended with precedent, building anticipation)
761. In what can only be an understatement, Spiderman is a blockbuster.
(metadiscourse that builds anticipation)

A sentence-initial *to* can build anticipation in the audience .

762. To come to the party underdressed embarrassed her.

For clauses often overlap with reasoning.

763. Alex got lost in the downtown area, for he had lost his map.
(The for clause signals cue reasons; this is common when it follows the main clause and is followed by a nominal subject and a finite verb.)

In sentence initial position, the *for-to* combination creates an anticipation for an extended noun phrase to come.

764. For it to have happened to Alex was unexpected!
765. For Alex to have lost his map was unexpected.
766. For him to have lost his map was unexpected.

When a sentence initial *to* clause is sufficiently drawn out, the audience can be left waiting to learn what action or event, if any, resulted from the purpose.

767. To find his way in the downtown area, Alex asked for help.
(The to clause signals project ahead or purpose; this is common when it precedes the main clause; when extended, it also affords an anticipation of what Alex did to find his way)

When used as a clausal instigator, questions words *(who, where, when, why what, how)* form the pseudo-cleft construction. They regularly build anticipation by delaying the meat of the sentence. Consider the following examples:

768. What they are expecting is a good contest.
(blends with inner thinking; builds anticipation for what to expect)
769. When it comes to suspects, he's at the top of the list.
(blends with specification; builds anticipation for the kind of suspect he is)
770. How she's done is something we are interested to find out.
(blends with uncertainty; builds anticipation for writer's interest in her)
771. Why it's happening is anyone's guess.
(blends with uncertainty; builds anticipation for writer's knowledge to answer why)

Dimension 12: Providing Linear Guidance

Like sidebars and call-outs within a visual layout, writers use strings from this dimension to drop navigational cues to help audiences anticipate what is to come and what has been covered. Expert writers, we have found elsewhere, make significantly more use of these navigational signals than do novices do, at least in some writing situations (Collins, Kaufer, & Neuwirth, 2002). Within our catalog, the dimension of linear guidance strings consists of five classes of strings: *metadiscourse, asides, follow-ups, cohesive pronouns, and external sources.*

Navigating the Audience

The following string classes help audiences navigate the linear stream of language.

Class 1: Metadiscourse In the literature (Crismore, 1989), metadiscourse constitutes a sprawling category that can include any marker in the stream of language that orients the audience. This broad view of metadiscourse cuts, a bit haphazardly in our view, across many of the various clusters, families, dimensions, and classes we have already examined. For example, Crismore's view of metadiscourse crosses what we have already characterized as the speaker or writer's epistemic and evaluative stances (under the thought cluster; see Hunston & Thompson, 2000) and the speaker or writer's efforts to share reasoning, social ties, and activities (under the relational cluster). In our catalog, we restrict metadiscourse to aids the speaker or writer provides to help the audience's linear navigation. More specifically, we restrict metadiscourse to strings that keep the audience "moving ahead" as it proceeds in real time through speech or text.

The speaker or writer can provide linear guidance to prepare the audience for an upcoming word, phrase, or clause, such as *more specifically, more technically, more generally, more concretely, in spite of, I want to underscore that* and so on.

Alternatively, he or she can provide a preview string that will aid the reader's movement over a much longer span (e.g., *the purpose of this paper is, my thesis is, you should skip to chapter 5 if you know chapter 4*).

When frequent enough, even metadiscourse with a small look-ahead window can influence the audience's perception of genre. Compare in the following how the small metadiscourse string *simply put* instructs the audience to approach the text less as a narrative than as information to process.

772. The construction schedule for the arena has been way behind. The city planners knew this would cost the taxpayers millions of dollars.
     (narrative, based on past tense and the implicit causality between the construction schedule and the inner thinking of the city planners)
773. The construction schedule for the arena has been way behind.
     Simply put, taxpayers will lose millions of dollars.
     (information-based; based on the metadiscourse string, simply put)

Example 772 tells a story to an unacknowledged audience about the events of an arena under construction and the nervousness of city planners because of delays. Carrying almost the identical semantic units, string 773 conveys information to an addressed audience about an impending threat to city taxpayers. The choice of tense and the metadiscourse string *simply put* are the only switches needed to transform information into stories and vice versa.

Let us put under the microscope some of the directional signals associated with different strings of metadiscourse:

774. as a matter of fact
     (you weren't expecting me to be more conclusive, but I can and will be)
775. briefly stated
     (there's a lot more to say than you will hear)
776. but inasmuch
     (I'm shifting direction and there's a reason coming why)
777. by contrast
778. (I'm shifting direction)
779. exactly what this means
     (What you've heard hasn't been pinned down. I'm getting to that)
780. generally speaking
     (there's a tendency here if not a formal generalization)
781. in a word
     (what you've heard isn't as succinct as what you will hear)

Although our identification of metadiscourse with linear navigation is narrower than the notions in much of the literature, we made constructive use of some of the literature for our catalog. For example, Crismore (1989), citing Lautamatti (1978), noted that writers use metadiscourse to direct the audiences' attention to ideas and to control their inferences about them (e.g., *this suggests, this suggests further that, which suggests that*). Vande Kopple (1985), also cited in Crismore (1989, p. 93), suggested that this type of metadiscourse provides a suggested reading procedure (e.g., *You might wish to read the last section first; if you already know X, you can skip this chapter*). More frequently, it assigns a parenthetical gloss to something already written so that the audience is primed to understand it in more familiar terms (e.g., *which means that, to put it more succinctly*).

Our catalog includes with metadiscourse the idea of issuing direct comments to audiences about what they are reading with phrases such as the following:

782. in this sense,
    (I'm continuing on with a smaller thread than I began with; overlaps with specification)
783. which means that…
    (I've told you what I've said…let me tell you what I mean by it)

The literature on metadiscourse accommodates the idea of providing audiences with previews for the language to come. Metadiscourse of this type is associated with the previewing functions of what Crismore calls "reportative metadiscourse." Examples of such previews are purpose statements *(My purpose is)* and discourse organizers *(firstly, secondly, in summary)*. The following are some canonical longer examples:

784. This paper discusses
785. in summary
786. To begin,
787. As I discuss below
788. What you will learn is…
789. firstly, secondly, thirdly *(overlaps with sequence)*

Like opening moves in a chess game, American elementary and middle school students learn this previewing metadiscourse as the opening moves of expository writing. They are the lexical formulae taught in school writing to help students appreciate their responsibilities to guide an audience. As opening moves, they are perhaps the most canonized strings in American writing curricula. Yet, the danger of canonization is that students can use them formalistically and mechanically, with little variation or artistic control. By middle school, teachers advise students to compose interesting introductions, lest they begin every paper with the stultifying, "My thesis/theme is…"

When they occur with regularity, metadiscourse that previews what is to come become indicators of texts used to inform. Writers cannot regularly forecast to audiences what is to come without bringing their own presence and plans (and, by implication, their information goals for audiences) to the conscious awareness of audiences. A high preponderance of preview strings, in other words, confers to a text the feel of overt exposition, the writer as visible informer. Compare:

790. I want to talk about the red dresser, which Uncle Charlie sold.
(*Previewing Metadiscourse ["I want to"], the writer is visible and the text feels informative as well as descriptive. The focus is on the writer's strategy for telling as much on the red dresser*)

Class 2: Asides   Speakers and writers employ asides, or digressions, to make the audience aware that the ideas of the moment are, decidedly, not the ideas of the whole speech or text. If the asides are functional—and they need not be—they are side notes that should sharpen the contours of the essential information. Speakers or writers digress either when they interrupt the main thread of ideas or when they signal a return to the main thread. Some signals that the speaker or writer is entering an aside are the following: *as an aside, let me digress, I digress by the way, incidentally, which, by the way.* Some signals that the writer is exiting an aside are the following: *in any case, but I digress, to return, anyway, anyways, in any event, at any rate.* When speakers and writers see a strategic purpose in making inessential points to reduce the chances of their audiences missing essential ones, they have good reason to digress.

English punctuation can create asides and, in so doing, can layer and differentiate the interactive effect on an audience. The English hyphen ("-"), parentheses ("( )") and some uses of the comma (",") allow the writer to segment the textual experience into central and side flows. The hyphen segments the flow into central and side information. Parentheses segment the audience into a central audience, one who may find the asides optional to read, and a more select audience who will find them essential reading. Consider the contrast:

791. I will talk about dogs—a collie in particular—as life long pets.
(*my specific reference to a collie is incidental to my overall topic of dogs as pets, but I mention it anyway*)
792. I will talk about collies as life-long pets.
(*not sure I can endorse other breeds, which is why you will hear about collies*)
793. I will talk about dogs (collies in particular) as life long pets.
(*my parenthetical reference to collies may interest some of you dear audiences, but not all, as most of you came to hear about dogs as pets, so I shall whisper collies. You collie lovers will not miss this whisper, as you know you are a special audience*)

As just mentioned, hyphens segment the textual flow into central and side channels of information. In string 791, the writer indicates, through hyphens, that the particularization of collies is not essential to the topic of dogs as pets. Were it otherwise, and collies the essential reference, string 792 would be the more efficient alternative. Parentheses create whispering asides and segment audiences into those who find the asides optional and those who find them essential reading (Nunberg, 1990). Example 793 indicates a writer who knows that some audiences will care that collies are the key example of the topic of dogs as pets, and other audiences will not.

Asides are relevant in disambiguating the English restrictive relative *(that)* from the nonrestrictive *(which)*. Contrast:

> 794. John yearned for the book that he was reading and hadn't finished.
> *(restrictive that; The properties of reading and not finishing are classifications of the book that are part of the yearning).*
> 795. John yearned for his favorite chair, which was oak with a smooth varnish.
> *(unrestrictive which; The oak and varnish are incidental properties of the chair, one that could change without affecting John's yearning.)*

As string 795 illustrates, the nonrestrictive *which* raises a property of John's chair (oak with a smooth varnish) as incidental to his yearning for it, and so an aside from the main business of describing that yearning. *Which* constitutes an aside, a purveyor of incidental information about an object; *that* signals a specification or classifier. It is clear that the restrictive and nonrestrictive distinction of *which* vs. *that,* assigned to grammar, is more a distinction of micro-rhetoric. It is a difference of priming actions carried through strings.

Class 3: Follow Ups   Follow-ups as a string class references a previous transaction with the audience. Some of these strings have become frozen into conventional openings for business correspondence:

> 796. Per your request...
> *(opening to business correspondence)*
> 797. I am getting back to you regarding the meeting.

Follow-up actions are typically blends of first person, inner thinking, and interactivity with, of course, some reference to the audience's previous communication as a writer or speaker. In this sense, follow-up actions often establish audience empathy, often in cases where the audience is a customer.

> 798. I appreciate your advice.
> 799. I appreciate your input.
> 800. I am listening to you.
> 801. I am sensitive to the fact that he wasn't invited.

Follow-ups can be signaled by the first person and perfect aspect *have,* similar to an autobiographical reference. However, they also have enough second person and verbs indicating recently completed action (e.g., *taken, done,* and *heard)* to reference a second round of exchange:

802. I have taken your advice.
     (follow-up to your advice)
803. I have therefore done what you asked.
     (follow-up to your request)
804. I have heard you.
     (follow-up to what you told me)

In professional discourse, writers use follow-ups to give authoritative weight to an opinion requested in a previous transaction. The writer signals the follow-up with thinking verbs referencing credentialed behavior (e.g., *examining, investigating, follow up, studying, reviewing, concluded),* often conjoined with the commonplace of common authorities *(it was determined that)* preceded by first person or the preposition *after.*

805. after examining, I have...
806. after the review, it was determined that...
807. after carefully reviewing your chart, I have...
808. I am following up on your...
809. I have concluded that...

Follow-up actions vary widely depending on the context in which the writer responds. In a context stressing customer service and satisfaction, follow-up actions overlap with acknowledgment actions, used not merely to orient the audience to a previous transaction, but to acknowledge the audience's positive input in causing the current one.

810. Thank you for your letter of April 16.
     (overlap with acknowledgment)
811. Per your letter of April 16, I am now...
     (personal but formal)
812. Based on customer feedback, prices have been cut.
     (institutional)
813. Your desire for better service is appreciated.
     (mixed personal/institutional)

Follow-up actions often express the audience's perspective through interactive pronouns *(you, your)* [examples 810, 811], juxtaposed with the writer's first person [string 811]. The personalization of follow-ups makes sense in letters to specific individuals. Examples 810 and 811 find their way into personal letters of correspondence seeking to create empathy.

However, to mass audiences, personalizing the empathic effect can seem contrived and false. In the impersonal, 812, the personal pronouns have been erased. The writer depersonalizes the audience's perspective into an abstract noun phrase (customer feedback). Furthermore, the writer depersonalizes his or her own perspective into the voice of institutional anonymity *(prices have been cut.)*

Example 813 reflects an interesting compromise between personalized and impersonalized forms of follow-up. The audience's perspective remains personalized whereas the writer institutionalizes his or her perspective. The relative effectiveness of personalized vs. depersonalized responsiveness remains a matter for further research.

Class 4: Pronoun Focus   Grammar books tend to characterize cohesive pronouns as words that refer (mainly)* back to nouns already referenced on the page. These pronouns range across personal *(him, her it, them)*, relative *(that, which)*, and demonstrative *(this, that, these, those)* pronouns. Cohesive pronouns are what linguists also call *anaphoric* pronouns (literally, referencing backward) and cohesive ties (Halliday and Hasan, 1976). As linear guides, cohesive pronouns allow writers to signal objects of reference that have persistence, that remain active in the working memory of the audience across the input stream and forms an anchorage for information to accumulate. Compare the following strings where persistence on a fixed source is maintained or broken:

814. David saw it was a beautiful spring day. He left his office.
(David making a decision based on what he saw; the lightness of the pronoun signals persistence of attention around which details of the story can accumulate)
815. David saw it was a beautiful spring day. David left his office.
(David involved in two unrelated acts, seeing and leaving; the reinsertion of the proper name inhibits the feeling of a persistent source around which information accumulates)

In string 815, the semantic "lightness" of the pronoun allows information to accumulate across a fixed source, which is David. In string 815, the reinsertion of the proper name (David) retards and, for some, even inhibits this effect. The audience is no longer invited to assume a fixed source around which information accumulates. The string more easily invites the audience to think that our attention must be shifting to a different David. Without the pronoun, we lose the primary signal of persistence and the implicit command to sustain our attention on a referent with working memory. The result is a feel of a connection and accumulation between David's seeing and leaving that strengthens more with than without the pronoun. Speakers and writers use cohesive pronouns precisely to keep aspects of the audience's attention persisting (about a source, say, David) so

---

* Although pornouns can refer forward, this is much rarer than backward reference or anaphoric pronouns. We catalogued only backward referencing pronouns.

that other, changing information (e.g., *seeing and leaving)* can connect and accumulate about it. Simply put, cohesive pronouns create both a feel of referential persistence and accumulation for the audience.

Our experience with textual genres suggests that referential persistence and accumulation are common in character-based fiction writing where the plotline revolves around the sustained thoughts and actions of a narrator and a few characters. Once the characters are established in the opening pages, much subsequent reference can be made through pronouns. We have also found referential persistence and accumulation less in evidence in information-dense, particularly scientific texts and legal discourse, where the stakes of ambiguous reference are so high that pronouns are considered high-risk linguistic maneuvers.

To avoid the risk of free-floating and ambiguous pronouns, legal and ceremonial discourse make use of formalized pronouns that take the spatial pronoun *there* as their base *(thereon, therein, thereupon, thereunto, therewith, therewithal, theretofore, thereafter, thereinafter).* The effect is to fix the syntactic case of the antecedent in relation to a spatial entity with a spatial position in the document. This, in principle, makes the identification of the antecedent more apparent at the very time it is pronominalized.

External Sources: Priming Multiple Voices in the Linear Stream

Through the linear channel of language, speakers and writers can thread not only their own voice but also the voices of various historical and contemporary external voices. Communicators recruit various string classes to accomplish this feat: *citations, quotations,* and *dialog cues.*

Class 5: Citations   Citations tell audiences that the ideas mentioned derive from an external source. Within academic writing, citations are signaled by a variety of expressions: *according to, in the words of, these ideas owe to/are due to, based on the work of, on the strength of the research of, tells, tells that, reports, reports, that, reported that, reports that, says that, said that, argues that,* and *contends that.* Geisler (1994) has shown that the acquisition of these strings is essential for academic literacy, where student writers learn to separate their distinctive ideas from inherited ideas.

What makes the above formulas of citation clear and unproblematic within academic writing is that they rely not only on verbs of public speech and writing (e.g., *tells, reports, says, argues, contends),* but also on the official products of such academic actions (e.g., *research, ideas).* In addition, the easy formulas of citation are often accompanied by further verbal cues of citation (e.g., *according to, in the words of).* In case law, the citation of previous cases is a primary mode of argument. Here the phrase, *the court ruled,* is understood to reference a previous decision as an indivisible historical act (e.g., *the court ruled in Roe vs. Wade that)* that furnishes indivisible decisions to draw on as premises or warrants for further claims.

Not All Cases of Citation Are Signaled

There is a rich overlap between verbs of citation and many verbs indicating private thought. To understand the basis of the overlap, imagine a teacher receiving a get-well card from a student and the teacher is overheard to say, "I really appreciate the card." If we are the ones overhearing and we then report to someone else, "The teacher appreciated the card," we are citing the teacher's previous remark. Now imagine we overheard no such thing and rather just saw the teacher smile at the card, with our inferring that the smile means appreciation. If we then report to a third party, "The teacher appreciated the card," we cannot be citing the teacher's speech. We are rather using our powers of personal acquaintance and inference to reconstruct and express the teacher's private thought.

Notice that whether a private thinking verb like *appreciate* contributes to the reconstruction of personal thought or to the citation of public communication depends entirely on the originating context being reported. English priming strings do not carry by themselves the contextual nuances of these originating contexts that decide the matter one way or another. The decision is made only by understanding the context-specific principles of citation within a particular domain of discourse (Hyland, 2001). The result is a substantial class of verbal phrases that overlap in their potential for reconstructing private thought or citing public communication. A comprehensive but hardly exhaustive list of such overlapping phrases includes the following: *appreciated that, apprehended that, caught on that, comprehended that, conceived that, considered that, contemplated that, dawned on her that, decided that, desired that, detected that, dreamed that, estimated that, expected that, fathomed that, figured that, guessed that, had the feeling that, heard that, imagined that, intended that, judged that, mused that, noticed that, perceived that, realized that, recognized that, reexamined that, saw to it that, thought that, wanted that, was aware that, and was mindful that.* Each of these verbal phrases can be used to reconstruct another's personal thought or to cite another's public communication. Yet, which function any of the above phrases serves depends upon the details of their context. In fiction, where authorial narrators often enjoy special access to the minds of characters, we do not need to hear the words of a character cited to believe the author's assertions about the character's mind. Citation thus does not pose the same evidentiary concerns in fictive writing as it does in non-fictive epistemic writing.

Class 6: Quotations   Although citation strings permit audiences to know that the ideas referenced derive from an external source, these strings do not necessarily determine by themselves whether the ideas referenced are paraphrases of the external source or verbatim borrowings. Quotation represents a further class of source strings that clinch the speaker or writer's attribution of ideas in a verbatim format. Quotation strings often involve verbs of saying, verbs that precede a comma, an optional that + quotation marks:

816. allege (that), "...
817. claim (that), "...
818. maintain (that), "...
819. declare (that), "...
820. affirm (that), "...
821. tells it (that), "...
822. in an official statement said (that), "...

Quotation also relies on various official verbs of reporting (*included, volunteered,* and *offered)* that, when co-occurring with quotation marks, that-complements, or both, imply official, on the record, speech:

823. She included that, "...
824. He volunteered that, "...
825. She offered that, "...

The mere presence of quotation marks in the linear stream is a discretionary rhetorical device—also called nonstandard quotation.

826. I have a "special" feeling about her.
(non-standard discretionary quotation—a quotation mark used to emphasize a word in the stream of text without functioning as a true attribution of an external source)

On the other hand, a single word or phrase emphasis in quote marks can convey a true quotation function when the words quoted truly belong to an external source:

827. Austin Powers was devastated when he lost his "mojo."
(a quotation mark used to emphasize a word in the stream of text that DOES function as a true quotation category, an attribution of an external source. This is because "mojo" is Austin's word, not a word shared in the vernacular by everyone, including the speaker)

The discretionary use of the quotation mark is an inconclusive and a highly ambiguous clue with respect to rhetorical priming. For this reason, we do not include in our catalog the mere presence of quotation in the surface text as a priming function in its own right. This does not mean that the various functions of discretionary quotation are bereft of rhetorical interest. Schneider (2002) recently studied the various rhetorical functions of student and professional writers who use quotation as a rhetorical device. She found, among other things, that both professionals and students use quotation to redefine popular terms into disciplinary terms and vice versa. They use quotes to indicate that certain words have been taken from verbal clichés or cultural commonplaces. They use quotes for straightforward, ironical, or whimsical emphasis, or use them to indicate that certain terms and their correct definition remains open to controversy. Scheider observed that while both students and professionals express some understanding of these various uses of quotation, the effective use of them ultimately depends on the writer's cultural and disciplinary experience. Simply put, Scheider reports that whereas both students and experienced writers use quotations in their writing, the experienced writers use them in more nuanced and appropriate ways.

Class 7: Dialog Cues   As the depiction of verbatim statements, quotations capture some of the auditory experiences of external source statements as they were originally voiced. However, quotations are important less for their immediate sensory value than for the writer's interest to inform the reader and credit the source.

Dialog cues are specialized subsets of quotation actions, residing in scenic description, that carry the reverse priorities of expository quotation. Dialog cues are more descriptive than informative. They are involved in scenic interplay to deliver to the audience an auditory sensation of "being on scene live." Dialog cues blend the attribution of words from external sources and the embedded scene in which these words are originally delivered. When writers quote language within a dialog, they are also adding to the spatial-interval effect of a text. Compare the following strings:

828. John said that he felt sick.
     (indirect quotation)
829. John says, "I'm feeling awful."
     (dialog cue)

Example 828 supplies a paraphrase of John's words. We know what John did but we must infer the actual physical sounds he used to do it. The direct reporting of string 829, by contrast, opens up the spatial-auditory interval of John's verbal behavior. Yet it leaves us to infer the general action John took through his words. For example, John may have filled the air with "I'm feeling awful" to indicate guilt, discomfort, or vague distress as well as illness. Example 828 forfeits spatial immediacy to stabilize the interpretation of what John did. Example 829 forfeits the stability of interpreting what John did in order to place the audience squarely in the auditory space of John's words. Novelists and short story writers are interested in the technique of dialog largely because it enhances the audience's feel of sharing auditory space with the characters.

The boundaries between expository quotation and dialog cues can become quite fine. However, the discerning reader can make some reliable distinctions between the two. Dialog cues are more restricted than normal quotation in three main ways. First, and probably most important, dialog cues are more likely to occur in textual contexts where the surrounding actions are descriptive, depicting scenes with the spatial extension necessary for richly textured talk to unfold. Second, dialog cues tend to focus less on generic saying or telling than on the expressive manner of the talk itself. They invoke a rich sensory spectrum of the various pitches in which the human ear can hear talk. These pitch differences are caught in the variability of verbs such as *utter, enunciate, enunciates intone, chatter, exclaim, babble, prattle, blurt, cry, fume, grumble, huff, rant, yell, rave, raves, shout, snap, sputter, grunt, groan, moan, murmur, stammer, stutter, whisper, whine, and interject.* Finally, dialog cues are more likely to co-occur with (conversational) sequence, pronouns and other cohesive ties (cohesive pronouns) that reference the interlocutors and their accumulation of shared information relative to one another.

Notice how we can turn what first appears as a series of quotations into a perceived dialog sequence by adding to 830 more richly expressive verbs of saying (from the generic *"said"* to *"shout"* and *"yell"*), more concrete sequencers (from *"and"* to *"and so then"*), and more scene-establishing spatial pronouns (from *"to the store"* to *"there too"*).

830. John said "Mary went to the store" and Bill said "Jim went to the store."
   (series of quotations, not perceived as connected dialog)
831. John shouted, "Mary went to the store," and so then Bill yelled back, "Jim went there too."
   (dialog cues)

9

Cluster 3:
External Perspectives

In this chapter, we turn to the third and final cluster of strings, external perspectives. This cluster comprises strings of English that a speaker or writer uses to describe the external world as "objectively" as possible, with few traces of an inner mind that can get in the way of the audience's direct experience of the world described. Sustained over a long enough course, these descriptive strings can make an audience feel it is not reading at all, but experiencing immersive situations firsthand.

Fiction and poetry are particularly well known for their high degree of external description. Much of the focus of a storyteller or creative writer's education is to create descriptions that plunge audiences seamlessly into scenes, imaged in photorealistic detail, temporally extended across other scenes, and held together in the sweep of a compelling story. Such description is the province of good fiction. Yet description is not bound to fiction. Description plays an important role in all written genres, from profiles and histories to instructions and argument. In the following sections, we review the two major families of English strings, extended space and extended time, that contribute to external description.

FAMILY 5. EXTENDED SPACE:
IMMERSING AUDIENCES IN SCENES

This family covers dimensions and string classes that prime an audience's feel of extended space.

Dimension 13: Word Pictures

This dimension covers visual nouns and verbs. The style manual for *The Wall Street Journal* instructs its reporters that the opening paragraphs of a story ought to provide the audience with a word picture. A word picture is an image that embodies all the major elements of the story. Offering the audience a word picture allows him or her to "see" the skeleton of the story in mental imagery before the skeleton is fleshed out in detailed exposition. Word pictures help the audience see the forest so that the audience can easily place the trees to follow. Word pictures also provide a motivation into the story. They offer the audience the concrete and visual stimulation to motivate listeners and readers into a story.

Therefore, when James S. Hirsch, then a reporter for *The Wall Street Journal,* did a story on the passing of a generation of strong and prideful women matriarchs who defined themselves as glue to their family, he begins with the recent passing of his own grandmother, Rose Simon.

> On my grandmother's 100th birthday, the family was to gather in St. Louis and pose for a photograph. It would be a fitting tribute to a woman who once bristled when someone tried to photograph her sitting alone. "By myself, I'm no one," she said, "but with my family, I'm everything." A week before her birthday on Dec. 25, Rose Simon weakened and entered the hospital. But she never lost her trademark wit and verve. "Mrs. Simon," a nurse said. "I hear you're going to be 100 years old next week." "Can't anyone keep a secret?" she mumbled.

Hirsch used word pictures, language stimulating our eye and ear, to capture the image of his grandmother's sense of family investment and pride, the premise on which the rest of his story hangs. How might we characterize the specific classes of word pictures Hirsch relied on to build imagery in the minds of his audiences? By trying to answer this question, we will understand not only our catalog dimension called word pictures but also the various string classes that constitute this dimension.

Whereas the provenance of word pictures are often objects we can see and name in the environment, they can also derive from states of mind that language communities have managed to reify into sensory objects through use.

832. We will have a good camp, provided we bring food.
  (provision of food as contingent thought)
833. Let's make sure we bring our provisions (pointing to food).
  (contingent thought reified into a word picture)

Class 1: Person Properties   Hirsch described Rose Simon's trademark *wit* and *verve.* These words are examples of a specific string class of word picture we call *person properties*. Such properties help audiences distinguish, through the five senses, one human being from the mass of human beings on the planet. Hirsch describes Rose in her youth as a *petite olive-skinned beauty at 4 feet 11 inches*. Person properties capture the visual and auditory features audiences notice, but seldom verbalize, when they come to know human beings through a face-to-face acquaintance. By including person properties as part of the language experience, speakers and writers are able to set in motion the audience's acquaintance with the persons in the writing.

Single-word examples of person properties s are *bearded, bedraggled, beefcake, pompadour, pouty-voiced*. Notice that these lexical items are more specific than the stereotypic adjectives (e.g., *nice, friendly, mean*) and generic classifier nouns (e.g., *liberal, teamster, teacher, homemaker*) that we normally use to describe and classify persons. Rather than a generic description — fancy hairstyle — which appeals to the imagination more than the eye, a person property lets the audience see a *pompadour* in his or her mind's eye and so leaves it to the audience to infer that it is a fancy way of wearing one's hair. Rather than a *strange voice,* which says too many possible things about a person, a person string expressing *pouty-voiced* lets audiences hear in their own auditory memory just what kind of strangeness is going on.

Person property strings are often adjectives and single or compound nouns that describe and classify persons. They can also consist of multi-word strings (e.g., *deflects credit*) that describe personal tendencies and individuating characteristics. In some cases, a person's properties reflect generalizations of abilities that people exhibit in time and place. For example, a person who, in local circumstances, exhibits spatial proximity to important persons can be attributed the general person property of *having access*. In such cases, as we saw, the line between descriptive properties and specifications becomes extremely fine.

Class 2: Sense Properties Sense properties are a second string class composing word pictures. These properties are not restricted to sentient beings but to objects and environments as well. The following examples are a small sample: *yellowing, grisly, gruesome, grumbling, grunting, gurgling, snow white, gushing, guzzling, gyrating, smooth to the touch, hacking, looking haggish*. There are overlaps between person and sense properties *Grunting* and *looking haggish* do not need to describe humans only; but they can describe a person's voice and appearance — and so legitimately resonate as both a person and sense property.

We also find natural resonances between sense properties and affect. *Grisly* and *gruesome* indicate negative affect and, in some contexts, intensity, as well as descriptive properties of sense. Narrative ambiguities can ride on whether the storyteller words a negative story element as primarily a property of sense (e.g., a *gruesome cut)* or words it as an overt negative commentary (e.g., *was gruesome)*. Compare the consequences of these slight variations in the following strings:

834. Jack's bandage covered a gruesome cut.

(gruesome = sense property; part of physical description; negative affect is encapsulated in the sensory world of the writing. The writing seems a description of something bad happening to John)

835. Jack's bandaged cut was gruesome to look at.

(gruesome = negative affect; part of authorial commentary imposed on the world of the writing. The writing seems a negative commentary)

The English word *garbled* is the single best example we could find of mixing sense properties and subjective uncertainty.

Class 3: Sense Objects Sense objects are a third string class behind word pictures. These are primarily noun-based visual objects, experiences, or events. They are sometimes stable as single words, but often need additional length to pin down stable descriptive objects and entities. A short list from our catalog includes the following: *snarled traffic, snow crystals, snow piles, smelly cigars, smoky smells, sloping terrain, slumping hillsides, small villages, smashed glass, smell of wood-smoke, skillet.*

The versatile *just* adds flexibility to strings indicating sense objects. Recall that in the case of reassuring a audience in written instructions, a *just* + *verb* string keeps the audience focused on a task that is smaller and less frightening than the task the audience fears having to perform.

836. Just stay with me on this.
837. I will just focus on the first menu.

There is an analogous use of the adverbial *just* + *a* + *sense object,* that is used to shift expectations in the context of storytelling, usually from anxiety to relief.

838. The soldiers heard stirring in the bushes. They were relieved to find it was just a mouse.

Style manuals routinely issue the caution to use specific, concrete words rather than abstract words. Jack Lynch (2001) wrote in his online style guide from Rutgers:

> Instead of "apparent significant financial gains," use "a lot of money" or "large profits." Instead of "Job suffers a series of unfavorable experiences," use "Job's family is killed and his possessions are destroyed."

Why is this good advice? Ostensibly because it makes a text more concrete. However, do we really want to say that concrete always means better? Granted, abstractions can be arcane and vague. However, in experienced hands, they can also be precise and exact. Abstractions, moreover, are not just sometimes nice.

They are sometimes necessary. Professionals in any field find it impossible to be precise and efficient in their communication to insiders without their technical terms of art. These terms of art are typically abstract concepts (such as mathematical concepts) and even when they not abstract (such as medical diseases), can be remote and inaccessible to lay audiences.

As general advice to writers taken uncritically, the replacement of abstract with concrete nouns is misleading. Something else is going on when style mavens rally for concrete language. More than concreteness for its own sake, they are rallying to change the fundamental linguistic experience constructed for the audience. Abstractions prime audiences to experience a text as a concept-container, one the writer fills and the audience empties. Concrete referents, by contrast, prompt audiences to follow a text as an unfolding array of story and scene. The text is no longer a container, but a window through which the audience can follow storylines. A more defensible reason for shifting from abstract to concrete language is to help a speaker or writer rescue a narrative effect from a linguistic experience of language as a concept dispenser (Williams, 2000). A bulky abstraction, like *apparent significant financial gains,* conceals all traces of a storyteller or a story. Revising to a more concrete paraphrase, *possible large profits,* keeps a story visible behind the summary.

Dimension 14: Spatial Intervals

A second dimension priming the experience of extended space is the spatial interval. English strings of this type create a feel of contiguous spatial experiences for their audiences. They allow audiences the experience of selectively scanning, zooming, and panning in the space within scenes. Spatial intervals can unfold in time as well as space but they remain bounded within the contours of scene. Consequently, they structure time for audiences as shifting windows of attention over a scene rather than dissolves across scenes.

Seasoned poets, fiction writers, literary journalists, professional storytellers, playwrights and screenplay writers must learn to master spatial intervals to create extended scenes in the reader's mind's eye. Spatial intervals are constructed through single words like *accompanied, adjacent, adjoining, adorned, decked out, approaching, cantilevered, bordering, resting, running, seated, arm in arm, hemmed in, rubbing, met,* and *riding.* These words take a spatial preposition (e.g., *by, to, on, with, over, against)* to help audiences pin down spatial relationships.

While English is particularly strong in naming objects, it is particularly restricted in naming intervals of space.* Although there are tens of thousands of object names, English relies primarily on a small handful of prepositions *(on,*

---

* Naming spacial intervals and evoking them needs to be distinguished. By describing concrete nouns and their properties, English is rich in evoking a reader's sense of space and space intervals. The point here is that English has relatively few wordes to name such intervals directly, as it names objects.

under, across, over, against, along, alongside, up, down, in front of, in back of) to denote relationships between objects occupying contiguous space:

839. Resting on
840. Running with
841. Seated next to
842. Arm in arm with
843. Rubbing against

As these and other examples suggest, audiences can frequently detect spatial intervals with a present tense progressive motion verb *(is + verb + ing)*, sometimes followed by the prepositional phrases, *around with or along with:*

844. Jack is partying with Mary.
845. Gus is coming along with the gang.

Spatial prepositions are relatively specific in helping a speaker or writer specify direction, but notoriously vague in helping specify distance. Both clouds and roofs *hang over* us, but at different distances that the English preposition *over* does not distinguish. Short of providing exact numerical modifiers for distance, English relies on a handful of spatial adverbs like *way, just, right, directly, immediately, barely,* and *well* to express the qualitative feel of relative distance (e.g., *way under, just under, just barely under, right under, directly under, immediately under, well under;* Jackendoff & Landau, 1995).

These generalizations about the communication of spatial relations hold most of the time. Nonetheless, one well schooled in them can still be surprised by the irregularities that sometimes violate these generalizations. For example, a writer can create a spatial relationship that, for whatever reason, stubbornly refuses a spatial preposition. One such case arises with the verb *ignore*. One can ignore a person only if one occupies space with that person and is not mindful of him or her. On the merits of spatial proximity, one would predict *ignore* accepts a spatial preposition. Alas, English does not allow us to *ignore with* someone. English seems rather to take an interest in persons being socially close before it lets us speak of them as spatially close. English phraseology pays scant attention to lovers who ignore one another; and equally small attention to strangers who room together. Strangers who share a space are literally "alone with one another." Yet, English reserves the expression *alone with one another* as an idiom referring only to intimates behind closed doors. English seems, at least on the small evidence of these cases, to require social closeness before it allows a spatial preposition to pin down a spatial experience.

Whereas the spatial preposition *with* carries social as well as spatial underpinnings, the operative scope of *with* within the social realm seems to change depending on whether the *with* is self- or other-directed. When other-directed, *with* is typically prosocial. We perceive *getting along with Fred* or *getting on with* Fred as a positive social expression. However, when self-directed, the social extensions of *with* are not as clear-cut. *Getting along with oneself* seems less overtly positive, indicating some past turbulence that is now in a process of reconciliation. We had suffered a setback that has alienated us from our own routine and sense of self. *To get on with one's life* becomes a resolution to pick up the pieces of the setback and to resume one's normal activities. The dynamics of sociality and spatiality in English priming strings and the conditioning of sociality on assumptions of self- and other-directedness are beyond our current scope and are matters for further research.

Furthermore, English furnishes us with a word that assumes a causal relation between spatiality and sociality. The word in question is *miss*. *Miss* implies physical closeness, albeit with the loss of a direct contact that had been part of a prior expectation.

846. John missed the ball.
   (John and the ball are spatially close)
847. Mary missed her bus.
   (Mary and the bus are spatially close)
848. Mary missed John in the airport.
   (Mary and John are spatially close)

Yet, with a proper name as direct object and no spatial preposition to indicate spatial proximity, the verb *miss* morphs from a spatial to an inner thinking verb, one conveying an agent's inner longing to overcome a perceived social (and implied spatial) distance:

849. Mary missed John.
   (inner longing caused by non-proximity or disaffection)

How can we explain the flexibility of *miss* to span spatial proximity and inner longing? We can experience space in memory as well as immediately. When *miss* primes an inner-thinking experience, the absence of contact no longer references objects in the same space but rather the displacement into memory of a once immediate space. From describing objects that managed, contrary to expectation, not to touch in a proximate space, *miss* now becomes the memory of agents who fulfilled the expectation of contact, who fulfill that expectation no longer, and who wish to restore it.

We can mentally miss not only other people, but also anything we can miss (as a verb of spatial proximity) in literal space:

850. Jeff and Kathy miss their house in Colorado.

There thus seems some deep general relationship between how objects we can miss in physical space become transformed into objects we can miss in memory. Objects require a certain favored way of cohabiting physical space before they can become candidates for "missing one another" or "being missed" in an inner longing, memorial, sense. The causal relationship seems unmistakable, but is beyond our scope to pursue further here.

Spatial intervals effects blend with other effects, such as positive and negative affect. The mouth receives delight from good food and this delight can be metaphorically transferred to the eyes to create positive and negative viewing spaces:

851. Her eyes feasted on the beauty of the new auditorium.
(spatial interval + positive affect)
852. All he could see around him was filth and squalor.
(spatial interval + negative affect)

Other blends of spatial intervals with affect arise when we say we are behind someone else. *Behind* can refer to physical orientation but also social support. *Behind* becomes a term of negative affect when used as a metaphor of concealment. In these instances, we accuse someone of being *behind* a plot or an unfavorable situation. As a spatial term, *behind* conveys the double sense of buttress and bulwark on the one hand and stealthy force hidden from view on the other. As this example suggests, spatial terms can become both prosocial and sinister and how they accommodate this mixed potential requires cultural and historical as well as further language research.

Let us now turn briefly to the interaction of spatial intervals and the adverbial *just*. The effect of *just* is generally to subjectify a spatial experience, to turn an outside experience inward. *Just + spatial interval,* for example, is an indication of a length or distance that is shorter than expected.

853. We will be living 30 miles apart.
(a geographical future fact)
854. We will be living just 30 miles apart.
(not as far as I feared; I can see you)
855. The log is 4 inches thick.
(a log fact)
856. The log is just 4 inches thick.
(not as thick as I thought; we can cut it)

Dimension 15: Motion

A third and final dimension contributing to the family of extended space experiences is motion.

Class 1: Motion   This string class invites audiences to build an image of a kinetic shape.

>857. He saw the person walking.
>   *(generic motion)*
>858. He saw the person toddling along.
>   *(specialized motion)*

Example 857 invites a generic theme of walking with no specialized image. However, the generic image can be filtered into specialized images of *leisure stroll, power-walking, puttering* and other specialized words and strings referencing kinetics. Therefore, for example, string 858 specializes the walk and the kinetic imagery describing it. Furthermore, of all rhetorical primings, motion appears to be among the more versatile in blending with other string classes in like and unlike dimensions and families. The examples here indicate only a few of the resonant overlaps that are typical of motion.

>859. shimmying up the tree
>   *(motion, space interval)*
>860. bursting into laughter
>   *(motion, positive affect)*
>861. eyes welling with tears
>   *(motion, negative affect)*
>862. the kidnapper stalked his prey
>   *(motion, negative affect, narrative event)*
>863. with hands trembling
>   *(motion, intensity)*
>864. he kept coughing all day
>   *(motion, sense property, ongoing action)*
>865. fishing in his pocket for a dime
>   *(motion, project ahead)*

The rich resonance of motion strings may explain why motion seems de rigueur for fiction writing. Spooning out detailed kinetic shapes induces the audience to see many layered aspects of the writer's world. It further prompts the spatial imagery of word pictures and spatial intervals, but now adds spatial action as a new element, with spatial action being the building blocks of spatial stories. Compare the progression from spatial information to spatial action as we enrich a spatial representation across words pictures, spatial interval, and motion:

>866. Jack saw the green fence.
>   *(word pictures)*
>867. Jack stood next to the fence.
>   *(word pictures + spatial interval)*

868. Jack walked up to the fence.
(walked up to = motion that completes spatial action)

Positive standards can sometimes evolve, as the Greeks believed, by freezing courageous action and marble-izing it in the language. Many of our lasting metaphors and moral lessons from childhood survive from small spatial stories with motion. Sticks are proverbial weapons and tools of primitive peoples. The surprise is that even in the space age, we use vestiges from the stone age to praise others and even ourselves — in the metaphorical bowels of language — for the skillful use of sticks. When we see friends making a valiant attack, we rally them *to stick it to* their enemies. When we defend weaker friends, we agree *to stick up for* them. When we feel fully determined yet overwhelmed, we reassure our friends we can *stick it out*. Perhaps a vestige from our primitive past, English still commemorates our kinetic skill with sticks as a positive standard.

The image of *stick* as a kinetics exported out of its spatialized context to hold down a variety of generalized priming functions is typical of hundreds of motion verbs within English. Turner (1996) has observed how many of the abstractive concepts of English started life as spatial stories, once, but no longer, confined within contiguous spatial boundaries to assume meanings that are more general. In our own cataloging of motion verbs, for example, we have noted how, in a short run, verbs of motion, like *cut* and *tear*, can prime similar kinetic concepts. The first evokes the kinetics of straight incision. The second evokes the kinetics of jagged incision.

869. Jack cut into the paper.
(severing a surface with a straight incision)
870. Mary tore into the paper.
(severing a surface with jagged incision)

Yet as runs with these motion verbs are extended beyond contiguous spatial contexts, the similar kinetics evolve into quite dissimilar generalized primings.

871. Jack cut into Bill's speech.
(cut into = interrupted, probably before the speech is completed)
872. Mary tore into Bill's speech.
(tore into = criticized, probably after the speech is completed)

Class 2: Motion Intervals Motion intervals are used to signal continuous motion across a spatial interval. Common patterns of strings from this class are *motion verbs + the progressive marker being* (e.g., *is being opened*) or process verbs with an *-ing* ending (e.g., *getting up*). The progressive marker *being* often indicates action unfolding in a spatial series:

873. The door being opened earlier, John didn't need his key.
874. The door is being opened.

Motion intervals also couple the progressive with the conjunction *while* (e.g., *while holding, while grabbing*) and often with a second person (e.g., *while you are holding, while you are grabbing*).

875. While examining the bumper, check for dents.
    (procedures; motion interval)
876. While holding the pot, stir slowly.
    (instructions; motion interval)

In our catalog of motion intervals, we also include a few strings with continuous adverbs, like *increasing* or *increasingly,* along with a common noun indicating the perception of motion (speed, rate).

877. increasing speed
    (motion interval)
878. increasing rate
    (motion interval)

Even here, we found we have had to be mindful of a fine line between an actual interval of continuous motion and the subjective perception of spatial intervals. Consider the contrast between:

879. Her yells became increasingly loud.
    (a perceived interval where her yells follow an accelerated trajectory; seems more descriptive than subjective)
880. Her yells became increasingly distressing.
    (a perceived interval where the speaker's perceptions follow an accelerated trajectory; seems more subjective than descriptive)

Both strings, no doubt, takes audiences on the scene of an interval of sound. However, the first string, better than the second, hides the fingerprints of the writer's mind.

FAMILY 6. EXTENDED TIME:
TRANSPORTING AUDIENCES ACROSS TIME

This family illustrates English's capacity to record events that audiences do not directly witness or no longer witness. Using utterances and texts to mark or commemorate unwitnessed or past events, especially myths and civic and commercial transactions, is among the oldest uses of written language (Olson, 1994). When discussing thinking ahead and thinking back as part of inner thinking, we discussed the human ability to think about past and future, about what could be and has been from the vantage of a single mind. We have yet to discuss how language and texts themselves create a public world of actual and sequenced happenings, how they can support dramatic events such as plot, story, and narrative.

Plot, story, and narrative all assume the elapse of time. Time elapses only when an event boundary has ended. Something must be over before we can proclaim it to have happened. This is why narrative typically assumes a narrator who knows how the story ends before beginning the tale. Without time elapsing and moving ahead in one irreversible direction based on events having completed, we are unable to form the idea of events or event sequences. In this section, we survey English strings that close and complete events.

Dimension 16: Past Events (Narrative)

This dimension of extended time signals the elapse of time through the expression of past events. Past events rely on string classes featuring the simple past, mainly through -*ed* action verbs (e.g., *came, saw, conquered*). Although the rule that the simple -*ed* verbs indicate events in English is sturdy, there are also many irregularities, resulting in -*ed* adjectives and passives that have lost their sense of plot action. We have glimpsed many of these exceptions when we discussed extended passives as anticipatory strings that make the audience wait. Moreover, there are many more cases where the -*ed* form of the verb does *not* signal the opening and completion of a single event. Consider the following examples:

881. He was always harassed.
    (recurring emotional property)
882. He stretched his legs.
    (motion)
883. She cooled her heels all day at the office.
    (time interval, idiomatic)
884. She mulled over the situation.
    (inner thought)
885. The creek murmured.
    (recurrent sense property)

These strings all illustrate -*ed* verbs that do not close off events in the way narrative requires. *Harassed* (881) and *murmured* (885) in these examples are adjectival properties, *mulled* (884) and *stretched* (883) mark past action so deeply interior or spatial that they resist public-event recording. Finally, the verbal *cooled* (883) is part of an idiom for a process verb, indicating waiting. The -*ed* form of the verb, in sum, is an unreliable indicator of a true simple past. Semantics, and more importantly considerations of discourse, must distinguish true from spurious cases of past events.

What are the semantic considerations that help us distinguish true from spurious narrative verbs? Hopper and Thompson (1980) link up the narrative concepts of foregrounding and backgrounding to the notion of verbal transitivity. We can understand narrativity by understanding transitivity. According to Hopper and Thompson, transitivity is not a uni-dimensional property of verbs but a multi-dimensional discourse property, based on a wide variety of features. For example, according to Hopper and Thompson, the feel of transitivity is enhanced when the verb conveys purposeful action, punctuality (the start and surcease of the action are immediate) volitionality, affirmative action, and realis mode (e.g., *Caesar came, saw, conquered* rather than *Caesar was to come, see, and conquer*). Within the terms of our catalog, these features are tantamount to saying that verbs are most likely to serve transitive (narrative) functions when they specialize for agency and external action and when they resist blending with internal or relational perspectives. Thus *believed* is a poor *ed-* verb for carrying a narrative because it overlaps too extensively with internal perspectives. In addition, *stated the case* is a poor verb phrase for narrative because it overlaps extensively with non-narrative relational perspectives generally and reportative functions specifically.

As Hopper has noted more recently (personal communication), witnessability tends to be another key feature of transitive events. Various pseudo-events reported in the *-ed* form are complex summaries of goings-on that are never witnessed.

886. Mary returned to her car.
     (witnessable, discrete, narrative)
887. We returned to the drawing board.
     (unwitnessable; summarizes across many potential occurrences)

Example 887 does not narrate as much as inform.

As an adjunct to the simple past, the adverbial just carries the idea of event recency. The event is closed, but its completion happened only shortly before the time of speaking or writing. Compare the following:

888. He arrived.
     (his arrival is done)
889. He just arrived.
     (his arrival has happened, but it hasn't been long in happening)

Dimension 17: Time Intervals

Time intervals are a second dimension of strings priming the feel of extended time.

Class 1: Time Intervals   This string class primes bounded intervals of time (e.g., *for months, every week*). English strings that support time intervals rely heavily on prepositions *(for, over, on, all, in;* and (notably) *during:* examples 890, 891, 892, 893, 894, 895 and 896), count numbers (e.g., *three)* adjacent to time periods (string 897), time-sequenced adverbs, like first and last (examples 898, 899) and temporal idioms (900).

890. The campaign dragged-out for months.
     (for + time period)
891. Over the last few years, I've been sick.
     (over the + time period)
892. I waited a few months for new shoes.
     (for + a few time periods)
893. On the third day, he left.
     (on + [sequence-number] time period; blends with sequence)
894. All day yesterday...
     (all + time period)
895. in its entirety...
     (in + abstract noun depicting temporal duration)
896. During the cold war, the arms race accelerated.
     (during + event depicting an interval framing other action(accelerated)).
897. It took him three weeks to recover.
     (count-number + time period)
898. The very last of the movie...
     (time-sequenced adverb + event; blends with sequence)
899. *I'll be there first thing in the morning*
     (time-sequenced adverb + event)
900. made a day of it...
     (idiom involving time period extension)

When projecting ahead to estimate the time it will take to get things done, we tend to estimate time intervals. Many of these strings overlap with the subjective perception of time. Consider the strings here:

901. in good time
     (when I am ready and events warrant)
902. in a split second
     (before you can blink; subjective time)
903. in due course
     (some time; subjective time)
904. in due time
     (some time; subjective time)
905. within a couple of weeks
     (before 14 days)

906. in a little bit
   (maybe a few seconds but before the day moves much farther; subjective time)
907. in a little while
   (maybe a few minutes but before the day moves much farther; subjective time)

In contemporary American English, we often interpret short time intervals, like those just mentioned, as intervals within which to promise and perform work. The result is that we often take the phrase within a few weeks as a plan or as part of a promise as much as an interval.

Other important markers of time intervals are the English conjunctions *while* and *as*. Both depict a time interval in which a state, event, or action is being reported. The writer who has mastered the subtle difference between these conjunctions knows that *while* is more flexible when it comes to referencing information within a time interval. *As* is restricted to time intervals that also frame interval motion. Compare the following string pairs:

908. While she was in high school, Mary ate at the school cafeteria.
   (acceptable English; while frames Mary's high school years)
909. While she was eating breakfast, Mary practiced her table manners.
   (acceptable English; while frames motion interval)
910. As she was in high school, Mary ate at the school cafeteria.
   (unacceptable English; writers might use as in this string to mean because, but that usage is awkward.)
911. As she was eating breakfast, Mary practiced her table manners
   (acceptable English. as can frame time intervals of motion interval)

Time intervals correspond with frames within which the action of a main clause takes place. Consider the following:

912. On Tuesday, I'll be going to Paris.
   (On Tuesday = time shift in discourse, indicating writer's anticipation. But also = time interval, frame within which writer will depart for Paris.)
913. I'll be going to Paris on Tuesday.
   (On Tuesday = time shift indicating writer's departure date. Moving 'on Tuesday' to end position weakens its effect as a framing interval. Tuesday has been reduced to a single point, a flight across the ocean.)

How, practically, do examples 912 and 913 differ? Suppose the writers of both work in the same office and the boss has just sent out a general e-mail that she wants to call a meeting for Tuesday. The writer of 912, leaving Tuesday open as an interval, implies that he may be able to make the meeting, depending on when (within the interval) of the day the meeting is called. The writer of 913, closing off Tuesday as an interval and reducing it to one point (a flight to Paris), indicates that attending the meeting is not possible.

Class 2: Generic Events   This class signals extended time intervals through the priming of generic events. Generic events are recurrent activities so stereotyped within cultural scripts that they can be referenced non-specifically (that is, generically) and the audience feels no loss of information. Examples consist of generic activity verbs *cooking* and *cleaning, vacationing, made reservations, made a phone call, read the newspaper, jogged* and generic settings that structure such activities (e.g., *in church, at school, at work*).

Class 3: Recurring Events   This string class consists of temporal adverbs used to mark event recurrence, such as *every, always, traditionally, customarily, regularly, frequently repeatedly, usually, on and off, typically, occasionally* do much of the work in English to convey event repetition. These adverbs of temporal recurrence indicate the repetitive nature of non-generic as well as generic events. Compare examples 914 and 915, which differ only in the time adverbial.

914. Smith presented his briefing Tuesday afternoon.
   (report of unique event)
915. Smith presented his briefing every Tuesday.
   (report of repeated event)

What a person does repeatedly often becomes a characteristic trait. For that reason, it is not surprising to find overlaps between repeated-events and person properties:

916. John always drove.
   (John is a habitual driver)
917. John regularly drove.
   (John drove a lot)
918. John seldom drove.
   (He loved walking)

English allows us to describe a person's interests by what he or she has done, and does, repeatedly. Repeated events also combine with think-back actions to create a combined effect of reminiscence about times past. The element of repetition, recruited with the aspectual auxiliaries of time past (e.g., *has had, have*), creates a sense of living recollection. Consider the similarities and differences between:

919. Mary made her bed.
   (historical reference of past action)

920. Mary would *(often)* make her bed.
   (reminiscence of repeated activity)
921. Mary had often made her bed.
   (reminiscence of repeated activity)

Example 919 references a past while 920 and 921 tend more to retrospect from eyewitness memories.

Dimension 18: Event Shifts

This final dimension in our catalog references shifts in events. In the physical world, time and spatial shifts co-occur. When one moves into another room, one necessarily changes location in time as well as space. This is an obvious fact of science, but English strings representing shifts in space and time are not scientific representations. English strings can separate shifts in space from shifts in time.

Class 1: Shifts Across Scenes   This string class allows speakers and writers to move a story along by dissolving from one scene to the next. Strings from this class entail breaking the boundaries of scene either by leaving scene or making reference to a (past, present, or future) scene as a holistic entity (e.g., *gone to a place where...*). We first discuss leaving a scene and later turn to referencing scenes holistically as a way of shifting scene.

English is rich with verbs that implicate a change of scene through unplanned and often undesirable conditions (e.g., *ensconce, flee, escape, and take refuge in*). It is also rich with verbs marking a scene change through deliberate transport (e.g., *move, trek, hike, drive, fly, sail, truck, motor, bus, walk, run, hop, skip, jump, high-tail, cruise, globe-trot, journey, voyage, walk, sled, ride, fly, come, arrive, migrate, emigrate, transfer, ramble, travel*). These verbs all carry high potential to change scene in the mind's eye of audiences.

Nonetheless, these verbs can all be creatively used to describe actions that do not break the contour of scene.

922. Fred motored from one end of the couch to the other.
   (normal change-of-scene verb with no change of scene; the result is to view "motor" as artistic metaphor)

Motor is marked as a scene-shifting verb and we perceive creative metaphor when it is used to describe in-scene motion. The three-word string *head over to* is like *motor.* It signifies deliberate transport toward a planned destination that breaks scene. If one from Chicago is referenced as *heading over to* Europe tomorrow, no one will expect sightings of the windy city once the journey begins. We thus recognize tongue-in-cheek creative expression should a speaker groan about having to *head over to* the television to change the channel. However, other motion verbs are more versatile in their potential to break or not break the contour of scene. Because of their versatility, using them to stay in scene or break it will not strike us as a creative extension. The string *go over to* has this versatility. A speaker can with equal ease reference *going over to* Europe and to the television for a channel change. Other motion verbs are constrained within scene and using them to break scene requires creative metaphor. *Reach over to* is only a body part away from *head over to*, yet it can't break scene. It assumes a distance sufficiently small that only the arms need to be in motion. The torso and legs can remain fixed. Carrying assumptions of immobility, a *reach over to* Europe reminds one of a phone commercial more than a plane ride.

When a subject of interest changes enclosures, the likelihood increases that the scene changes when the enclosure changes. It is as if the audience's eye, tracking the subject from a rear camera, knows to associate a new enclosure with a interior director's cut or dissolve.

923. Cecil ran out of the house and into the woods.
(Cecil shifts scenes with a shift of enclosures. Audiences lose sight of him in the new enclosure and the writer needs to haul the camera into the woods to continue to track him.)
924. Cecil ran above the house and over the woods.
(Cecil in a spatial interval, perhaps on a bridge overlooking a house in the woods. Cecil stays in scene because the spatial prepositions, above and over, do not change enclosures.)

As is clear from many of the previous examples, markers of spatial shifts often involve directional prepositions, notably *from* and *to*. Both break the bounds of scene from different points of view. However, not all directional prepositions work symmetrically in breaking scene. The directional phrases *up to* and *down to* are not symmetric in this regard. This is particularly true in the context of specific verbs, like *walk*. *Walk up to* implies a destination that never leaves the speaker's line of sight. *Walk down to* implies a departure whose destination carries beyond the speaker's vantage.

925. John walked up to the bar.
(The bar is in view as the approach is made; no scene shift)
926. John walked down to the bar.
(The bar is an out of view destination; scene shift)

Other spatial-shift strings involve adverbs that cut to another scene (e.g. *meanwhile*) or that create spatial dislocation from the current scene (e.g., *miles away, a way from here, up north, down the street, on the next block*). Still other spatial-shifts juxtapose the prepositions *from* and *to* with common destination nouns (e.g. *from school, to Paris*). Longer spatial-shift strings rely on extended verb phrases:

made the excursion to, made the long trek to, exported to, traveled a long distance to, made the excursion, hauled all the way from.

Curiously — a curiosity for which we have no good explanation — *enter* with a spatial preposition like *in* or *into* is just as likely to signal starting an abstract relationship as it is to signal a shift of scene.

927. Mary entered the room.
     (common English)
928. Mary entered into the room.
     (stilted English)
929. Mary entered into a new relationship with John.
     (less stilted than above)

The capacity of scene-shifting *enter* to indicate more abstract information when accompanied by a spatial preposition also applies to otherwise spatial verbs like *turn, come, enter,* and *fall.*

The preposition *with* often depicts spatial contiguity and simultaneity while *at* tends to depict temporal and spatial dislocation from the writer:

930. John is with Bill.
     (John and Bill share the same space at the same time)
931. John is at Bill's.
     (John is at Bill's—and so not here with me).

These differences matter when creating subtle shadings that border between an over-time change of scene and a sceneless shift of time. Consider the subtle shading differences between:

932. John turned up with Bill.
     (invites a picture of John's spatial contiguity with Bill before, as well as after, the time of showing up; shift of time implies John and Bill's joint shift of scene)
933. John turned up at Bill's.
     (invites no spatial picture of John prior to showing up at Bill's; shift of time does not imply shift of scene. Just describes the narrative event of John's arrival)

The *with* in 932 invites the reader to construct a mental picture of John and Bill together both prior to and at the time of their showing up together. The shift in time implies a shift in scene. The *at* in 933 does not invite such a spatial hint and summons only a narrative event, John's arrival at Bill's.

Take is another verb that makes shifts in scenes, but only in certain forms. *Take* reliably shifts scene with a direct object followed by the preposition *to.*

934. John took Mary to the prom.

However, surprisingly, the string *take to* can't shift scene as comfortably. It more commonly conveys the idea of attraction to a person or activity. In the following examples, only *John took to the streets* retains some hint of scene-shifting and even here the sense of John's continued attraction to street life overshadows the idea that John made a unique sojourn to the streets.

935. John took to Mary.
936. John took to gambling.
937. John took to the streets.

The only other instance we could find of *take* supporting scene-shifting activity is when it is used to specify the portability of someone or something to some destination.

938. Mary is someone John could take to the prom.
939. A good book is something you can always take to the beach.

As we mentioned at the start of this section, a speaker or writer can prime a shift in scene simply by referencing a scene holistically. Consider the contrast between shifting scene by referencing a place holistically (e.g., *a place where*) and referencing within a scene.

940. The place where I like to run.
    (scene shift achieved by referencing a place holistically)
941. Mary was running in place in her living room.
    (spatial interval with no shift in scene)

Class 2: Shifts in Time   This string class marks the shifting of events either back or ahead in time: *a long while back* (back), *a year before* (back), *an hour earlier* (back), *a week later* (ahead), *a few minutes ago* (back), *two days afterwards* (ahead), *a harbinger of things to come* (ahead), *a long time from now* (ahead).

942. From now to then, we have much work to do.
    (Time shift: Shift from a time of less work to more)
943. Now as then, we have much work to do.
    (Time shift + resemblance: Our work ethic in the past resembles our work ethic now)
944. The Carter family always was and will be a proud lot.
    (Time shift + resemblance: The Carter family's future resembles its past—it won't change)

In the course of telling a story, a speaker or writer will often tell the story shifting back and forth through time. Time shift actions are important devices for the writer's storytelling. When paired with time shifts, the adverbial *just* reliably indicates a perceived shortening of the shift.

945. a few weeks ago
 (time shift)
946. just a few weeks ago
 (it feels like days)

Examples like 946 overlap with the subjective feel of time. We classify them as temporal shifts because of their capacity to move a story along.

Time shifts also take place in biographical time, the major events or milestones that mark transitions in the life of an individual. These strings overlap with autobiographical reference and time intervals to indicate periods of life. They also overlap with person description and subjective perception to indicate why a milestone was never reached. (e.g., *too short to play college basketball)* or why it was (e.g., *devoted enough for graduate school)*. Blending time shifting with person description and subjective perception are common techniques in biography and autobiography. Time shifts can also be voiced by an omniscient narrator, generalizing on an entire life through quick-shifts through different horizons of time. These blends are common in personal reminiscences and memoirs.

947. in my early years, I often…
 (time shift + time intervals to indicate early habits)
948. had never been kissed
 (time shift + thinking back + to indicate the absence of an experience)
949. went on to college
 (time shift + narrative past to indicate life passage)
950. at 16, she was now old enough to drive
 (time shift with person property to indicate why a milestone is enabled)
951. never to see her again
 (time shift + generalization + think ahead + recurrence to indicate across the future from the present)
952. Years later, I would learn that his visits to my house always followed his mother's tongue-lashings.
 (time shift + think ahead + think back + narrative past to indicate retrospective hindsight)
953. best time he ever had
 (time shift + think back + generalization + positive affect to indicate generalizing over periods of life)

One workhouse for shifting time in English is the string *a time.* Yet when this string is preceded by a specific number + *at,* it indicates simultaneity of action within a scene and not time at all!

Chapter 9

954. He remembered a time when he had a good job.
   (shift in time)
955. She saw the racers taking their laps, four at a time.
   (interval in space)

III

Implications and Applications of Rhetorical Priming Theory

10

Using Priming Strings to Analyze Corpora of Texts

To this point in the book, we have described a framework of rhetorical priming and a catalog of strings derived from that framework to help us understand everyday language and its rich and diverse role in priming audience. Let us shift gears and now consider the proven and potential implications of a rhetorical priming framework on the study of English texts. In the most extensive study to date, Jeff Collins (2003) combined the framework described in this book and the catalog derived from it with methods of discourse analysis (Johnstone 2002) and corpus linguistics (Biber, Conrad & Reppen, 1998) to identify and confirm stable usages of specific combinations of our priming strings in two broad corpora of published texts. Collins' results suggest the usefulness of the priming theory at associating different functioning texts with differences in the combinations of primings on which they rely. His results further point toward a heretofore hidden layer of "languaging" (Becker, 1991) that is evidently part of the professional writer's craft.

Of course, the full impact of any newly conceived framework will not be immediately apparent — particularly in the humanities and social sciences — and is best judged by the thinking, insights, and writing it enables future scholars. Such is the nature of ideas and of scholarship and, in this regard, we expect the theory offered in this book to be no different.

In this final chapter, we describe some of the insights gained by considering language strings as instruments of rhetorical priming. Alongside our students, we have made discoveries about the way people use language. We have detected significant and interesting differences based on writer, topic, and other aspects of the rhetorical situation. We now review just how powerful exploring language as priming strings can be.

The notion that small, systematic differences in language choice accumulate into large, important differences is not particularly new. In some sense, our approach is a rhetorical interpretation of a view of language usage that has been on the radar screen of applied linguists (see, e.g., Biber 1988) and even some rhetorical theorists (Hart, 2000). What we bring to these existing approaches is a rhetorical-linguistic framework and systematic string collection method that allows a systematic consideration of everyday English as acts of symbolic action.

We developed a coding scheme based on our language theory and have been using this scheme to examine the priming strings in collections of texts. This method of inquiry places us in the company of empirically minded discourse analysts. In this tradition, we present the following findings tentatively, with the hope our empirical insights will pique the interests of other language scholars and will be suggestive of the insights our language theory may unlock when applied to the study of English texts.

A note about our methods: In the following sections, we compare groups of texts to one another. We chose this mode of presentation because it helps demonstrate the potential impact of our language theory on the study of texts. Toward this end, we emphasize the qualitative differences revealed by a close examination of the texts and the priming strings found within them. We also quantify our comparisons in the following sections because such quantifications serve as persuasive evidence of our theory's efficacy and serve as useful guides to understanding how our theory leads to the qualitative insights presented.

The tables in the sections below include the mean and standard deviation scores on each of the 18 language dimensions presented in this book. The mean score indicates the average percentage of text devoted to the dimension. The standard deviation indicates the variability within each group of texts on that dimension. In other words, a low mean score indicates a low percentage of strings in the texts are devoted to priming that dimension. A low standard deviation indicates the texts in the group have similar percentages of strings devoted to the dimension.

In addition, we quantify the differences between the groups by using the statistical process of analysis of variance (ANOVA). This process is useful because it compares the scores of the groups, takes account of each group's variability, and provides an indication of how confident we can be that the differences between the scores is due to group membership and is not the result of random variation. The ANOVA process yields a statistic known as the F-score, which we have provided for each dimension. The higher this score, the more likely the differences between the groups is statistically significant on that dimension.

From the F statistic we also calculated the p-value, which further describes the confidence warranted by the results of the analysis. The p-value quantifies the probability of finding is a random occurrence. That is, a low p indicates a low probability the difference is due to random error: a p-value less than 0.05 is commonly accepted as an indication of statistical significance.

TO REASON WHY: DIFFERENCES IN SHAKESPEARE'S HISTORIES AND COMEDIES

Many writers write across ranges of textual genres: take George Orwell or Joyce Carol Oates, writing both memorable fiction and succinct, biting short essays on a variety of subjects; or consider Peggy Noonan or Carolyn Curiel, writing presidential addresses and newspaper editorials on topics across the spectrum of political interest. Rhetoricians have long been interested in understanding how such authors' rhetoric changes when their genre or topic of writing changes. Using our language theory and software to examine texts, we gain insight into such questions.

An interesting, well-known case for exploration of such an author is William Shakespeare. One of our colleagues, an expert on the rhetoric of Shakespeare (Witmore, 2001), asked if our techniques could help detect differences across Shakespeare's works from a rhetorical point of view. We turned this curiosity into a classroom assignment for our students.

After running our string-matching software to count the number of language strings in an electronic version of Shakespeare's plays (Hylton, 2000),* our students found interesting differences. For example, Shakespeare uses several categories of priming strings differently in comedy and history plays (indicated in table 10.1, by low p-scores in the right-hand column).

One probably will not find it surprising that the comedies have more positive affect priming stings than the histories. Likewise, the histories, with their tales of regicide and combat, have, on average, more "think negative" than the comedies. These findings coincide with what you might expect, based on what you already know about comedies and about the language theory discussed in the previous chapters of this book. On the other hand, our students were initially surprised to find little difference in the amount of text the histories and comedies devote to priming retrospection. They expected the history plays to use more "think back" and "past events" priming strings because, after all, the histories tell tales of events long ago. Upon reflection, the students reassessed their assumptions as they realized Shakespeare's plays transport the audience through time, asking the audience to experience history as an eyewitness. Shakespeare doesn't describe the events of history as a history textbook might ("The English army attacked Harfleur a second time"), but as a playwright ("King Henry: Once more unto the breach, dear friends, once more!").

More interestingly, the comedies have more strings priming "reasoning" than do the histories. It seems that in most of Shakespeare's comedies, the masking and unmasking of characters and the tangling and resolution of deceits necessitates reasoning between the characters. Take, for example, the resolution of the romantic comedy *As You Like It*. In the end, the couples sort themselves out

---

* All subsequent quotations fron the plays come from this electronic source.

Table 10.1: Comparison of language feature scores for Shakespeare's comedies and histories

Variable	Comedies[a] (n=13)		Histories[b] (n=10)			
	mean	s.d.	mean	s.d.	F	P
First Person	3.713	0.576	3.252	0.408	4.600	0.044
Inner Thinking	2.942	0.254	2.633	0.200	10.000	0.005
Think Positive	1.546	0.473	1.141	0.177	6.570	0.018
Think Negative	1.610	0.227	2.271	0.489	18.740	<0.001
Think Ahead	1.062	0.066	1.104	0.073	2.050	0.167
Think Back	0.150	0.038	0.151	0.057	<0.001	0.960
Reasoning	3.147	0.363	2.721	0.108	12.780	0.002
Share Soc Ties	1.988	0.367	2.421	0.264	9.910	0.005
Direct Activity	0.489	0.130	0.447	0.059	0.900	0.353
Interacting	3.729	0.408	2.704	0.408	35.700	<0.001
Notifying	1.338	0.164	1.292	0.148	0.490	0.490
Linear Guidance	3.575	0.317	3.468	0.359	0.570	0.459
Word Picture	4.636	0.509	5.551	0.621	15.110	0.001
Space Interval	0.875	0.186	0.922	0.115	0.500	0.488
Motion	0.554	0.139	0.582	0.066	0.350	0.561
Past Events	1.137	0.124	1.211	0.139	1.810	0.193
Time Interval	0.538	0.069	0.540	0.047	0.010	0.928
Shifting Events	0.557	0.112	0.597	0.049	1.100	0.305

df=(1,21)

a Comedies: All's Well, As You Like It, Comedy of Errors, Love's Labours Lost, Measure for Measure, Merchant of Venice, Merry Wives, Midsummer Night, Much Ado, Taming of the Shrew, Troilus and Cressida, Twelfth Night, Two Gentlemen of Verona

b Histories: King John, Richard II, Henry IV (parts 1-2), Henry V, Henry VI (parts 1-3), Richard III, Henry VIII

appropriately and all is happy, but the humor and dramatic irony across the play depends on the audience understanding the varied misconceptions of the characters on stage. To achieve such understandings for the audience, Shakespeare has his characters reason with one another (priming assertions and logical connections, as discussed in the context of relational and reasoning strings) and thereby reveals his characters' points of view to the audience. For example, notice the reasoning cues in these lines from Act III as Celia and Rosalind concoct a disguise for themselves:

Celia: What shall I call thee when thou art a man?
Rosalind: I'll have no worse a name than Jove's own page;
      And therefore look you call me Ganymede.
      But what will you be call'd?
Celia: Something that hath a reference to my state
      No longer Celia, but Aliena.

In using such priming, Shakespeare signals the audience to pay attention to the gender-bending deceits that will be important later in the play. Furthermore, these lines remind the audience that the actor playing Celia is Celia and is going to remain a woman in the upcoming farce, a reminder that would be especially important when male actors are cast in the part. We see more explicit reasoning as Adam works to persuade Orlando to allow him to be servant and, thereby, signals the character's motivation and role to the audience:

Let me be your servant:
Though I look old, yet I am strong and lusty;
For in my youth I never did apply
Hot and rebellious liquors in my blood,
Nor did not with unbashful forehead woo
The means of weakness and debility;
Therefore my age is as a lusty winter,
Frosty, but kindly: let me go with you;
I'll do the service of a younger man

Likewise, in an explicit aside to the audience Touchstone, the court jester, explains his motivation for taking a particular course of action that might otherwise seem improbable to the audience or, at least, would not be immediately apparent:

I am not in the mind [to go to the priest to be married again] but I were better to be married of him than of another: for he is not like to marry me well; and not being well married, it will be a good excuse for me hereafter to leave my wife.

Meanwhile, Shakespeare's histories show significantly fewer instances of language that primes reasoning. To help make this clear, we graphed the plays' normalized scores on the "reasoning" and "think negative" dimensions in figure 10.1. The texts to the right side of the graph contain a higher percentage of "reasoning" strings than the texts to the left. Likewise, texts toward the top of the graph have a higher percentage of "think negative" strings than the lower texts. So, for example, *King John* has a higher percentage of "think negative" than *Henry V* and both of these have a higher percentage than *As You Like It*.

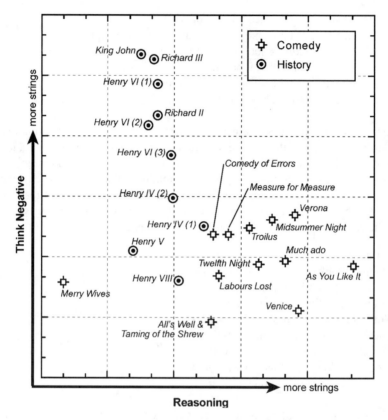

Figure 10.1: Normalized "Reasoning" and "Think Negative" scores of Shakespeare's history and comedy plays

Notice how the Bard's Histories fall into a relatively narrow vertical band on the graph. This indicates they all have a similar percentage of "reasoning" strings, also indicated by the histories' low standard deviation score on this dimension. Notice, also, the history plays fall to the left of most of the comedies. This means that, except for the *Merry Wives of Windsor,* the individual histories in Shakespeare each have a lower percentage of "reasoning" strings than the individual comedies.

We hypothesize one reason behind this finding to be that Shakespeare's histories generally have fewer situations where explicit reasoning and explanations need to be shared with the audience. The actions in the histories unfold onstage with fewer twists than the comedies. The audiences of the histories thus require less revelatory reasoning to stay abreast of all that's happening in the dramatic situations.

This is not to say the histories have no reasoning cues. An average of 2.7% of the text in history plays is devoted to "reasoning" priming stings. Dramatized histories are, after all, interesting in part because they reveal otherwise hidden motivations of the characters. They provide the author's answer to the essential "why" question of historical research: the dialog reveals some of the motivations of history. For example, King Henry V explains his reasoning for hanging Bardolph, a drinking friend from his younger, wilder days who had stolen a trinket from a French church:

> We would have all such offenders so cut off: and we give express charge, that in our marches through the country, there be nothing compelled from the villages, nothing taken but paid for, none of the French upbraided or abused in disdainful language; for when lenity and cruelty play for a kingdom, the gentler gamester is the soonest winner.

Later in the play, King Henry walks disguised among his soldiers the night before the major battle of the play. In having the king do so, Shakespeare lets the audience function as eyewitnesses to see how the men think about the war in contrast to the King.

> King Henry V (disguised): ...methinks I could not die anywhere so contented as in the king's company; his cause being just and his quarrel honourable.
> Williams: That's more than we know.
> Bates: Ay, or more than we should seek after; for we know enough, if we know we are the king's subjects: if his cause be wrong, our obedience to the king wipes the crime of it out of us.
> Williams: But if the cause be not good, the king himself hath a heavy reckoning to make, when all those legs and arms and heads, chopped off in battle, shall join together at the latter day and cry all "We died at such a place."

Shakespeare provides his audience further understandings of the king's religious beliefs and motivations in his quite explicit answer to Bates and Williams' reasoning:

> Every subject's duty is the king's; but every subject's soul is his own. Therefore should every soldier in the wars do as every sick man in his bed, wash every mote out of his conscience: and dying so, death is to him advantage; or not dying, the time was blessedly lost wherein such preparation was gained: and in him that escapes, it were not sin to think that, making God so free an offer, He let him outlive that day to see His greatness and to teach others how they should prepare.

Revealing such reasoning in the histories enhances the dramatic effect and provides important answers to why what happened happened as it did.

Nonetheless, reasoning plays an even more fundamental role, arguably, in the comedies, where the what of dramatic action is none other than the why of the character's often faulty and incomplete reasoning and assumptions. Without characters laying bare their reasoning in the plays, there is no plot. Our Shakespearean colleagues have been encouraged with the initial results of our quantitative analysis and have been applying our categories to answer other research questions in their research about the Bard.

FICTION AND NONFICTION: DIFFERENCES IN GENRES OF PUBLISHED WRITING

Since Carolyn Miller's (1984) influential essay about genre, many language scholars have come to view genre as fundamentally a rhetorical notion: genre is an indication of how a text performs action in the world. It should thus not be surprising to learn that our approach to English strings may offer powerful insights in the study of textual genres.

Some genres, such as journals, diaries, memoirs, and reflections, might be expected to emphasize strings of the writer's inner mind over other dimensions. For example, when reading a memoir one would expect to find out how the author felt about coming upon a glorious field of poppies during a pitched battle in a Viet Nam jungle. Yet, in other genres, such as fieldguides or nature writing, authors would probably emphasize descriptive strings. One would not expect these genres to focus on the writer's feelings or poignant thoughts about the poppies. Instead, they would probably describe the sensory information observed with visual nouns, motion verbs, and spatial intervals. In still other genres, such as popular accounts of science, journalism, or public relations writing, authors might be expected to include more relational strings, perhaps relying on interactivity and social ties to build shared curiosity with the audience. For example, one might find sentences like this: "You have probably never imagined the beauty of a field of red and orange poppies laced against the dense greens of an Asian rain forest. Where might you find such beauty at a reasonable price and only footsteps away from your hotel?"

In his dissertation, Collins (2003) explores the connections between the language theory presented in this book and textual genre by analyzing two corpora of written American English, known as the Brown and the Frown corpora (Francis & Kucera, 1979; Hundt, Sand, & Siemud, 1998). These parallel, million-word corpora are each comprised of 500 texts, sorted into some common fiction and non-fiction genres of professional writing (listed in table 2 2). The texts in each corpus were randomly selected and were meant by the original compilers of the corpora to represent all major professionally published writing. Although, as Collins points out (Chapter 3), the corpora genres and their division is certainly dated, the distinctions drawn by the readers who compiled the corpus and sorted the texts into the genres may be still useful for some textual explorations of genre.

Table 10.2: List of the genres in the Brown and Frown corpora

Non-Fiction Genres[a]	Fiction Genres
Press Reportage	General Fiction
Press Editorials	Mystery and Detective Fiction
Press Reviews	Science Fiction
Religion	Adventure and Western
Skills and Hobbies	Romance and Love Story
Popular Lore	Humor
Belles Lettres, Biography, Memoir	
Miscellaneous	
Learned	

a The division of genres into fiction and nonfiction was made by the group of linguists who originally compiled the Brown corpus, not by the current authors. See Francis & Kucera (1979).

Telling insights are found by comparing the usage of priming strings between the fiction and nonfiction genres of the corpora. As we have been arguing in this book, English depends on the usage of priming strings for achieving robust understandings among readers. The authors of the texts in the fiction categories of the two corpora used the majority of language dimensions differently than did the writers of nonfiction texts. This is indicated by the priming categories with very low p-scores in the right-hand column of table 10.3. For example, in an academic essay in the Brown corpus by B. Blanshard, Blanshard tries to convince the reader of his point by evoking "social ties," a priming characteristic of many nonfiction forms of argumentation:

> The [emotive] theory claims to show by analysis that when we say, "That is good," we do not mean to assert a character of the subject of which we are thinking. I shall argue that we do mean to do just that.
>
> Let us work through an example, and the simpler and commoner the better. There is perhaps no value statement on which people would more universally agree than the statement that intense pain is bad. Let us take a set of circumstances in which I happen to be interested on the legislative side and in which I think every one of us might naturally make such a statement.

Strings invoking social ties with the reader are found more often in the nonfiction texts than in the fiction texts. The empirical observation of such differences tends to support Kaufer and Butler's (2000) argument that overtly building ties with readers is a necessity for much information and instructional writing. Writers of legal briefs, academic papers, and other explicit arguments depend on social ties, directives to the audience, and reasoning cues to achieve the engagement needed to bring an audience along on the writer's rhetorical journey.

Table 10.3: Comparison of fiction and non-fiction genres in Brown and Frown corpora of English texts

Variable	Non-Fiction (n=748)		Fiction (n=252)		F	P
	mean	s.d.	mean	s.d.		
First Person	0.366	0.688	1.515	1.456	280.180	<<0.001
Inner Thinking	2.571	0.841	2.839	0.718	20.540	<0.001
Think Positive	0.758	0.415	0.773	0.364	0.260	0.609
Think Negative	1.254	0.753	1.349	0.490	3.490	0.062
Think Ahead	1.212	0.494	1.068	0.323	18.530	<0.001
Think Back	0.482	0.283	0.742	0.379	132.800	<<0.001
Reasoning	2.530	0.805	2.578	0.699	0.720	0.397
Share Soc Ties	2.315	0.995	1.253	0.410	271.380	<<0.001
Direct Activity	0.282	0.269	0.236	0.180	6.520	0.011
Interacting	0.437	0.599	1.402	0.872	381.630	<<0.001
Notifying	2.823	0.607	2.052	0.413	351.750	<<0.001
Linear Guidance	3.940	1.460	7.640	1.960	1015.110	<<0.001
Word Picture	4.884	2.121	6.758	1.946	153.250	<<0.001
Space Interval	1.001	0.543	2.008	0.700	555.720	<<0.001
Motion	0.400	0.339	0.743	0.374	183.750	<<0.001
Past Events	1.732	0.786	3.154	0.880	579.940	<<0.001
Time Interval	1.390	0.550	1.045	0.330	88.290	<<0.001
Shifting Events	0.733	0.313	0.993	0.295	133.760	<<0.001

$df=(1,998)$

Authors of fiction texts, on the other hand, compose from external perspectives significantly more frequently than do authors of nonfiction. More specifically, authors of fiction make more use of strings priming visual imagery, as illustrated in this passage from "Rattlesnake Ridge" by P. Field:

> He tramped out of the Miners Rest with his hopes plummeting, and headed doggedly for the Palace Saloon, the last place of any consequence on this side of the street. The Palace was an elaborate establishment, built practically on stilts in front, with long flights of wooden steps running up to the porch. Behind its ornate facade the notorious dive clung like a bird's nest to the rocky ribs of the canyonside. Russ ran up the steps quickly to the plank porch. The front windows of the place were long and narrow, reaching nearly to the floor and affording an unusually good view of the

interior. Heading for the batwings, Cobb glanced perfunctorily through the nearest window, and suddenly dodged aside. Nerves tight as a bow-string, he paused to gather his wits.

This is not to suggest the fiction genres do not make use of relational strings to build engagement. In his Rhetoric of Fiction, Wayne Booth (1961) showed the surprising extent to which authors insert themselves overtly into the descriptive world of the novel in order to sway the audience's opinions. Not even so-called escapist literature leaves the audience free of authorial intervention. Fiction texts make regular use of strings within the relational perspective to help make the authors' points, as is shown by the mean scores on these dimensions in table 10.3.

In our rhetorical analysis course, we ask students to write three initial essays with a minimum of writing instruction and before we teach them the language dimensions described in this book. First, we ask them to introduce themselves to the class in a short acquaintance paper. Second, we have them describe their dorm room. Lastly, we have them write a paper that teaches the reader to do something the student knows a lot about. After the students have written the three papers, we teach them to analyze all of the papers statistically for differences, applying a procedure called "factor analysis" (Kachigan, 1991, chapter 7).

Without getting overly technical, factor analysis is a multivariate statistical technique for making sense of interactions among variables. We teach the technique to our students because it clarifies the relationship among the language dimensions in ways that often bring about qualitatively useful textual insights. The procedure works by mathematically reducing the dimensions into super-variables, called "factors." Each of these factors indicates how correlations among the dimensions in our theory contribute to the overall variation in the group of texts being studied. This means that each of the factors encompasses several dimensions and the factors may often be used to separate texts and understand some of the underlying rhetorical moves the authors have made.

Students are surprised to discover that the factor analysis procedure reliably divides the class's papers according to the assignments they completed. That is, without explicitly intending to do so, the students all used similar combinations of language strings in a way that even the dumb computer is able to discern using relatively simple mathematics. This demonstration exercise not only helps the students understand a rhetorical basis of genre, but it also supports our notion of patterned aggregations of English strings contributing to readers' deep understandings of texts and their rhetorical operation in the world (see also Collins, 2003).

ADVERTISING AND PRESIDENTIAL INAUGURALS: ADAPTING THE MESSAGE TO THE TIMES

As rhetoricians interested in the study of genre have consistently indicated, many aspects of the rhetorical situation affect genre. Genres are not static categories of text, but are built of texts generated by readers' and authors' responses to previous texts and current situations (Bazerman, 1994; Berkenkotter & Huckin, 1995; Freeman & Medway, 1994). Such studies have demonstrated that genres guide writers—writers must operate within and against a genre when composing texts—but genres are also built by the writers acting in the moment and evolve (or dissipate) with each new writing.

Table 10.4: Comparison of cigarette ad copy from two decades of Life Magazine

Variable	1940s (n=28)		1950s (n=23)			
	mean	s.d.	mean	s.d.	F	P
First Person	0.436	1.030	0.410	0.846	0.010	0.924
Inner Thinking	3.409	1.623	3.403	2.243	<0.001	0.991
Think Positive	3.551	1.367	5.477	3.151	8.540	0.005
Think Negative	0.980	1.165	0.487	0.754	3.060	0.086
Think Ahead	0.764	1.144	0.592	0.839	0.360	0.552
Think Back	0.207	0.411	0.210	0.470	<0.001	0.982
Reasoning	2.998	1.966	3.193	2.298	0.110	0.746
Share Soc Ties	1.371	1.213	1.936	1.644	1.990	0.164
Direct Activity	0.494	0.803	0.413	0.862	0.120	0.731
Interacting	2.890	1.936	2.953	2.174	0.010	0.913
Notifying	1.802	1.141	2.052	1.619	0.420	0.522
Linear Guidance	4.636	2.031	4.596	1.387	0.010	0.936
Word Picture	7.533	2.350	7.911	2.660	0.290	0.593
Space Interval	0.804	0.965	0.422	0.833	2.230	0.142
Motion	0.584	0.994	1.168	1.455	2.890	0.096
Past Events	0.622	0.817	0.652	0.978	0.010	0.904
Time Interval	0.896	0.795	0.693	0.820	0.800	0.376
Shifting Events	0.519	0.598	0.340	0.528	1.260	0.267

df=(1,49)

As we indicated in the previous section, we have begun to discover genres as varying combinations of priming strings. Adventuresome writers combine elements of pre-existing genres, putting the language dimensions together in new ways. These blends become the basis of emergent genres. Imagine, for example, an instruction writer writing a text on how to use a word processor. We might not expect the instruction writer to include a personal autobiography—itself a combination of inner mind and strings indicating historical recollection—but some creative instruction writers do just that. They might explain, in brief or at length, their first experiences with what they will teach. Perhaps the instruction writer would try to build motivation by explaining, "I've composed with a computer since the mainframe days and the austere 'vi' text editor. Today's word processors support you in ways I would have never dreamed possible." In such moments of authorial inspiration and inventiveness, new genres emerge and old ones change. Authors use priming in surprising and (perhaps) effective combinations that will be taken up (or not) by future writers.

To help our students begin to understand genres as dynamic entities, we ask them to complete a classroom exercise comparing tobacco advertisement copy in *Life* from the early 1940s with copy from the mid-1950s (Wooden, J. A., DeVore, J., Graef, C., & Westman, L., 1998). Many aspects of this particular genre remain quite stable across the two periods, as indicated by the relatively high p-values for most dimensions in the right-hand column of table 4. Nonetheless, the "think positive" and "think negative" dimensions are exceptions to this stability.

The tobacco ad copy of the 1950s uses, on average, more strings priming positive feelings than the advertisements of the 1940s. For example, this 1950s text accompanies a picture of a male lifeguard (figure 10.2) holding a cigar (calling all Freudians!) while blowing his whistle:

He alone rules the happy chaos of a million beach-goers every summer. It's a job that takes skill and patience. And like men everywhere, he makes the going easier by enjoying the cigar that's one in a million-mild, yes tastefully mild-Dutch Masters.

Contrast that image of male responsibility over "happy chaos" with the image of responsibility conveyed by the following 1940s ad copy, which accompanied the image shown in figure 10.3:

Figure 10.2: 1950s tobacco advertisement

He's a Bombardier. He's the business man of this B-17E bomber crew. His office is the "greenhouse" of transparent plastic in the nose of the ship. And he works there on split-second time. But when those office hours are over-well, just look below and watch him enjoying a Camel-the favorite cigarette on land, sea, and in the air.

Figure 10.3: 1940s tobacco advertisement

Related differences are also prevalent in the ads' use of strings involved in positive and negative priming. Consider the positive affect primed in this 1950s ad that attempts to engender a sense of scientific progress:

> Only Chesterfield is Made the Modern way-with AccuRay. Discover for yourself what modern science can do to increase your cigarette enjoyment ....You'll marvel at the extra flavor that comes through. Yet because the measurably better cigarette smokes more slowly you enjoy a cool mildness never possible before.

Contrast that copy with a 1940s ad that also aims toward the scientific register, but includes "think negative" priming strings in the text:

> When you inhale-and all smokers do, some of the time-there's increased chance of irritation. So, be guided by the findings of eminent doctors. They discovered: On comparing the irritant quality in the smoke of the four other leading brands was found to average more than three times that of the strikingly contrasted Philip Morris and the irritation lasts more than five times as long! Philip Morris brings you the delightful flavor and aroma of the world's finest tobaccos-with never a worry about throat irritation.

The 1940s ads use, on average, twice as much "think negative" as the 1950s ads. This negative priming comes through in strong images of wartime duties as well as in ad copy that attempts to claim new features or manufacturing processes that overcome some of smoking's deleterious effects; effects rarely mentioned in 1950s advertising even when new "scientific" processes are advertised.

This exercise leads our students to ask the quite sensible question, "Why do these changes occur?" with some attendant possibilities: Is this change in genre due to ads' tendency to reflect their own audience? Did post-war Americans want a positive view of themselves and were the advertisers happy to comply? Did the world events of the 1940s make Americans suspicious of overly positive claims that led advertisers to limit their priming of positive feelings during that decade? Or did the advertising itself change America's self-perception, doing more than simply reflecting consumers' desire and, instead, prompting some change in America's world view?

We are pleased our students begin to ask such questions of texts. Some of them are disappointed (as you may be also) when we answer, "We don't know and can only speculate." Such is the limitation of purely textual research into genres. This is an excellent lesson for our students to learn at the beginning of the rhetorical analysis course.

Our purpose in presenting these examples (both to our students and in this chapter) is to spawn interest in beginning to ask and answer such questions. Although we are convinced the language theory presented in this book can be helpful to such scholarship, we fully recognize explanations need to extend well beyond the text. Expert insights on popular culture and history are needed to explain (or discount) the textual findings revealed by our close examinations. Full explanations would need to characterize other important aspects of the rhetorical situation and extend into the culture(s) surrounding the texts. We maintain, however, that careful study of text can be (and should be) an important part of such explanations. We offer the language theory in this book as a potential contribution to this effort.

In another consideration of genre, we examined the presidential inaugural address, arguably one of the most carefully crafted textual genres in politics. These addresses provide the chief executive of the United States the opportunity to set forth his or her vision of what is to be accomplished during the president's tenure. Like texts in other genres-such as the tobacco ads just considered -we would expect the inaugurals to be affected by various aspects of the rhetorical situation and to reflect the times in which they were delivered. We might expect the addresses to change with the answer to questions such as these: At the time of the address is the country facing or already embroiled in a diplomatic crisis? Is the economy booming or are Americans having trouble finding work and earning enough to feed their families? Was the previous president booted out of office by an unhappy electorate or narrowly defeated or die while in office?

Another, perhaps less obvious, situation that might affect the address is whether the president has delivered such an address before. To find an answer to this question, we divided electronic versions of the inaugural addresses (Kibler & van Leeuwen, 2002) into two groups: first and subsequent inaugural addresses. The first group is comprised of addresses delivered the first time a president is elected to office. The "subsequent" group is comprised of addresses delivered by presidents who had already delivered at least one previous inaugural address.* For example, President George Washington (a founder of the inaugural address

---

* Franklin D. Roosevelt is the only president to have delivered more than two inaugurals. He delivered four of them. The inaugural addresses included in the "subsequent" group are listed at the bottom of table 10.8.

genre, as well as the country) delivered two inaugural addresses, one in 1789 and a second in 1793. His 1789 address is part of the "first" group and his 1793 address is included in the "subsequent" group of addresses.

After counting the occurrences of the priming strings in the addresses, two of the dimensions, "think positive" and "time interval," show significant differences whereas a third, "reasoning," is marginally significant, as shown in table 10.5. Interestingly, it appears inaugurals delivered by a president who already delivered one tend to be less positive yet more invested in referencing "time intervals." The subsequent addresses also tend to use fewer markers of explicit reasoning.

Table 10.5: Comparison of first and subsequent U.S. presidential inaugural addresses

Variable	First (n=37) mean	s.d.	Subsequent[a] (n=17) mean	s.d.	F	P
First Person	0.965	0.654	0.982	0.654	0.010	0.933
Inner Thinking	2.575	0.585	2.551	0.585	0.020	0.887
Think Positive	1.281	0.394	1.013	0.394	5.620	0.022
Think Negative	1.358	0.412	1.346	0.412	0.010	0.928
Think Ahead	1.845	0.373	1.919	0.373	0.380	0.542
Think Back	0.578	0.297	0.637	0.297	0.510	0.478
Reasoning	3.217	0.714	2.806	0.714	3.390	0.071
Share Soc Ties	5.834	1.169	5.297	1.169	2.600	0.113
Direct Activity	0.521	0.287	0.469	0.287	0.430	0.513
Interacting	0.408	0.357	0.395	0.357	0.020	0.885
Notifying	2.390	0.421	2.317	0.421	0.270	0.606
Linear Guidance	3.056	0.528	3.091	0.528	0.040	0.847
Word Picture	2.922	0.873	3.181	0.873	1.040	0.313
Space Interval	0.741	0.257	0.884	0.257	3.370	0.072
Motion	0.184	0.112	0.171	0.112	0.140	0.713
Past Events	1.085	0.327	1.146	0.327	0.290	0.592
Time Interval	1.175	0.319	1.540	0.319	11.800	0.001
Shifting Events	0.582	0.170	0.585	0.170	<0.001	0.959

df=(1,52)

a The "subsequent" group includes inaugurals from Washington (1793), Jefferson (1805), Madison (1813), Monroe (1821), Jackson (1833), Lincoln (1865), Grant (1873), Cleveland (1893), McKinley (1901), Wilson (1917), FDR (1937, 1941, 1945), Eisenhower (1957), Nixon (1973), Reagan (1985), and Clinton (1997)

While only painstaking historical research can truly answer these questions, theories of rhetorical priming can supply a layer of statistical fact that become the basis for historical hypothesis generation and testing. It is interesting in this regard to consider the possibilities for explaining the statistical differences between an inaugural given the second time versus a President's maiden inaugural address.

Perhaps presidents become world-weary during their first terms and, therefore, just naturally reduce positiveness in their second inaugural. Or perhaps—after being reelected—they wish to avoid seeming to brag about their previous accomplishments and, therefore, tone down the positive so that it not be mistaken for gloating. For example, near the opening of his first inaugural in 1801 (Kibler & van Leeuwen 2002), Thomas Jefferson uses effusive, positive terms to tell the audience of his awe at contemplating his vision:

> A rising nation, spread over a wide and fruitful land, traversing all the seas with the rich productions of their industry, engaged in commerce with nations who feel power and forget right, advancing rapidly to destinies beyond the reach of mortal eye-when I contemplate these transcendent objects, and see the honor, the happiness, and the hopes of this beloved country committed to the issue and the auspices of this day, I shrink from the contemplation, and humble myself before the magnitude of the undertaking.

But in his 1805 address, Jefferson avoids effusive description. He takes up where he left off, but offers a modest recounting of his administration's accomplishments by avoiding language too overtly positive:

> On taking this station on a former occasion, I declared the principles on which I believed it my duty to administer the affairs of our commonwealth. My conscience tells me that I have, on every occasion, acted up to that declaration, according to its obvious import, and to the understanding of every candid mind. In the transaction of your foreign affairs, we have endeavored to cultivate the friendship of all nations... At home, fellow citizens, you best know whether we have done well or ill. The suppression of unnecessary offices, of useless establishments and expenses, enabled us to discontinue our internal taxes.

Another possible explanation is that reelected presidents owe part of their reelection to political circumstances that stressed both them and the nation. To the extent a president exploited these stresses to gain reelection, to that extent it might seem unpresidential not to tackle these stresses head on in the second inaugural.

Yet another possibility is that presidents delivering second inaugural addresses are increasingly concerned about their future legacies and, therefore, tend to use their second inaugural to address their place in posterity (requiring "time interval" priming strings) and to frame their to a more severe universal audience rather than to an electorate who had just made him a winner.

For example, near the beginning of Ronald Reagan's second inaugural address (1985) he evokes comparisons with the distant past in beginning to suggest a bright future for Americans:

> This is, as Senator Mathias told us, the 50th time that we the people have celebrated this historic occasion. When the first President, George Washington, placed his hand upon the Bible, he stood less than a single day's journey by horseback from raw, untamed wilderness. There were 4 million Americans in a union of 13 States. Today we are 60 times as many in a union of 50 States. We have lighted the world with our inventions, gone to the aid of mankind wherever in the world there was a cry for help, journeyed to the Moon and safely returned. So much has changed. And yet we stand together as we did two centuries ago.
>
> When I took this oath four years ago, I did so in a time of economic stress. Voices were raised saying we had to look to our past for the greatness and glory. But we, the present-day Americans, are not given to looking backward. In this blessed land, there is always a better tomorrow. Four years ago, I spoke to you of a new beginning and we have accomplished that. But in another sense, our new beginning is a continuation of that beginning created two centuries ago when, for the first time in history, government, the people said, was not our master, it is our servant; its only power that which we the people allow it to have.

As with the other examples presented in this chapter, we introduce these textual observations about inaugural addresses as a way to pique interest and not settle matters of criticism. To answer definitively would require historical research and understandings far beyond the scope of rhetorical priming.

Earlier in this chapter, we briefly described the multivariate process of "factor analysis" and what it can indicate about genres. An interesting exercise is to develop a factor for all the inaugural addresses and then plot the factor scores over time, as we did in figure 10.4.

The factor depicted in Figure 10.4 must be interpreted and it requires extensive historical investigation, beyond our scope, fully to interpret it. However, we do in the text below hint at what this factor is by comparing an early Presidential inaugural (Madison, 1809) who scores very high on it and a much later Presidential inaugural (Clinton, 1993) that scores very low.

Looking at Figure 10.4, one can see a definite historical trend for inaugurals to have steadily declined on this factor over time*

---

* We can calculate this trend mathematically. The formula for the trend line is $yt=1.163 + (?1.38E?02)t+(?7.38E?04)t2$. The line described by this formula results in a mean squared deviation (MSD) = 0.167 when compared with the inaugural speech data.

Remember that a factor represents a combination of the different dimensions that account for the variance within the speeches. By showing the trend of the inaugural address scores over time, figure 10.4 suggests measurable evidence of a steady change of this genre over the last two centuries. That is, despite the vagaries of time and marked changes in the rhetorical situation surrounding each specific speech, we see evidence of a slow, steady change in this genre.

As we mentioned, factors are developed through a statistical process and, in our context, factors represent combinations of the language dimensions described in this book. These combinations are described by a series of numbers—called the factor loading scores—with one loading assigned to each language dimension. Factor loadings can be thought of as a recipe put together by mixing in dimensions in different combinations as if they were different ingredients. The ingredients for our factors are the 18 language dimensions of our catalog. The amount of each dimension within a factor is specified by the loading score for the particular dimension. Dimensions with large factor loadings are important for understanding the overall factor.

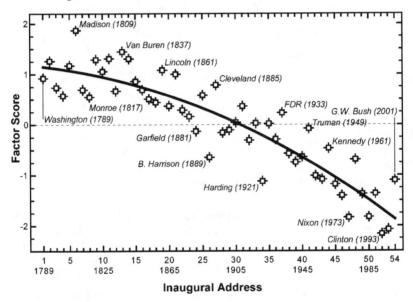

Figure 10.4. Historical change of U.S. presidential inaugurals on one factor

Table 10.6 lists the dimensions and loading scores for the factor we have used to organize the presidential inaugurals in figure 10.4. You will notice that the factor loading scores have both positive and negative signs. A positive sign means that having large amounts of the dimension also means having a high score on the factor. A negative sign means that having large amounts of the dimension means having a low score on the factor.

225

Close inspection of the table below reveals that the early presidential inaugurals had a high tendency to be first person, positive, and to provide audiences with lots of linear guidance to aid their navigation through the inaugural. Yet the historical trend has been to see these dimensions weakening over time in favor of inaugurals that are more descriptive, reportative, and even more directive with audiences. These trends are all made visible by the single factor used to organize the inaugurals.

As humanistic readers, we can learn how to make more sense of these over-time results by comparing sections from two inaugural speeches with widely varied placement on the graph, namely James Madison's (1809) and William J. Clinton's (1993) first inaugural addresses.

Table 10.6 Factor loadings for the factor plotted in Figure 10.4

Dimension	Factor Loading Score
Linear Guidance	0.640
First Person	0.518
Think Positive	0.397
Direct Activity	-0.611
Word Picture	-0.599
Time Interval	-0.489
Motion	-0.478
Space Interval	-0.427
Notifying	-0.420

In their inaugurals, the two presidents express gratitude to the electorate and to presidents who went before. They also both present a thumbnail sketch of where the nation stands in relation to the rest of the world. Notice, first, Madison's usage of "first person" strings in opening his speech as he says:

Unwilling to depart from examples of the most revered authority, I avail myself of the occasion now presented to express the profound impression made on me by the call of my country to the station to the duties of which I am about to pledge myself by the most solemn of sanctions.

In contrast, Clinton uses "first person" strings only 12 times in his entire first inaugural address. As an alternative to first person, he opens his speech by giving voice to the notion of generational change many perceived his election to represent.*

In contrast to Madison's use of "first person" priming strings, Clinton uses inclusive priming ("we speak," "we feel," "we show") to bring his audience into his vision:

My fellow citizens: Today we celebrate the mystery of American renewal. This ceremony is held in the depth of winter. But, by the words we speak and the faces we show the world, we force the spring. A spring reborn in the world's oldest democracy, that brings forth the vision and courage to reinvent America. When our founders boldly declared America's independence to the world and our purposes to the Almighty, they knew that America, to endure, would have to change. Not change for change's sake, but change to preserve America's ideals-life, liberty, the pursuit of happiness. Though we march to the music of our time, our mission is timeless. Each generation of Americans must define what it means to be an American. On behalf of our nation, I salute my predecessor, President Bush, for his half-century of service to America. And I thank the millions of men and women whose steadfastness and sacrifice triumphed over Depression, fascism and Communism.

Madison also acknowledges his predecessor in his speech, but he does so at the end and, even while doing so he uses more introspective, almost self-congratulatory language:

It is my good fortune, moreover, to have the path in which I am to tread lighted by examples of illustrious services successfully rendered in the most trying difficulties by those who have marched before me. Of those of my immediate predecessor it might least become me here to speak. I may, however, be pardoned for not suppressing the sympathy with which my heart is full in the rich reward he enjoys in the benedictions of a beloved country, gratefully bestowed or exalted talents zealously devoted through a long career to the advancement of its highest interest and happiness.

Another area of difference between the two speeches is found in the thumbnail sketch of the world they provide and the way they couch their prescribed remedy. Madison uses many strings involving "linear guidance" whereas Clinton does not and, instead, is directive in his prescription. These evident differences reflect the language in use at the time. Madison's "linear guidance" priming was necessary to keep his audience with him as his sentences twist and wind along their way:

* Clinton was the first "baby boomer" president, defeating George H. W. Bush, the last president to have fought in World War II.

227

The present situation of the world is indeed without a parallel and that of our own country full of difficulties. The pressure of these, too, is the more severely felt because they have fallen upon us at a moment when the national prosperity being at a height not before attained, the contrast resulting from the change has been rendered the more striking.

And near the end of his speech, Madison gives his prescription, relying on cabinet officers, Congress, and state governments for help:

But the source to which I look or the aids which alone can supply my deficiencies is in the well-tried intelligence and virtue of my fellow-citizens, and in the counsels of those representing them in the other departments associated in the care of the national interests. In these my confidence will under every difficulty be best placed, next to that which we have all been encouraged to feel in the guardianship and guidance of that Almighty Being whose power regulates the destiny of nations, whose blessings have been so conspicuously dispensed to this rising Republic, and to whom we are bound to address our devout gratitude for the past, as well as our fervent supplications and best hopes for the future.

In contrast, Clinton's thumbnail of the world is not as complex and does not require the navigational help that Madison provided his audience:

Today, a generation raised in the shadows of the Cold War assumes new responsibilities in a world warmed by the sunshine of freedom but threatened still by ancient hatreds and new plagues. Raised in unrivaled prosperity, we inherit an economy that is still the world's strongest, but is weakened by business failures, stagnant wages, increasing inequality, and deep divisions among our people. When George Washington first took the oath I have just sworn to uphold, news traveled slowly across the land by horseback and across the ocean by boat. Now, the sights and sounds of this ceremony are broadcast instantaneously to billions around the world. Communications and commerce are global; investment is mobile; technology is almost magical; and ambition for a better life is now universal. We earn our livelihood in peaceful competition with people all across the earth.

And in a passage that sounds remarkably similar to the 1985 Reagan inaugural, Clinton provides his remedy using "direct activity" strings ("we must," "we pledge") that Madison avoided. Perhaps Madison avoided such usage because implying the American presidency could be a monarchy, capable of royal pronouncement was still a fresh fear in the minds of early 19th century Americans listening to the speech. In Clinton's remedy, the language of directed activity is prevalent as he commands his audience:

Our democracy must be not only the envy of the world but the engine of our own renewal. There is nothing wrong with America that cannot be cured by what is right with America. And so today, we pledge an end to the era of deadlock and drift-a new season of American renewal has begun. To renew America, we must be bold. We must do what no generation has had to do before. We must invest more in our own people, in their jobs, in their future, and at the same time cut our massive debt. And we must do so in a world in which we must compete for every opportunity. It will not be easy; it will require sacrifice. But it can be done, and done fairly, not choosing sacrifice for its own sake, but for our own sake. We must provide for our nation the way a family provides for its children. Our Founders saw themselves in the light of posterity. We can do no less.

What can be seen by the steady decline of the speeches' scores on this factor is the movement away from language like those in Madison's speech and toward language like those found in Clinton's speech. As with the other examples presented in this chapter, there are several plausible explanations for this observation. A satisfying explanation would need to extend far beyond the study of the texts themselves (to which our analysis is limited) and would need to be placed in the context of the political and linguistic changes in the United States since its establishment. We hope, however, this example has further demonstrated the potential of carefully assessing textual genres based on the authors' usage of rhetorical priming strings within it.

ADAPTING THE AUDIENCE TO A MESSAGE: DIFFERENCES IN INDIVIDUAL WRITERS' LANGUAGE CHOICES

Several times in this chapter, we have generalized about the types of strings writers use based on the genre in which they write. As you would expect, genre is not the only factor that might influence a writer's usage of the language dimensions. Our colleague, Barbara Johnstone (1996) has observed and described some potential relationships between social and psychological factors-as well as the rhetorical situation-that might lead individuals toward a particular linguistic behavior. Disentangling the social from the individual determinants is difficult, if not impossible.

An exercise we use to introduce such individual variance to our students is to ask them to compare the audience-priming choices of different career writers. Some might call this a comparative "style" analysis of a writer, but the idea of style is very nonspecific compared to our catalog of English strings. We ask the students to make head-to-head comparisons between a series of essays by two professional opinion columnists, Mary McGrory and Michael Kinsley. Both writers take a left-leaning view and often write on the same political topics.

229

Nonetheless, McGrory and Kinsley, our students discover, routinely provide their audiences with starkly different reading experiences, as shown in table 10.7.

McGrory's texts tend to withhold her mind and inner thought and interaction with the audience. She offers audiences experiences that are constructed to seem relatively objective descriptions of realities, relying on word pictures and letting readers infer her opinion through these pictures. In a column of February 25, 2001, she portrays George W. Bush as a butcher of English pronouns:

> Bush's news conference provided more heartburn for language lovers: "Laura and I are looking forward to having a private dinner with he and Mrs. Blair." This was in the Style section's "Reliable Source" column. It was Page 1 material. The news conference also brought an acute moment of what grammarians call "pronoun confusion." Asked what he would tell his family about seeking a pardon from him, he said, "My guidance to them is behave yourself. And they will." In two short sentences, he swung from the plural to the singular and back to the plural.

Although it may not be immediately clear that McGrory concealed her internal perspective and involvement with the audience, this becomes strikingly apparent when we contrast her prose with that of Michael Kinsley, also writing on George W. Bush and language. Kinsley's mind is visible in his texts and that visibility is part of a signature style. Furthermore, his use of first person coupled with thinking verbs, subjective perception, and interactive questions assures that he is always in his audience's face. Read Kinsley regularly and you will be struck not only by his interior and subjective thinking, but also by his frequent engagement with the audience in this representative column of January 26, 2001:

> When did they pass the constitutional amendment requiring every president and would-be president to end every speech with the words, "God bless you and God bless America"? Even a nonbeliever cannot reasonably object to the sentiment. If I turn out to be mistaken about the central question of the universe, I'll be happy enough that others were doing some celestial lobbying on my country's behalf.

Another interesting activity to tease out pattern contrasts among career writers is to compare their approaches when asked to address a common rhetorical situation. This approach served Berkenkotter and Huckin (1995) well when they reviewed variations across conference abstracts for a particular conference. We found it useful to use the dimensions presented in this book to analyze fifty-seven authors contributing to "The Writers on Writing" series. *The New York Times* has published the series since 1997. The series was the brainchild of the *Times'* culture editor, John Darnton. A Pulitzer winner for fiction and a Polk Award winner for journalism, Darnton reported that he had struggled with his

Table 10.7: Comparison of opinion articles by two columnists

Variable	Kinsley (n=32)		McGrory (n=33)		F	P
	mean	s.d.	mean	s.d.		
First Person	0.345	0.336	0.458	1.013	0.360	0.553
Inner Thinking	4.010	0.698	2.388	0.592	102.260	<0.001
Think Positive	0.814	0.424	1.054	0.485	4.500	0.038
Think Negative	1.830	0.829	1.909	0.932	0.130	0.718
Think Ahead	1.387	0.482	1.211	0.422	2.440	0.123
Think Back	0.440	0.313	0.576	0.249	3.780	0.056
Reasoning	4.118	0.908	2.275	0.578	95.810	<0.001
Share Soc Ties	3.183	1.124	2.099	0.576	24.190	<0.001
Direct Activity	0.323	0.199	0.246	0.188	2.560	0.115
Interacting	1.624	0.869	0.506	0.434	43.440	<0.001
Notifying	3.028	0.533	2.526	0.559	13.760	<0.001
Linear Guidance	4.326	1.196	5.447	1.265	13.460	0.001
Word Picture	3.988	1.120	6.253	1.264	58.330	<0.001
Space Interval	0.662	0.311	1.032	0.349	20.290	<0.001
Motion	0.441	0.260	0.393	0.198	0.700	0.405
Past Events	1.216	0.489	1.916	0.769	19.050	<0.001
Time Interval	1.044	0.534	0.969	0.371	0.430	0.512
Shifting Events	0.661	0.289	0.817	0.302	4.500	0.038

df=(1,63)

first novel and found he was endlessly curious to know the secrets of successful writers. He devised the Writers on Writing series to satisfy his own (and he hoped the audiences') curiosity about writing.

By analyzing the texts using the categorized strings in this book and factor analysis-as just described Kaufer (forthcoming) discovered that the authors vary according to whether they offer lessons to the audience dialogically or monologically. Dialogical lessons involve interacting with the audience directly and empathically, meaning a high degree of second person involvement and interactivity. The audience portrayed is an eager and engaged apprentice with the writer as the master, dispensing advice in a studio setting. For example, the most dialogical of lesson givers is Allegra Goodman. Speaking about her own experience with writing anxiety, she uses the second person, and interactive questions to tele-graph her empathy for the audience suffering from the same anxiety she faced:*

> The specter of the third-grade teacher who despaired of your penmanship. The ghost of the first person who told you that spelling counts. The voice of reason pointing out that what you are about to attempt has already been done and done far better than you might even hope. So why bother? Why even begin? It is, after all, abundantly clear that you are not Henry James. Your themes are hackneyed, your style imitative. As for your emotions, memories, insights and invented characters, what makes you think anyone will care? These are the perfectly logical questions of the famous, petty and implacable inner critic.

The audience Goodman evokes seeks interactive coaching in writing. And responding to these audience expectations, Goodman does not hesitate to confront her audience with tough-love questions:

> But take a step back. What are you really afraid of here? When you come down to it, this is just a case of the inner critic masquerading as public opinion, and playing on your vanity.

Using familiar sense objects, the second person, engaged questioning, and confrontation, Goodman engages her audience as a concerned and involved tutor.

Monological lessons, by contrast, involve keeping one's distance from the audience. The lessons dispensed come across as aloof lectures on writing to an audience sitting in a lecture hall, not a writing studio. One of the more monolog-ical of lesson-givers is Edmund White. His contribution to the Times' series observes what the novelist must do. Yet he makes his observations with no acknowledgment of an audience anxious to learn or practice. He provides lessons on writing based on analogies with music. Although the analogy provides an interesting read, it also keeps a noninteractive distance from the reader.

> Just as the novelist must keep all his strategies aloft and not allow the reader to forget a character or lose sight of the house, the ha-ha or the wilderness beyond, or skip over a crucial turn in the plot, in the same way the composer must teach the listener to recognize the key themes, the shifts in harmonic progression and the division of the composition into parts.

The language is reportative and inert, rather than interactive and engaged. It features the heavy syntax of information writing and inner speculative thought and contrasts markedly with writers who respond to the situation as Goodman did.

---

* All the quotes fron the Time series are also cited in Kaufer, forthcoming.

FINAL THOUGHTS

Our overriding aim in this book has been to report on a framework, theory, and method to study everyday language and its rich and diverse role in audience priming. The results of our approach have been a systematic catalog for how to think about everyday English strings as acts of symbolic action. The burden of this book has been to report on this organized catalog of micro-rhetorical action in detail. We indicated in this last chapter how we use our catalog, along with computer and statistical methods, to study the rhetoric of everyday language in texts found in common usage.

Although there are many similarities between how rhetoricians and empirically minded linguists look at language, rhetoricians, we dare say, are often so (justifiably) impressed with the contingency of language that we despair (less justifiably we think) about that contingency and its systemic roots in empirical description. Few rhetorical accounts of language stop at what speakers and writers actually do in the contexts of interest. Following Aristotle's dictum that rhetoric involves "all the available means" of persuasion, rhetorical analysts are more inclined to look at the speaker or writer's behavior in the context of all the options available and in the context of how actual performance sizes up against the possible.

It is this sense of rhetorical contingency that we have tried to build into our approach to rhetorical priming and our methods of textual analysis. The final compatibility between a rhetorical approach like ours and more standard rhetorical and linguistic approaches to language remain to be seen. We believe this will be a fruitful, worthwhile exploration.

REFERENCES

Austin, J. L. (1997). *How to do things with words*. Oxford: Oxford University Press. New York, NY: Norton.

Altenberg, B. (1990). Speech as linear composition. In G. Caie, K. Haastrup, A. L. Jakobsen, A. L. Nielsen, J. Sevaldsen, H. Specht, & A. Zettersten (Eds.), *Proceedings from the Fourth Nordic Conference for English Studies, Vol 1*. (pp. 133-143). Copenhagen: University of Copenhagen.

Bainton, G. (1890). (Ed.), *The art of authorship: Literary reminiscences, methods of work, and advice to young beginners, personally contributed by leading authors of the day*. New York: D. Appleton and Company, 1890.

Bazerman., C., & Russell, D.R. (Eds.) (2002). *Writing selves/Writing societies: Research from activity perspectives. Perspectives on writing*. Fort Collins, CO: The WAC clearinghouse and Mind, Culture, and Activity. Retrieved August 1, 2003, from http://wac.colostate.edu/books/selves_societies/

Bazerman, C. (1994). Systems of genres and the enactment of social intentions. In A. Freedman & P. Medway (Eds.), *Genre and the New Rhetoric* (pp. 79-101). London, UK: Taylor & Francis.

Becker, A.L. (1991). A Short essay on languaging. In F. Steier (Ed.), *Research and Reflexivity* (pp. 226-234). Thousand Oaks, CA: Sage Publications.

Bell, M. S. (1997). *Narrative design: A writer's guide to structure*. New York, NY: Norton.

Berelson, B. (1952). *Content analysis in communication research*. New York, NY: Free Press.

Berkenkotter, C., & Huckin, T. (1995). *Genre knowledge in disciplinary communication: cognition/culture/power*. Mahwah, NJ: Lawrence Erlbaum & Associates.

Berthoff, A. (Ed.). (1991). *I. A. Richards on rhetoric: Selected essays, 1929-1974*. New York, NY: Oxford University Press.

Biber, D. (1988). *Variation across speech and writing*. Cambridge, UK: Cambridge University Press.

Biber, D., Conrad, S., & Reppen, R. (1998). *Corpus linguistics: Investigating language structure and use*. Cambridge, UK: Cambridge University Press.

Bleich, D. (1998). Know and tell: *A writing pedagogy of disclosure, genre, and membership*. Portsmouth, NH: Heinemann-Boynton/Cook.

Booth, W. (1969). *The rhetoric of fiction*. Chicago, IL: University of Chicago Press.

Buranen, L., & Roy, A. M. (Eds.). (1999). *Perspectives on plagiarism and intellectual property in a postmodern world*. Albany, NY: State University of New York Albany Press.

Burke, K. (1969). *Rhetoric of motives*. Berkeley, CA: University of California Press.

Burton, G. (1996) *Silvae Rhetoricae*. http: //humanities.byu.edu /rhetoric/silva.htm

Chafe, W. (1994). Discourse, consciousness, and time: The flow and displacement of conscious experience in speaking and writing. Chicago, IL: University of Chicago Press.

References

The Chicago Manual of Style (14th ed.) (1993). Chicago, IL: University of Chicago Press.

Channell J. (2000). Corpus-based analysis of evaluative lexis. In Hunston & Thompson (Eds.), *Evaluation in text: Authorial stance and the construction of discourse* (pp. 38-55). Oxford, UK: Oxford University Press.

Chomsky, N. (1957). *Aspects of the theory of syntax.* Cambridge, MA: MIT Press.

Clark, H. (1996). *Using language.* Cambridge, UK: Cambridge University Press.

Collins, J. (2002, March). Tuning the ear for words: Capturing reading experience through visualization technology. Paper presented at the Conference on College Composition and Communication, Chicago.

Collins, J. (2003). *Variations in Written English: Characterizing the Authors' Rhetorical Language Choices Across Corpora of Published Texts.* PhD thesis, Carnegie Mellon University.

Collins, J., Kaufer D., Neuwirth, C. M., Hajduk, T. J., & Palmquist, M. (2002). Representational differences in the writings of experts and novices. Unpublished manuscript, Pittsburgh, PA.

Coulson, S. (2001). Semantic leaps: Frame shifting and conceptual blending in meaning construction. New York, NY: Cambridge University Press.

Coulson, R., & Oakley, A. (2000). Blending basics. *Cognitive Linguistics, 11*, 175-196.

Croft, W. & Cruse, D.A.. (In press). *Cognitive Linguistics.* Cambridge, UK: Cambridge University Press.

Crismore, A. (1989). *Talking with readers: Metadiscourse as rhetorical act.* New York, NY: Peter Lang Publishing.

Day, R. (2001). *The modern invention of information: Discourse, history, and power.* Carbondale, IL: Southern Illinois Press.

Didion, J. (1979). *The white album.* New York, NY: Farrar, Straus & Giroux

Ede L., & Lunsford, A. (1990). *Singular texts/plural authors: Perspectives on collaborative writing.* Carbondale, IL: Southern Illinois University Press.

Elbow, P. (1991). Some thoughts on expressive discourse: A review essay. *Journal of Advanced Composition, 11*, 83-93.

Fauconnier, G. (1994). *Mental Spaces: Aspects of Meaning Construction in Natural Language.* NewYork, NY: Cambridge University Press.

Fauconnier, G. (1997). *Mappings in Thought and Language.* New York, NY: Cambridge University Press.

Fauconnier, G. & Turner, M. (1998). Conceptual Integration Networks. *Cognitive Science 22*, 133-187.

Fauconnier, G., & Turner., M. (2002). The way we think: Conceptual blending and the mind's hidden complexities. New York, NY: Basic Books.

References

Faust, M. (2000). Reconstructing familiar metaphors: John Dewey and Louise Rosenblatt on literary art as experience. *Research in the Teaching of English, 35*(1), 35-65.

Faigley, L., & Witte S. (1986). Analyzing revision. *College Composition and Communication, 32*, 400-414.

Fairclough, N. (1989). *Language and power.* London, UK: Longman.

Fillmore, C., Kay, P., Michaelis, L., & Sag, I. (In press). *Construction Grammar.* Stanford, CA: CSLI Publications.

Firbas J. (1992). *Functional sentence perspective in written and spoken communication.* Cambridge, UK: Cambridge University Press.

Fish, S. (1980). *Is there a text in this class? The authority of interpretive communities.* Cambridge, MA: Harvard University Press.

Fitzmaurice, S. (2002). Intersubjectivity and the linguistic construction of addressee/interlocutor/reader stance. Paper presented at the Modern Language Association Conference, New York, December 28.

Fletcher, R. (1992). *What a writer needs.* Portsmouth, NH: Heineman.

Flower, L., Hayes, J. R., Carey, L., Schriver, K. & Stratman J. (1986). Detection, diagnosis, and the strategies of revision. *College Composition and Communication, 37*, 16-55.

Foley, M. (1997). *Anthropological linguistics: An introduction.* Oxford, UK: Basil Blackwell.

Foucault, M. (1977). What is an author? In D. F. Bouchard (Ed.). *Language, counter-memory, practice* (pp. 124-127). Ithaca, NY: Cornell University Press.

Francis, W. N., & Kucera, H. (1979). Brown corpus manual. Available online at http://www.hit.uib.no/icame/brown/bcm.html .

Freedman, A., & Medway, P. (1994). Locating genre studies: Antecedents and prospects. In A. Freedman & P. Medway (Eds.), *Genre and the new rhetoric* (pp. 1-22). London, UK: Taylor & Francis.

Galbraith, D., & Torrance, M. (1999). Conceptual processes in writing: From problem solving to text production. In M. Torrance & D. Galbraith (Eds.), *Knowing what to write: Conceptual processes in text production* (pp. 1-12). Amsterdam, Netherlands: Amsterdam University Press.

Geisler, C. (1994). *Academic literacy and the nature of expertise.* Mahwah, NJ: Lawrence Erlbaum Associates.

Gere, A. (2001). Revealing silence: Rethinking personal writing. *College Composition and Communication, 53*, 203-223.

Goldberg, A. (1995). *Constructions: A construction grammar approach to argument structure.* Chicago, IL: University of Chicago Press.

Gurak, C. (2001). *Cyberliteracy: Navigating the Internet with awareness.* New Haven, CT: Yale University Press.

Hale, C. (1999). *Sin and syntax: How to craft wickedly effective prose*: New York, NY: Broadway Books.

Halliday, M.A.K. (1994). *An Introduction to functional grammar*. (2nd Ed.). London, UK: Edward Arnold.

Halliday, M.A.K., & Matthieson, C. (1999). *Construing experience through meaning*. New York, NY: Cassell.

Halliday, M.A.K., & Hasan, R. (1976). *Cohesion in English*. London, UK: Longman.

Hart, R. (2000). *Campaign talk: Why elections are good for us*. Princeton, NJ: Princeton University Press.

Harvard, U. (2001). *Close reading guidelines*, [URL]. Harvard University Writing Center. Available online at http: //www.fas.harvard.edu /~wricntr/.

hooks, B. (2000). Rhapsody remembered: Dancing with words. *Journal of Advanced Composition, 20* (1), 1-8.

Hopper, P. (1999a). *A short course in grammar*. New York, NY: Norton.

Hopper, P. (1999b). Was Bakhtin a proto-integrationalist? Paper presented at MLA Conference. Washington , D.C.

Hopper, P. & Thompson S. (1980) Transitivity in grammar and discourse. *Language 56* (2): 251-299.

Hopper, P., & Traugott E. (1993) *Grammaticalization* (Cambridge Textbooks in Linguistics). Cambridge, UK: Cambridge University Press.

Hopper, P. (2002). Hendiadys and auxiliation in English. In J. Bybee & M. Noonan (Eds.), *Complex sentences in grammar and discourse: Essays in honor of Sandra A. Thompson* (pp. 145-174). Amsterdam: John Benjamins.

Howard, R. (1999). Standing in the shadow of giants: Plagiarists, authors, collaborators. Stamford, CT: Ablex.

Hunston, S., & Thompson, (Eds.). (2000). *Evaluation in text: Authorial stance and the construction of discourse*. New York, NY: Oxford University Press.

Hundt, M., Sand, A., & Siemud, R. (1998). Manual of information to accompany the Freiburg-LOB corpus of British English. Available online at http://www.hit.uib.no/icame/cd.

Hyland, K. (2000). Disciplinary discourses: Social interactions in academic writing. New York, NY: Longman.

Hyland, K. (2001). Bringing in the reader: Addressee features in academic article. *Written Communication, 18*, 549-574.

Hylton, J. (2000). Complete works of William Shakespeare. Available online at http://the-tech.mit.edu/Shakespeare/works.html.

Iser, W. (1978). *The act of reading: A theory of aesthetic response*. Baltimore, MD: Johns Hopkins University Press.

Jackendoff, R. (1999). The representational structures of the language faculty and their interactions. In C. M. Brown & P. Hagoort (Eds.), *The neurocognition of language* (pp. 37-71). Oxford, UK: Oxford University Press.

Jackendoff, R., & Landau, B. (1995). Spatial Language and Spatial Cognition. In R. Jackendoff (Ed.), *Languages of the mind: Essays on mental representation* (pp. 99-124). Cambridge, MA: MIT Press.

Johnson, T.R. (2003). *A rhetoric of pleasure: Prose style and today's composition classroom.* Portsmouth, NH: Boynton Cook.

Johnstone, B. (1996). *The linguistic individual: Self-expression in language and linguistics:* Oxford: Oxford University Press.

Johnstone, B. (2002). *Discourse analysis.* London, UK: Blackwell.

Kachigan, S. K. (1991). *Multivariate statistical analysis* (2nd ed.). FDR Station, NY: Radius Press.

Kaufer, D. (2000).White Paper on Flaming: Research behind the MoodWatch flame detection program. Available from the author.

Kaufer, D. (forthcoming). The public and the private in the New York Times writers and writing series. In T. Kent & B. Couture (Eds.), *The private, the public, and the published: Reconciling private lives and public.* Carbondale, IL: Southern Illinois University Press.

Kaufer, D., & Butler, B. (1996). *Rhetoric and the arts of design.* Mahwah, NJ: Lawrence Erlbaum & Associates.

Kaufer, D., & Butler, B. (2000). *Designing interactive worlds with words: Principles of writing as representational composition.* Mahwah, NJ: Lawrence Erlbaum & Associates.

Kaufer, D., & Carley, K. (1993). *Communication at a distance: The influence of print on sociocultural change.* Mahwah, NJ: Lawrence Erlbaum & Associates.

Kaufer, D., & Geisler, C. (1989). Novelty in academic writing. *Written Communication, 6,* 286-311.

Kaufer, D., Hayes, J.R., & Flower, L. (1986). Composing written sentences. *Research in the Teaching of English, 20,* 121-140.

Kaufer, D., Ishizaki, S., Ishizaki, K., Butler, B., Collins, J., Vlachos, P. K., & Ritivoi, M. (2002). Docuscope. Available online at http://betterwriting.net/docuscope.

Kibler, J., & van Leeuwen, S. H. (2002). Inaugural addresses of the presidents of the United States. Available online at http://www.bartleby.com/124/index.html.

Kolln, M. (1999). *Rhetorical grammar: Grammatical choices, rhetorical effects* (3rd ed.). Needham Heights, MA: Allyn & Bacon.

Kucera, H., & Francis W. (1967). *Computational analysis of present-day American English.* Providence, RI: Brown University Press.

Lakoff, G. (1987). *Woman, fire, and dangerous things: What categories reveal about the mind.* Chicago, IL: University of Chicago Press.

References

Lakoff, G., & Johnson M. (1980). *Metaphors we live by.* Chicago, IL: University of Chicago.

Langacker. R. (1987). *Foundations of Cognitive Grammar, Volume 1: Theoretical Prerequisites.* Stanford, CA: Stanford University Press.

Langacker, R. (1990). *Concept, Image, and Symbol.* Berlin, Germany: Mouton de Gruyter.

Lanham, R. (1999). *Revising prose* (4th Ed.). Boston, MA: Allyn & Bacon.

Lautamatti, L. (1987). Observations on the development of the topic in simplified discourse. In U. Connor & R. B. Kaplan (Eds.), Writing across languages: Analysis of L2 texts (pp. 87-113). Reading, MA: Addison-Wesley (Originally published 1978).

Lippman, W. (1927). *The phantom public.* New Brunswick, NJ: Transaction Press.

Locker, K. (1999). Factors in reader responses to negative letters: Experimental evidence for changing what we teach. *Journal of Business and Technical Communication, 13,* 5-48.

Lynch, J. (2001). On-line style guide: Rutgers University. Retrieved Sept 1, 2002, from http://newark.rutgers.edu/~jlynch/Writing/

Manning C. D., & Schutze, H. (2001). *Foundations of statistical natural language processing.* Cambridge, MA: MIT Press.

Manovich, L. (2001). *The language of the new media.* Cambridge, MA: MIT Press.

McGann, J. (2001). Reading fiction, teaching fiction. *Pedagogy, 1,* 143-165.

Melville H. (1856). *Benito Cereno.* Available online at http: // books.mirror.org/melville/benitocereno/s006.html, accessed July 3, 2003.

Miller, C. (1984). Genre as social action. *Quarterly Journal of Speech, 70,* 151-167.

Myers, B. R. (2001, July/August). A reader's manifesto: An attack on the growing pretentiousness of American literary prose. *The Atlantic Monthly,* 104-122.

Nunberg, G. (1990). *The linguistics of punctuation.* Palo Alto, CA: Center for the Study of Language and Information.

Olson, D. (1994). *The world on paper.* New York: Cambridge University Press.

Ong, W. (1975). The writer's audience is always a fiction. *PMLA, 90,* 9-21.

Ong, W. (1982). *Orality and literacy: The technologizing of the word.* New York, NY: Routledge.

Parsons, T. (1990). Events in the semantics of English: A study in subatomic semantics. Cambridge MA: MIT Press.

Perelman, C., & Olbrechts-Tyteca, L. (1969). *The new rhetoric: A treatise on argumentation (J. Wilkinson & P. Weaver, Trans.).* South Bend, IN: University of Notre Dame Press.

Quinn, A. (1993). *Figures of speech: 60 ways to turn a phrase.* Davis, CA: Hermagoras Press.

References

Reddy, R. (1979).The conduit metaphor–A case of frame conflict in our language about language. In A. Ortony (Ed.), *Metaphor and thought* (pp. 284-324). Cambridge, UK: Cambridge University Press.

Richards, I. A. (1950). *Practical criticism.* New York, NY: Harcourt Brace (originally published 1929).

Richards, I. A. (1974). Meanings as instruments in A. Berthoff (Ed.), *Richards on rhetoric.* New York, NY: Oxford University Press.

Roberts, C. (1997). A theoretical map for selecting among text analysis methods. In C. Roberts (Ed.), Text Analysis for the social sciences (pp. 275-283). Mahwah, NJ: Lawrence Erlbaum Associates.

Rosenblatt, L. A. (1978). *The reader, the text, the poem: The transactional theory of the literary work.* Carbondale, IL: Southern Illinois University Press.

Schneider, B. (2002). Nonstandard quotes: Superimpositions and cultural. *College Composition and Communication, 54*, 188-207.

Schryer, C. (2000). Walking a fine line: Writing negative letters in an insurance company. *Journal of Business and Technical Communication, 14*, 445-497.

Schwanenflugel, P. J., & White, C. R. (1991). The influence of paragraph information on the processing of upcoming words. *Reading Research Quarterly, 26*, 160-177.

Scott, M. (1998) The WordSmith Program. Oxford, UK: Oxford University Press.

Sinclair, J. M. (Ed.). (1995). *Collins COBUILD English dictionary.* London, UK: HarperCollins.

Sinclair, J. M. (1991). *Corpus, concordance, collocation.* New York, NY: Oxford University Press.

Smagorinsky, P., & Smith. M. W. (2000). Special Issue on "Is there a text in this study?" *Research in the Teaching of English, 35*, 1-20.

Spears, R.A. (2000). *NTC's American idioms dictionary* (3rd ed.). New York, NY: Oxford University Press.

Swales, J. (1990). *Genre analysis. Analysing academic and research texts.* Cambridge, UK: Cambridge University Press.

Turner, M. (1996). *The literary mind.* New York, NY: Oxford.

Turner, M. (2001). *Cognitive Foundations of Social Science.* New York; Oxford University Press.

Vongvipanond, P. (1994). Linguistic perspectives of Thai Culture. Paper presented to a workshop of teachers of social science organized by the University of New Orleans. Retrieved March 1, 2003, from http://www.thaiarc.tu.ac.th/host/thaiarc/thai/peansiri.htm

Warner, M. (2002). Publics and counterpublics, *Public Culture, 14*, 49-90.

Webster's New International Dictionary of the English Language Unabridged (1948). 2nd edition. Springfield, MA: G. & C. Merriam.

Wierzbicka, A. (1992). *Semantics, culture, and cognition.* New York, NY: Oxford University Press.

Witmore, M. (2001). *Culture of accidents: Unexpected knowledges in early modern England.* Palo Alto, CA: Stanford University Press.

Williams, J. (2000). *Style: Ten lessons in clarity and grace* (6th ed.). New York: Longman.

Williams, J. (1981a). The phenomenology of error. *College Composition and Communication, 32,* 152-168.

Williams, J. (1981b). Literary style: The personal voice. In T. Shapen & J.M. Williams (Eds.), *Style and variables in English* (pp. 116-126). Cambridge, MA: Winthrop.

Winsor, D. (1999). Genre and activity systems. *Written Communication, 16,* 200-224.

Wolf, G. (1999). An introduction to essays on integrational linguistics in the context of 20th-Century theories of language. *Language & Communication, 19,* 1-8.

Wooden, J. A., DeVore, J., Graef, C., & Westman, L. (1998). Truth in advertising: Vintage cigarette and tobacco ads. Retrieved August 1, 2003, from http://www.chickenhead.com/truth/index.html .

Woodmansee, M. (1996). *The author, art, and the market.* New York, NY: Columbia University Press.

Woodmansee, M., & Jaszi, P. (Eds.). (1994). *The construction of authorship: Textual appropriation in law and literature.* Durham, NC: Duke University Press.

Wray, A., & Perkins, M. (2000). The functions of formulaic language: An integrated model. *Language & Communication, 20,* 1-28.

Yovel, J. (2002). Rights and Rites: Initiation, Language and Performance in Law and Legal Education *Stanford Agora 2* (formerly the *Stanford Journal of Legal Studies*). Retrieved July 5, 2003, from http://agora.stanford.edu/agora/volume2/yovel/shtml.

AUTHOR INDEX

Author Index

SUBJECT INDEX